Japan and the Global Automotive Industry

The Japanese automotive industry enjoyed spectacular success in the 1980s. This was largely due to the so-called "lean production system" – the combination of an efficient production system, an effective supplier system, and a product development system. In the 1990s the industry fell on hard times because of the Japanese asset price bubble and extreme currency appreciation. In this book, eminent industry specialist Koichi Shimokawa draws on his thirty years of research and fieldwork with Japanese and US firms to show how the Japanese automotive industry has managed to recover from this difficult period. He shows how firms like Toyota were able to transfer Japanese systems to overseas plants and how they have changed in order to compete in increasingly globalized markets. In addition, the book addresses the two major challenges to the current industry model: the rise of China and the environmental and energy supply situation.

Koichi Shimokawa is Professor in the Faculty of Business Administration at Tokaigakuen University and Emeritus Professor at Hosei University, Japan. He is one of the world's leading researchers on the automotive industry and is a leading member of the International Motor Vehicle Program. He is the author of several books on Japanese business and the automotive industry, including *The Japanese Automobile Industry* (London: Athron Press, 1994).

Japan and the Global Automotive Industry

KOICHI SHIMOKAWA

CAMBRIDGE
UNIVERSITY PRESS

CAMBRIDGE
UNIVERSITY PRESS

University Printing House, Cambridge CB2 8BS, United Kingdom

One Liberty Plaza, 20th Floor, New York, NY 10006, USA

477 Williamstown Road, Port Melbourne, VIC 3207, Australia

314-321, 3rd Floor, Plot 3, Splendor Forum, Jasola District Centre, New Delhi - 110025, India

79 Anson Road, #06-04/06, Singapore 079906

Cambridge University Press is part of the University of Cambridge.

It furthers the University's mission by disseminating knowledge in the pursuit of education, learning and research at the highest international levels of excellence.

www.cambridge.org
Information on this title: www.cambridge.org/9780521866873

First published 2010
Reprinted 2011
First paperback edition 2012

A catalogue record for this publication is available from the British Library

ISBN 978-0-521-86687-3 Hardback
ISBN 978-1-107-41268-2 Paperback

Contents

Figures

Tables

Preface

This book describes the turbulent thirty-year history of the auto industry, while illustrating its important phases from a cross-sectional and a bird's-eye view. The auto industry has globalized rapidly in the past three decades, but now we have reached a time of world financial crisis. General Motors (GM) reigned as the world's top producer in the auto industry for seventy years, yet now has gone through bankruptcy restructuring. Nobody expected such a dramatic change. However, thirty years ago, nobody could have guessed that this would be a global industry and would be significantly linked with the fate of our new civilization at the beginning of the twenty-first century. A quarter of a century ago, in other words before the end of the 1970s, the automotive industry was only a local or regional industry which was independently established, although it was already an industry that represented regions and nations, particularly in the advanced countries. Certainly, no one expected that this industry would develop in Asian countries to such an extent that South Korea, China, and India would become countries which annually produce 3.3 million, 10 million, and 3 million cars respectively. Of course, even during this period, there were multinational companies in the industry, such as the US's Big Three, which produced cars in the US and Europe. But there was almost no business affiliation between these two areas.

However, automotive production, especially in Asia, is increasing significantly. It is only a matter of time until the production performance of China exceeds Japan's domestic production. The current situation in Japan shows that, in comparison with domestic production, the volume of overseas automotive production is increasing every year. In North America, the biggest foreign market, the annual production volume of cars has reached nearly 4 million, twice as much as Japan's export volume. Today, the automotive industry cannot exist without practicing global corporate behavior and strategies. This means that the operation of the industry should be available at any place of demand in the world, and this includes the construction of global product development, parts procurement, and production systems. At the same time, we should not forget that as the globalization of the automotive industry progresses, the industry has to face up to the issues of the civilized world, that is, to morph into an industry which takes responsibility in such areas as energy, resource, and environmental issues, which are becoming more and more serious.

The automotive industry in the twentieth century started with car-manufacturing craftsmen in Europe, before developing along the paradigm of mass production and mass sales, of which the Ford System and GM's Sloanism are representative. It was believed that if the car-ownership ratio increased along with the cost reductions created by mass production, and as long as a replacement demand was created by the diversification of products and model changes, then society would be enriched. However, there was a trap hidden in the paradigm of mass production, and this gradually became clear as we came closer to the end of the twentieth century. This became particularly apparent when the sense of value that mass production and mass consumption would bring to people's lives collapsed. In other words, the automobile industry has been caught up in the problems of energy, resources, and traffic, and now it has to face up to social requirements for building energy-saving cars, clean-energy cars that do not rely only on fossil fuel, cars which recycle resources, fail-safe cars, and a traffic system that can dramatically reduce traffic accidents. The fact is that the automotive industry faces these serious problems along with the impact of the globalization of the industry; these relations are neither too close nor too remote from each other, and the challenge of solving these problems has just begun.

When we consider the globalization of the automotive industry in the light of these challenges, we can see that a great change is needed in the automotive makers' business processes: development, production, procurement, and sales. This upheaval is equivalent to the introduction of mass production and mass volume production which was the basic paradigm for the twentieth century's automotive industry as it developed mass production, mass sales, and mass consumption. This led to the emergence of a lean production system which could perform flexibly with changes in demand and which operated through all the processes of development, production, procurement, and sales. MIT's International Motor Vehicle Program (IMVP) in the US, which I have been involved with for twenty years, made the paradigm of the lean production system known to the world, and it is believed that this paradigm started in the Japanese automotive industry in the 1980s. Today, it is universally recognized that auto makers everywhere are racing to adopt this business system.

The aims of this book are to show how the world's automotive industries went global over the past thirty years and how the change-over to this important paradigm was made. These questions will be examined based on data from field surveys conducted over the years and on the knowledge I have gathered from my involvement with two big international projects: MIT and Groupe d'Etudes et de Recherches Permanent sur l'Industrie et les Salariés de l'Automobile (GERPISA). Chapter 1 of this book discusses how a reversal occurred in the competitiveness of the Japanese and US automotive industries, of which a key factor was the oil crisis in 1979, and how the international comparison of productivity and Japan's comparative advantage were made possible.

Chapter 2 covers the internationalization of Japan's automotive industry, which gained momentum from the mid 1980s, and the situation of local production overseas, which symbolizes internationalization. This part also shows how the lean production system or the Japan-style production system, which developed in Japan, was transferred to local plants and how they in turn adapted it to suit the local situation. This part also examines how this move made an impact on the US's Big Three, especially on the systems of their plants.

Chapter 3 offers a multidirectional analysis into the reality of global competition in the 1990s, and this is a significant chapter, as it looks toward the future. This chapter covers the revival and reinstatement of Europe and the US's automotive industries in the 1990s, as well as the IT revolution and the realities and problems of global strategies which made the revival of the automotive industries possible. Furthermore, this chapter summarizes the deterioration of the international competitiveness of Japan's automotive industry and its restructuring. These happened because of the appreciation of the yen and the collapse of the bubble economy in the first half of the 1990s, something the Japanese automotive industry had not experienced before. This part also shows what Japanese auto makers learned from this bitter experience and how they went global. Chapters 4 and 5 cover the global reconstruction of the automotive industry, and the relocation of the auto-parts industry. These chapters analyze how the *keiretsu* auto-parts transaction, which was one of the strong points of Japanese manufacturing, changed.

Chapters 6 and 7 examine auto-related business in Asia, which has drawn particular attention in recent years. The examination starts with ASEAN, where Japan has a strong presence, and then it looks into the prospects for China's automotive industry (where the influence of Japan's automotive industry is becoming apparent, especially in recent years), and the strategies adopted by Japan's auto makers against China.

Based on this discussion, in Chapter 8 special consideration is given to the future prospects for and tasks of Japan's automotive industry. A historical summary and a retrospective of the automotive industry in the world are attempted, while acknowledging the important changes that are taking place.

The last quarter of the twentieth century was an era in which the world automotive industry experienced a period of dynamic and dramatic change before it went global. Change occurred in various areas, including the engineering of cars, production systems, development systems, supplier systems, sales/distribution systems, the social system around cars, and the business system which utilizes this social system. A number of field surveys, including factory studies and interviews, in addition to both domestic and international documents, were needed for organizing the history of the ever-changing auto industry before it was globalized. I had no opportunity to visit the US until April 1977, just after I published my book *The Business History of the U.S. Automobile Industry* (Toyo Keizai Shinpo-Sha, 1977). This opportunity was realized through support from the senior and junior members of Hosei University. During the stay, I studied under Professor A. D. Chandler, the leading authority on US business history, at the Harvard Business School, and with Professor W. J. Abernathy I began fact-finding surveys about friction in the Japan–US auto industry as well as international competition. Sadly, Professor Abernathy passed away in 1983 and I lost an important colleague. However, based on the awareness I shared with the late Professor Abernathy, I joined the IMVP at MIT, and at the same time I conducted field surveys by visiting auto makers in the US, Europe, and Japan.

Conducting such field surveys, I received understanding and cooperation from almost all of the auto makers inside and outside of Japan as well as from their suppliers, and I could share knowledge and awareness with them. Since the 1990s, as a member at the GERPISA convention, I have had close communications with researchers of the European auto industry through research presentations and field surveys.

My thirty-year field surveys and the research outcomes of two international automobile research projects are reflected in this book. For this, I would like to express my thanks to GM, Ford, DaimlerChrysler AG, VW, BMW, Renault, PSA, Fiat, Hyundai, Kia, Toyota, Nissan, Honda, and other Japanese auto makers, and suppliers including Delphi, Visteon, Bosch, Denso, NHK Spring, and Akebono Brake Industry. All of these companies kindly helped me in door-to-door surveys and factory studies. I would also like to express my thanks to Professors D. Roos, J. P. McDuffie, and M. Freyssenet, who were in charge of the two international projects, and the other researchers who were the main members of the projects.

Here, I would like to emphasize the fact that without instruction and help from the Japanese government, industrial circle, and my research partners, I could not have completed this book. I was able to continue my research and along with many other young researchers I shared in the bounty of a Grant-in-Aid for Scientific Research and International Academic Research from the Grant-in-Aid for Scientific Research of the Ministry of Education and Science. I would like to express my thanks to the Japan Society for the Promotion of Science.

Professor Takahiro Fujimoto of the Graduate School of Economics, Faculty of Economics, University of Tokyo was my research partner for more than thirty years and he supported my research surveys and provided me with much shrewd knowledge. My gratitude to him is beyond all description. I worked with him on the two projects and the field surveys which were conducted both inside and outside of the country, and he stimulated me greatly. He has become a world-class Japanese researcher, and I wish him continuing outstanding success. I would also like to thank the young researchers of the Fujimoto Office for their support.

My co-researchers supported me in the two projects under the grants for scientific research, and I have received valuable teaching in particular from Professor Akira Takeishi of Kyoto University, Professor Kentaro Nobeoka of Hitotsubashi University, Kiyohiko Nishimura, a former Professor of Tokyo University and Deputy

Governor of the Bank of Japan, Professor Hiromi Shioji of Kyoto University, and Associate Professor Masataka Morita of Meijigakuin University.

I wish to thank the research members and other members of the industrial circle who are involved with my research groups, especially the "Study group of the future of the production system" and the "Japan study group on car distribution." I also thank the members of The Japan Association for the Research on Automotive Affairs, where I have acted as chairman for a long time, and also Ryuji Fukuda and Tetsuo Kubo, who have supported the head office of The Japan Association for the Research on Automotive Affairs.

Many senior members and associates of the academic meetings I have been involved with have been very supportive. Tadashi Mito, a senior member of the study group of my late teacher Katsuzo Baba, taught me a kind of ethos in academic research. I would also like to express my thanks to emeritus Professor Minoru Harada of Kyushu University, emeritus Professor Yasuo Okamoto, graduate school Professor Ikujiro Nonaka of Hitotsubashi University, graduate school Professor Takayuki Itami of Hitotsubashi University, the four previous presidents of Japanese Business History Society, Professor Keiichiro Nakagawa, Professor Hidemasa Morikawa, Professor Hiroaki Yamazaki, Professor Mataro Miyamoto. And I am very thankful to Professor Kazuo Wada of Tokyo University, emeritus Professor Moriaki Tsuchiya, Professor Yotaro Yoshino of the Harvard Business School, and graduate school Professor Hirotaka Takeuchi of Hitotsubashi University.

I would like to thank the Japan Automobile Manufacturers Association, Inc., the Japan Auto Parts Industries Association, the Japan Automobile Dealers Association, former Chancellor Tadao Kiyonari of Hosei University, everyone in the Faculty of Business Administration of Hosei University, and everyone in the Innovation Management Research Center. I would like to express my thanks to Chancellor Tadao Murase of Tokaigakuen University and everyone in the Faculty of Business Administration and the Secretariat of the same university. I hope for the further prosperity of this university, which carries the theory and academic culture of human coexistence based on the Jodo shu of Buddhism.

Also, I would like to thank Dr. Hajimu Ikeda of Union Press for his negotiations with Cambridge University Press, and Dr. Hiroshi Ikeda,

Ms. Kako Richards, and Professor Ian Richards, who were engaged in the production of the English manuscript of this book.

Finally, I would like to thank my family, especially my wife, Michiko, Masatoshi Hirabayashi (my son-in-law), Momoko (my daughter), and Hanako (my grand-daughter), who have been supporting my research and field surveys for a long time. Without their encouragement and support, especially since my illness three years ago, I could not have completed this book.

Koichi Shimokawa

Introduction

The world's automobile industry was on the verge of significant change at the start of the twenty-first century. Automobile industries, typically in developed nations, accounted for 10 percent or more of each nation's gross national product (GNP), and the industry as a whole marked its 100th anniversary in 1985.[1] Over the years, the global automobile industry has experienced perpetual change.

Although the automobile was invented in Europe, mass production as the basis for mass marketing was developed and established in the United States. Everyone would agree that the Ford System of mass production was the influence behind the beginning of mass marketing. The Ford System, initiated by the emergence of the Ford Model T in 1908, was established by 1913. It later became the fundamental paradigm for production systems in the US automobile industry and was then transferred to advanced countries, including those in Europe, Japan, and other Asian nations, and adapted into its current state. In the US, mass production inherited from the Ford System was followed by a more marketing-oriented paradigm shift, from the simple mass production system limited to manufacturing a single model like the Model T to the full-line mass production system created by A. P. Sloan of GM, which responds better to a mature market. Some regard it as the "coexistence of Fordism and Sloanism."[2] The US automobile industry developed under these two paradigms. Europe, meanwhile, was influenced by the Ford style of mass production, yet maintained a tradition of craftsman-like automobile manufacturing to a certain extent, which today remains in the manufacture of luxury models and sports cars. While accepting Ford-style mass production, European automobile manufacturing mainly concentrated on compact vehicles with monocoque bodies.

In contrast to the mass production models that were developed in Western countries, the automobile industry in Japan, which was the last to join the developed nations, gathered mass production manufacturing techniques from both the European and US systems, but generated a production system different from both. This is called the Japanese production system or just-in-time (JIT) manufacturing. A further development based on this system is lean manufacturing, which took shape by absorbing automotive product development systems and supplier systems of *keiretsu* companies. In this book, lean manufacturing and just-in-time are treated as synonyms to describe the Japanese production system. Similarly, although Toyota refined this system to a higher level, we also regard production systems by Nissan, Honda, and other Japanese automobile manufacturers as practiced systems, though achievements and activities vary. It is well known that the Japanese production system had a huge impact and created a paradigm shift in the world's automotive manufacturing in the last quarter of the twentieth century.

The significance of the Japanese production system is its antithesis, which exposed the ill effects of mass production with high-volume manufacturing focusing only on economy of scale, rather than the elimination of wasted resources through streamlined production. How the Japanese production system came to overtake the prevailing Ford-style mass production system is described later in this book. The Japanese system, which began by committing to just-in-time production and synchronized manufacturing that manufactured what, when, and how much was necessary and eliminated wasteful processes and stock, brought a new paradigm. This ended the vicious cycle of stockpiles and forecast-based production characterized by the chain reactions of mass production and mass sales, and dissolved the rigidity of production where only existing products continued to be manufactured with existing technology. The Japanese production system also came to greatly influence parts manufacturers, trading systems, and even lean product development.

When taking a bird's-eye view of the global automobile industry in the last quarter of the twentieth century, the impact of lean production on international competition should be highlighted, emphasizing that the system itself was faced with internationalization/globalization, challenged in its international universality, and had to evolve and transform as it was transferred across national boundaries. Looking back on the past twenty-five years, history reveals the US automotive industry's critical phase in the early 1980s, triggered by the second oil crisis, the Japan–US inversion, the internationalization period among Japanese automobile manufacturers as they built plants in other countries in response to the automobile trade conflict between Japan and the US, and the strong yen appreciation following the Group of Five agreement in September 1985. In the 1990s, we can see that globalization of the world's automobile industry had become inevitable, and the revival of automobile manufacturers in Western nations, especially those in the US, is noteworthy. The key elements of their successful revival were their adoption and adaptation of the lean production system, their prompt adoption of Information Technology (IT) innovations, and their development of global strategy-building capabilities. Japanese auto makers that seemed to have reached the top of the world experienced a relative decline in international competitiveness in the first half of the 1990s due to a second period of strong yen, the collapse of the "bubble economy," and paralyzed financial systems. Although the level of decline varied from one Japanese manufacturer to another, in general what made a difference was the lack of strategy-building capabilities, which was due to ignoring changes in the global environment and the IT revolution.

When global restructuring of the world's automobile industry arrived as an extension to the revival of European and US automobile manufacturers in the 1990s and their new global strategies, two points of view emerged among journalists and academics, both within and outside Japan. One was that the world's automobile manufacturers would be aggregated into four or five manufacturers, and the accompanying economies of scale beyond national borders would have absolute meaning. This evolved into a "4 million unit scale club" theory that concluded that only those manufacturers with an annual production capacity of 4 million vehicles could survive. This theory spread on its own, without a clear source or authenticity.[3] The other view was that lean manufacturing would became a thing of the past as new business models emerged due to the IT revolution.[4]

However, the recent status of the world's automobile industry seems to display the flimsiness and the fallacy of these arguments. For example, how did Ford and GM, which individually acquired so many overseas brands, dip so far into the red? Why was it necessary for the two companies to implement corporate downsizing of their North US businesses in order to extricate themselves from the red, despite the fact that the North US market did not show the expected considerable decline in the aftermath of the terrorist attacks of 9/11? Why are we not seeing any

discernible results coming out of the Daimler–Chrysler merger, which
was a major focus of global restructuring? More specifically, why is the
North American Chrysler division in the red? On the other side, how
have the Japanese automobile manufacturers as a whole (not just the top
companies like Toyota and Honda), which only recently caught up with
the IT revolution and are rebuilding lean manufacturing, increased profits and gained their largest share ever in North America?

Looking at these very recent trends, these phenomena are not simply
incidental or temporary – no one could deny that at the depth of the
phenomena, the paradigm proposed by lean production still exists.

In this book, the author examines the generation and the progress of
lean production in the last quarter of the twentieth century and attempts
to demonstrate the process of its globalization, incorporating the competitive relationships and strategies among the automotive industries in
Japan, Europe, and the US. The author also aims to explore the most
desirable evolutional direction of lean production as the world's automobile industry faces a turning point in the twenty-first century. The
author humbly admits that it is beyond his ability to write a complete
treatise on a theme of such magnitude in one attempt, yet wishes to
approach it by reflecting as much as possible on the knowledge gained
through research, studies, and numerous international conferences,
both within and outside Japan over the past twenty-five years.

The automobile industry in the twenty-first century faces challenges
that extend beyond the framework of automotive technology, such as
the prevention of global warming by committing to zero emissions as
part of a concerted effort toward issues concerning the global environment, eradication of wasted resources and environmental degradation
through mass production, sales, and disposal, and the realization of a
fail-safe transportation system. It is necessary to cooperate in establishing the automobile industry in developing countries in areas such as
Asia, while at the same time preventing environmental destruction and
damage. A new evolution is required, where lean production can be
implemented beyond the realm of technological innovation to contribute to reforming distribution, logistics, recycling, and even social
systems. As a new paradigm develops with global universality, the
automobile industry can establish a new industrial system and paradigm that adds social responsibility to its automobile civilization.

Under such a vision, Chapter 1 examines how Japan gained a competitive edge at the beginning of the 1980s by comparing productivity

between Japanese and US automotive industries and by exploring the factors that drove improvements in Japanese productivity and quality.

Chapter 2 focusses on the second half of the 1980s and analyzes the real status of internationalization of the Japanese automobile industry and offshore production, including the transfer of Japanese production systems to overseas plants, with case studies based on field surveys. In the analysis, the author provides a generalized view on the beginnings of overseas production, the localization of management, the expansion of local parts-procurement ratios, and the localization of product development, based on many field surveys and interviews conducted between the second half of the 1980s and the first half of the 1990s. In Chapter 3, the author analyzes the impact of local production and lean production on the production, supplier, and development systems of the Big Three plants.

Chapters 4 and 5 reveal the background behind the birth of lean production, which drew the world's attention while the Japanese automotive industry was internationalizing. The international penetration of this system and its evolutionary process are also discussed, relating these issues to current problems such as automation of manufacturing processes.

The remainder of the book deals with the changes the automotive industry went through during the acceleration in global competition during the 1990s, and reveals how the automobile manufacturers of the West regained their strength and how the Japanese production system played a role in the recovery of Western automobile manufacturers. It also reveals the global restructuring of the automobile industry and the reality of the structural transformation in the automotive parts industry. Changes in supplier systems and, in relation to those changes, how businesses among *keiretsu* companies that used to be regarded as the strength of Japan are changing are analyzed. Based on the author's field surveys, the real condition of the European automobile industry, which is rebuilding its strategy after entering the globalization era, is examined, and the current situations, problems, and outlook for the Chinese and Asian automobile industries, which are considered to have the largest potential for growth, are explored.

Having examined the very dynamic developments in the world's automotive industry during the quarter century from the second half of the 1970s, the book concludes by examining the twenty-first century outlook for the world's automobile industry in a time of complete globalization and problems for the Japanese automobile industry. The author admits that the research subject of this book is too broad; however, there are a few key words that appear frequently, namely "production system" and "supplier system," which are aspects of the Japanese automobile industry that support its competitiveness even today. "Distribution and sales system" can be added to the list, as there are many associated unsolved/untapped issues with the advent of the information age. The author asks the reader to consider that a consistent theme of competitive strategy analysis – the impact of globalization/internationalization on Japanese as well as the world's automobile manufacturers – exists throughout this book, and invites the reader to join in considering what changes and evolutions the automobile industry of Japan, a latecomer to the industry, has been going through, what these changes mean, and what problems the industry will face in the future.

Notes

1. Although there are several stories concerning the birth of the automobile, Europe leads the invention efforts. Among the European inventors, Karl Benz and Gottlieb Daimler of Germany were the first to present to the world a car powered by an internal combustion gasoline engine. In 1885 a prototype was built, hence the basis for claiming it is the year the car was invented (K. Shimokawa, *The Business History of the U.S. Automobile Industry*, Toyo Keizai Shinpo Sha, 1977, p. 12). In 1985, Daimler-Benz held a sizable ceremony in Germany in commemoration of the one hundredth anniversary of the invention and invited individuals involved in the automotive industry from all over the world.

2. The first person to use these terminologies was Emma Rothschild. See her only work concerning the US automotive industry, *Paradise Lost – The Decline of the Auto Industrial Age*, Random House, 1973, pp. 33–51. Her book is mentioned in detail in Chapter 7 of the author's own book introduced above, where the author quotes her. Emma Rothschild's terminologies were also quoted by Robert Boyer, the leading member of the French Regulation School and a leading figure of GERPISA.

3. Jack Nasser, the former chief executive officer (CEO) of Ford Motors, reportedly said in a press conference at the Detroit Motor Show that the automobile industry of the world would be aggregated into four or five companies. Undoubtedly, at some point many other leaders of the industry as well were influenced by this thought. For arguments concerning this point, see T. Fujimoto, "Economics class column, Automobile industry: quality first," *Nihon Keizai Shimbun*, April 19, 1999; K. Shimokawa,

"Global amalgamation and flexible production system," *Daily Automotive Newspaper*, May 15, 1999.

4. Martin Kenney, in a book he coauthored (M. Kenny and M. Florida, *Beyond Mass Production*, Oxford University Press, 1993), presents his excellent study on production systems and supplier systems of overseas factories of Japanese companies. However, he expresses his lack of interest in the Japanese-style production system, as it was a thing of the past, in a return email to the author's invitation to a symposium sponsored by the Industrial Information Center of Hosei University in 1999.

1 | Comparing productivity of the Japanese and US automobile industries

This chapter was first published in 1982. Though more than twenty years have passed since its publication, there is still significant meaning in the author's analysis and the indications made by W. J. Abernathy and others about the reversion of competitiveness in the Japan–US automobile industry and the factors caused by the reverse in the view of Japan–US comparisons in productivities. The history of international competitiveness in the Japan–US automobile industry since then, and the contemporary lessons from the theory put forward by Abernathy, are briefly described in the addendum.

1. Introduction

The US automobile industry deteriorated markedly in the early 1980s due to the effects of the first oil shock of 1973, fuel regulations introduced under the 1975 energy conservation law, and the second oil shock in 1979. During 1980 and 1981, the Japanese automobile industry reached production levels of 100 million units per year and became a strong international competitor, resulting in increased protectionism in the US and Europe.

While struggling to protect themselves against Japanese competition, US and European auto manufacturers began to search for the reasons behind Japan's success. Even though the deterioration in the competitive power of the US automobile industry could be directly attributed to the energy crisis, government policies, and changes in the US market environment, it was widely agreed in business and industrial circles and amongst scholars that the resulting fall in productivity was clearly due to structural causes.[1] Furthermore, this was not limited to the automobile industry but also included iron and steel, textile, electric, and other industries. The need to learn from Japan was recognized, and this led to the subsequent influence of lean production revolution systems in US business circles.

How did the productivity gap between the two countries emerge? What new features of the competition between the US and Japan made this gap so conspicuous? To investigate and compare all aspects of automobile production in both countries, it is important to analyze the characteristics of the automobile industry overall as well as to study how each country addressed productivity problems during that period. But while the automobile industry overall can be used to represent the productivity of each country, there are numerous, inextricably linked factors that underlie that productivity. At the root of the productivity gap between Japan and the US in the early 1980s lay differences in production methods and in industrial behavior. We also have to consider these issues in the light of abrupt changes in automobile technology and technological innovations, and the fact that, in response to the oil shock, intensifying worldwide competition was centered on inexpensive small cars.

This chapter begins with the analysis of a set of indices that is thought to relate to productivity in the US and Japan, and goes on to discuss the reasons why the gap in productivity occurred. The significance of the new technological competition is explored by relating these indices to investment behavior and innovations in process technology. The conditions under which the Japanese auto industry might sustain its relative comparative advantage, and those under which it might break down, are examined. International adoption of the Japanese production and supplier systems, including localized manufacturing by Japanese industries in the US and US–Japan joint ventures, is discussed from the perspective of its impact on the recovery of US manufacturing industries.

2. Japanese automobile production from the viewpoint of economic indices

When discussing automobile production in the US and Japan, the indices most often used are sales volume, investment capital, or profit. The indices of sales volume and worldwide profit rankings have always been an issue, and it is only recently that the investment capital and scale of business have started to be considered as symbolic of international competitiveness. However, if we equate the marked fall in business performance with the fall in competitiveness of the US automobile industry in the early 1980s, it becomes quite clear why we cannot depend on nominal quantitative indices to predict the competitiveness of a business or industry.

In 1981, the true state of affairs was that GM, with a world ranking of number one, faced losses of $800 million; Ford, the second largest automobile maker in the world and ranked fifth in sales, faced a deficit of $2 billion; and Chrysler, which had been in the best ten in the world for the previous three years, had a cumulative deficit of $4 billion. Until 1978, three years earlier, it was widely thought that the high-profit financial structure of the US automobile industry was associated with a high level of technological achievement and high productivity. However, looking at the very serious deficits accumulating in Detroit at this time, one cannot help but think that the reality was radically different. Even if one accepts that the industry was affected by strict government policies regarding fuel efficiency and the rapid shift toward small cars in the US market, the question is then whether, if the standards of technology and productivity had been higher to start with, the situation would not have been so grave.

So what drove the high-profit financial structure of the US automobile industry until that period? In short, it was the oligopolistic structure in Detroit, which supported the production of large vehicles for the US market.[2] The high profit margin on large cars, of at least 18–24%, and the absolute profit figures of over three times, were guaranteed because the three car makers had a monopoly on large-car production.[3] Automobile production, under the umbrella of the Detroit monopoly, was protected from international competition, so poor technological standards and falls in productivity were hidden behind the high-profit structure.

In comparison with the situation in the US, the Japanese automobile industry was showing remarkable growth and international competitiveness, and was establishing a reputation for high productivity and high quality. Mass production of passenger cars in Japan had started after the Second World War, strengthening from the latter half of the 1950s. Although car production in Japan started to develop much later than in Europe and the United States, the Japanese domestic market grew rapidly from the late 1960s until the first oil shock of 1973, and the late 1970s saw a rapid increase in exports, especially to the US, growing to about 1 million vehicles per year. The Japanese automobile industry thus became the strongest automobile industry in terms of international competitiveness.

Of course, Japan's strong international competitiveness was founded on high technical standards and high productivity, but to compare productivity and manufacturing in Japan and the US using business indices means we have to decide how to define productivity and what kind of business indices to fit on to it. The concept of productivity itself is governed by various factors, such as the progress of the information society, social costs, and increases in environmental costs. There is also a trend to use ambiguous aspects such as work ethics and group management as indices, which cannot be quantified.

It is important to keep in mind the various elements that prevent simplistic comparisons. Among the differences in production methods between Japan and the US, the most typical is the percentage of parts produced in-house and the relationship between the maker and the various parts manufacturers. Furthermore, even within the same automobile industry there are other confounding elements, such as the industries that produce raw materials, the relationships between other related industries, labor–management relations, differences in work practices, etc., which make quantification and standardized comparisons difficult. However, here we will use simple and realistic elements, and define productivity as value added per person, as shown in the box below. In this case, value added has varying definitions, but here our premise is to add business profits, financial income, and depreciation as well as labor costs. (I am grateful for the cooperation of Yukio Suzuki of Nomura Souken in the use of this framework and calculation.)

Premise and framework of comparison of productivity of Japanese and US automobile makers

1. Framework of analysis

   Labor productivity = Value added / Labor = Production volume / Personnel / (number of vehicles per person) × value added / production volume / (value added per vehicle) = Production volume / Personnel / number of vehicles per person × Sales / number of vehicles / (sales per average number of vehicles) × value added / sales / rate of value added = value added / sales × production equipment / personnel × sales / production equipment

   value added / sales = (Percentage of value added)

   production equipment / personnel = (Labor equipment ratio)

   sales / production equipment = equipment utility ratio

2. Prerequisite conditions
   (1) Based on Toyota Automobile company, Nissan Automobiles
       security report
   (2) GM, Ford based on annual report
   (3) Toyota Automobile company
       (a) Final accounts as of May (74/5) for fiscal year 1973; for
           fiscal year 1974 final accounts of 13 months
       (b) Figures from Toyota Motor Sales Co. are excluded.
           Consequently, as for personnel, the 5,000 employees from
           Toyota Motor Sales Co. are excluded and so is the difference
           in sales (includes sales profit and financial commissions for
           sales) for Toyota Motor Sales Co. and Toyota Motor Co.
   (4) Business profit + financial income + depreciation + labor costs

First of all, if we look at the transition of the two companies representative of Japan and the US for value added for each employee, we get something like Figure 1.1, which shows remarkable growth for Toyota and Nissan from 1974 onwards. In contrast, GM and Ford stand out for their remarkable deterioration from 1978.

Next, comparing the production volume per employee as per Table 1.1, which also involves differences in in-house parts production percentage between Japan and the US as well as greater numbers of parts and processes for large vehicles for the US, we see that Japan, with its far lower number of employees (in 1979 Toyota had over 45,000 workers and Nissan 55,000, whereas GM had over 300,000 employees and Ford over 200,000), has by far the greater production volume. Furthermore, what is worthy of notice is that there was an 80 percent increase in growth of per head production, with Toyota showing an increase in per head production from 39.7 vehicles to 70.8 vehicles (68.7 vehicles in 1980), and Nissan showing an increase in per head production from 25.5 vehicles to 45.7 vehicles (50.54 in 1980). In contrast to this, the per head production for GM and Ford was 9–11 vehicles, or around a standard of 11–12 vehicles (9.5 vehicles, 10.1 vehicles in 1980). For domestic production in the US, GM showed a very minor and slow increase from 11.9 vehicles to a maximum of 15.4 to 12.7, and Ford from 13.7 to a maximum of 18.3 to 13.4. (We should note that the figures for Toyota were influenced by the fact that it separated into two companies during that time, Toyota Sales Company and Toyota

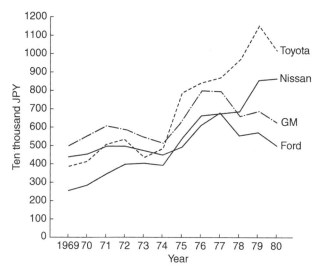

Figure 1.1 Comparison of two companies each for Japan and US for value added

Motor Company, hence the lower number of employees at Toyota. It is also important to take into consideration other makers, such as Hino Automobile Company, Daihatsu Company and Toyota Body Company, and the increase in outsourcing to related makers.)

Next, if we look at the value added per vehicle converted into Japanese yen, the increase for GM is from ¥300,000 to ¥600,000, and for Ford it is from ¥220,000 to ¥450,000, which is very high compared with the two Japanese makers at around ¥100,000 to less than ¥190,000. The remarkable difference is the prevalence of mass production of large vehicles, which gives the US the advantage. From this we can infer that the per head value added for Japan by far exceeds that of the United States, while the value added per production volume/unit for the United States is better than that of Japan. Thus we can deduce that the reason the US came top in productivity or competitiveness was due to the value added productivity per unit and scale of mass production.

Looking at the percentage of value added from Figure 1.1 (=value added/sales), the gap between the US and Japan is very large. Whereas for the two companies in Japan it is 19–15 percent vehicles, for GM it is 40 percent units and for Ford it is 30 percent units. The disparity between these figures reflects the trend of rapidly increasing sales for the two

Table 1.1 *Productivity-related indices for two US and two Japanese automobile makers*

Year		1969	1970	1971	1972	1973	1974*	1975	1976	1977	1978	1979	1980
Value added (A) (¥1 million)	Toyota	155,447	176,583	216,905	232,724	204,610	271,184 (250,324)	353,496	381,161	398,095	445,396	543,895	493,648
	Nissan	120,138	143,646	176,752	206,399	216,394	208,001	281,262	347,796	365,889	373,809	484,507	482,176
(A)/personnel (¥1 million/person)	Toyota	4.07	4.30	5.23	5.42	4.63	6.08 (5.01)	7.85	8.51	8.81	9.85	11.56	10.12
	Nissan	2.53	2.96	3.50	4.02	4.10	4.03	5.47	6.61	6.72	6.88	8.54	8.57
Per person production volume (units/person)	Toyota	39.7	42.9	48.8	51.9	49.0	54.3 (50.1)	54.6	58.3	63.4	65.0	70.8	68.7
	Nissan	25.5	29.2	33.0	37.0	37.8	35.9	41.0	43.8	43.3	42.6	45.7	50.54
Value added per person (¥)	Toyota	10.25	10.04	10.73	10.45	9.45	11.20	14.57	14.60	13.89	15.16	16.32	14.75
	Nissan	9.93	10.11	10.61	10.84	10.84	11.24	13.32	15.11	15.55	16.17	18.70	16.95
Average unit price yen/unit	Toyota	51.7	52.5	53.6	55.4	62.6	69.0	82.2	87.6	91.4	95.4	99.3	104.7
	Nissan	55.3	56.2	58.9	61.8	63.7	77.2	83.8	88.0	95.4	97.2	105.7	106.0

Table 1.1 (*cont.*)

Year		1969	1970	1971	1972	1973	1974*	1975	1976	1977	1978	1979	1980
Percentage of value added (%)	Toyota	19.8	19.1	20.0	18.8	15.1	16.2	17.7	16.7	15.2	15.9	16.4	14.1
	Nissan	18.0	18.0	18.0	17.5	17.0	14.5	15.9	17.2	16.3	16.6	17.7	16.0
Labor equipment ratio ¥1 million/person	Toyota	9.37	11.30	11.77	12.39	14.73	16.62	17.38	19.23	21.77	23.81	25.13	29.16
	Nissan	6.53	7.85	8.53	9.41	10.78	12.24	12.85	13.99	15.05	16.57	18.04	20.44
Machine utilization level (no. of times/year)	Toyota	2.19	1.99	2.22	2.32	2.08	2.26	2.58	2.66	2.66	2.60	2.80	2.47
	Nissan	2.16	2.09	2.28	2.43	2.23	2.26	2.68	2.75	2.74	2.50	2.68	2.62
Wage per person (¥1 million/year)	Toyota	1.15	1.32	1.59	1.89	2.32	3.04 (2.81)	3.07	3.46	3.76	4.12	4.46	4.74
	Nissan	0.99	1.20	1.44	1.67	2.07	2.52	2.94	3.42	3.71	3.95	4.27	4.83

Table 1.1 (*cont.*)

Year		1969	1970	1971	1972	1973	1974*	1975	1976	1977	1978	1979	1980
Value added (A) ($1 million)	GM	11,308	8,479	13,562	14,606	16,655	13,146	14,633	20,344	23,855	26,971	26,922	20,792
	Ford	5,443	5,587	6,191	7,503	8,451	7,487	7,077	9,383	12,351	13,607	12,837	9,386
(A)/personnel ($1,000/person)	GM	14.24	12.18	17.54	19.22	20.54	17.91	21.49	27.20	29.93	32.15	31.56	27.87
	Ford	12.48	12.96	14.30	16.94	17.83	16.10	17.01	21.13	25.78	26.84	25.93	22.00
Per person production volume (units/person)	GM	9.0 (11.9)	7.6 (10.3)	10.1 (13.6)	10.3 (13.9)	10.7 (14.6)	9.1 (12.3)	9.7 (13.2)	11.5 (15.4)	11.4 (15.2)	11.3 (14.8)	10.5 (13.8)	9.5 (12.7)
	Ford	11.1 (13.7)	11.1 (14.0)	11.4 (14.9)	12.6 (16.5)	12.4 (16.9)	11.3 (15.9)	11.0 (14.9)	12.0 (16.2)	13.4 (18.3)	12.7 (17.5)	11.7 (15.2)	10.14 (13.4)
Value added per person ($1,000/unit)	GM	1.58	1.60	1.74	1.87	1.92	1.97	2.21	2.37	2.63	2.84	2.99	2.93
	Ford	1.12	1.17	1.26	1.34	1.44	1.42	1.55	1.77	1.92	2.11	2.21	2.17
Average unit price ($1,000/unit)	GM	3.39	3.53	3.63	3.91	4.12	4.72	5.39	5.51	6.06	6.67	7.37	8.13
	Ford	3.04	3.14	3.33	3.61	3.92	4.49	5.25	5.44	5.89	6.62	7.49	8.57

Table 1.1 (*cont.*)

Year		1969	1970	1971	1972	1973	1974[*]	1975	1976	1977	1978	1979	1980
Percentage of value added (%)	GM	46.5	45.2	48.0	48.0	46.5	41.7	41.0	43.1	43.4	42.7	40.6	36.0
	Ford	36.9	37.3	37.7	37.2	36.7	31.7	29.4	32.5	32.6	31.8	29.5	25.3
Labor/equipment ratio $1,000/yen/person	GM	16.00	19.46	18.39	19.41	19.26	22.90	25.70	24.32	24.92	26.28	29.17	39.23
	Ford	15.54	16.72	17.68	18.54	18.64	20.38	23.82	23.08	23.21	24.54	28.82	36.46
Labor/equipment ratio converted to yen (¥1 million/per person)	GM	7.00	6.44	5.97	5.21	6.66	7.60	7.19	6.67	5.51	6.38	8.89	5.76
	Ford	6.01	6.18	5.71	5.05	5.93	7.05	6.83	6.22	5.15	6.31	8.24	5.59
Machine utilization level (no. of times/year)	GM	1.91	1.38	1.98	2.06	2.29	1.88	2.04	2.59	2.77	2.87	2.67	1.97
	Ford	2.18	2.08	2.15	2.46	2.60	2.49	2.42	2.81	3.40	3.44	3.05	2.38

Table 1.1 (*cont.*)

Year		1969	1970	1971	1972	1973	1974*	1975	1976	1977	1978	1979	1980
Wage per person ($1,000/ unit)	GM	7.93	8.99	10.37	11.41	12.71	13.31	14.73	17.26	19.16	20.50	22.10	26.06
	Ford	11.04	11.65	13.05	15.18	16.11	16.94	17.46	19.91	23.65	25.61	26.21	29.16
Wage per person converted to yen (¥1 million/ year)	GM	2.85	3.23	3.62	3.51	3.44	3.87	4.36	5.10	5.13	4.30	4.83	5.89
	Ford	3.97	4.19	4.56	4.67	4.36	4.92	5.16	5.89	6.33	5.37	5.82	6.59
Exchange rate (¥/$)		360.0	360.0	350.74	308.0	271.22	291.51	296.80	296.55	268.51	210.47	219.17	226.74

* Balance sheet calculated 13 months; within brackets is balance for 12 months.

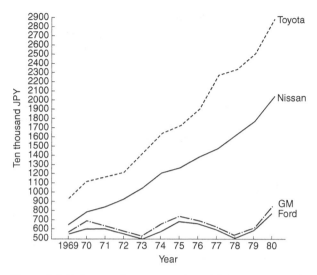

Figure 1.2 Labor equipment rate (trend for two companies each for US and Japan)

Japanese companies and the high profit structure compared with sales in the US. It is not therefore possible to compare the strength of business or productivity between Japan and the US because, when the increase in sales is considerable, it should be reflected in a fall in the rate of value added. In other words, when improvement in productivity is reflected in increased sales, there is a fall in the percentage of value added.

Figure 1.2 and Table 1.1 also give us the labor equipment ratio, which is expressed in the production equipment value per head. Converting the values to Japanese yen for GM and Ford, we see relatively low-range fluctuations, going from 5.76 and 5.59 million respectively in 1969 to peaks of 7.60 and 7.05 million respectively in 1975 and then falling again until 1978. In contrast to this, the labor equipment ratios for Toyota and Nissan in 1969 were 9.37 million and 6.53 million respectively, and these more than doubled in just ten years, rising to 23.8 million for Toyota and 16.57 million for Nissan. The largest gap in the labor equipment ratio was in 1980 and 1981, after which time US car makers started to make extensive investments in modernizing plant and building factories to produce small cars. Figures have been corrected to take account of disparities such as the large-scale layoffs due to economic recession and the closing of old production plants and idling of equipment.

Lastly, comparing Japan and the US in terms of equipment utilization rate, we can see greater increases for the two US companies than for the two Japanese companies, with GM going from 1.38 to 2.87 and Ford from 2.08 to 3.44, whereas Toyota's equipment utilization rate increased from 1.99 to 2.60, and Nissan's from 2.09 to 2.74. It is not possible to acknowledge a definite gap between the US and Japan regarding these figures, because, for the US companies, the absolute value of production equipment as well as sales were centered on production of large vehicles.

It is also worth noting from the absolute values of production equipment and tangible fixed assets shown in Table 1.2 and Figure 1.3 that, in 1969, the figure for GM was thirteen times that of Toyota, and for Ford was eight times that of Nissan. Over a span of ten years, this gap was largely reduced, and by 1978 GM had dropped to four and a half times that of Toyota and, in 1979, Ford was three times that of Nissan.

However, it is self-evident that it is not possible to judge the relative differences in productivity on the basis of a simple comparison of production equipment value. This is because factors such as the frequency of renewal of production equipment, the ratio between new and old equipment, the genuine production capacity of the equipment, and equipment productivity measured in terms of effective labor hours are not reflected by the monetary production equipment value. There is the tacit implication that the reason why the gap in production equipment value between the US and Japan decreased rapidly was due to the fact that, despite the small scale of the Japanese businesses, the latter invested in relatively new equipment with high efficiency. In comparison with this, as documented in a large number of publications and surveys, the US automobile businesses continued to focus on trying to preserve old plant facilities, replacing machine tools used to produce large vehicles when it came to renewing equipment, or simply increasing the models in order to continue variety marketing.[4]

We can therefore see several limitations when comparing business indices concerning productivity obtained from public-domain financial charts. These arise from the fundamental differences in the prerequisites of these values,[5] and the fact that the indices themselves cannot be directly connected to productivity and efficiency. The Japanese automobile makers were able to establish a lead over their US counterparts in terms of labor productivity ratio and per person production volume,

Table 1.2 *Trends for the two companies each of US and Japan for production equipment, tangible fixed assets*

Year	1969	1970	1971	1972	1973	1974	1975	1976	1977	1978	1979	1980
GM ($1m)	12,700	13,546	14,242	14,748	15,616	16,808	17,504	18,192	19,861	22,052	24,879	29,269
GM (¥1m)	4,572,000	4,063,800	4,984,700	4,542,300	4,231,900	4,891,100	5,181,100	5,384,800	5,322,748	4,630,900	5,448,500	6,699,063
Ford ($1m)	6,776	7,207	7,657	8,212	8,837	9,476	9,908	10,248	11,116	12,444	14,264	15,567
Ford (¥1m)	2,439,300	2,162,100	2,679,900	2,529,200	2,394,800	2,748,000	2,932,700	3,033,400	2,979,000	2,613,200	3,213,800	3,533,709
Toyota (¥1m)	357,763	463,479	488,033	531,911	651,321	740,764	772,934	861,249	984,143	1,077,187	1,182,735	1,421,580
Nissan (¥1m)	309,649	381,787	430,336	483,577	569,282	631,474	661,005	735,574	818,650	923,849	1,022,758	1,150,712

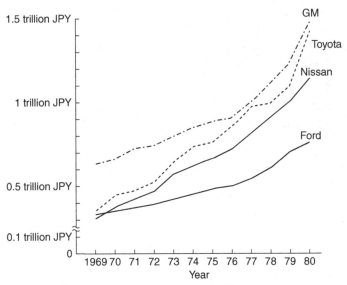

Note: The US was measured at 4.4 times that of Japan

Figure 1.3 Trends for the two companies each of the US and Japan for production equipment and tangible fixed assets

and this was despite the fact that Japan fell far below the mark with respect to the absolute value of production equipment. Both Japanese companies were able to overtake the US companies with respect to value added per person, or labor productivity.

The predominant viewpoint was that Japan achieved superior labor productivity because wages were lower, despite the impact of drastic land subsidies in Detroit. However, if we take the manpower cost of employees including managers and divide it and assign it per employee, then we see that the gap of nearly three times in per head yearly wages that existed in 1969 was between ¥4 million and ¥5 million per head, approaching 80% of the US wages (Table 1.3 and Figure 1.4).

We should also keep in mind that the reduction in manpower due to huge layoffs in 1980 contributed to the rise in per head wages for the two companies in the US. If we base our comparisons on documents/ materials from the labor union for labor union members, the monthly wages, though dependent on the type of work, show similar trends (Tables 1.4, 1.5, and 1.6).

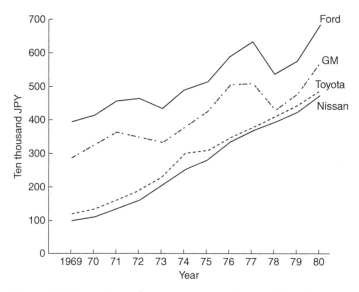

Figure 1.4 Comparison of two companies each in the US and Japan for trends in per head wages

Now let us look at other US–Japan automobile production data that relate to wages for comparing labor distribution rates where labor distribution rate = labor cost (encompasses fringe benefit cost) / rough value added × 100 and capital share = (financial expenditure – financial revenue + dividend distribution + small stock holder + write-offs) / rough value added × 100. The gap in the labor distribution rate reduced from 1972 over the next six years, even though it increased for Japan, but upon reaching 1975 completely reversed and continued to fall until the close of 1980 (see Table 1.5). The rise in wages in Japan is reflected in the narrowing of the gap in labor distribution rate between Japan and the US. The reversal of capital share in Japan reflects the constraints in dividend distribution and the shrinking of allotment due to increases in the proportion of self-financing. Compared with this, the US showed an increase in financial costs and dividend payout ratio.

Going beyond the automobile industry to include the wage index, labor productivity index, and wage cost index for the US and Japan from 1970 until 1978 using 100 as the baseline index for 1970 gives us more information (see Table 1.6). Here it is clear that the increase in the

Table 1.3 *Trends in average monthly wages of eleven automobile makers in the US and Japan*

(Units: yen in upper rows and dollar in lower rows)

	1970	1971	1972	1973	1974	1975	1976	1977	1978	1979	1980
Monthly wages	89,795	101,637	118,644	145,735	179,279	192,279	220,696	249,269	265,803	288,753	308,682
	249.4	291.6	390.0	534.3	611.7	646.6	741.6	924.8	1,399.0	1,312.5	1,265.1

Source: Japan Auto Workers' Union data

Table 1.4 *Trends in wages of UAW standard union members*

		1975	1976	1977	1978	1979
Assembly	Hourly wage	5.43	6.89	7.09	7.30	9.13
	Monthly (USD)	868.80	1101.600	1134.40	1168.00	1460.80
	Monthly (yen)	257,800	327,000	305,000	221,900	321,200
Tool manufacture	Hourly wage	7.01	8.66	9.02	9.29	11.19
	Monthly (USD)	1121.60	1385.60	1443.20	1486.40	1790.40
	Monthly (yen)	332,900	411,300	388,100	282,300	393,800

Source: Japanese Auto Workers' Union "Organization and Operation of U. A. W.," p. 43

Table 1.5 *Trends in US–Japan labor and capital distribution rate*

		1972	1973	1974	1975	1976	1977
Distribution to labor (%)	Average of two Japanese companies	34.51	42.50	57.72	45.56	42.10	44.74
	Average of three US companies	59.91	62.74	71.61	67.42	59.69	60.66
Distribution to capital (%)	Average of two Japanese companies	22.21	19.48	26.29	16.63	9.31	8.68
	Average of three US companies	17.53	16.61	18.55	18.91	17.80	17.12

Source: Japanese MITI Industrial Policy Bureau "Finance Analysis of World Enterprise," 1975, pp. 77–78

wage rate was almost double for Japan, and yet the rise in wages and the labor productivity matched, whereas this was not the case in the US, thus confirming that, compared with the increase in the wage index, the productivity index showed a tendency to remain stagnant.

Table 1.6 *Japan–US comparison of wage labor productivity*

	Japan			United States		
Year	Wage index	Labor productivity index	Wage cost index	Wage index	Labor productivity index	Wage cost index
1970	100.0	100.0	100.0	100.0	100.0	100.0
1971	115.6	103.4	111.8	106.6	105.4	101.1
1972	134.6	113.8	118.3	114.1	110.9	102.9
1973	166.6	131.2	126.9	122.1	114.1	107.0
1974	219.1	133.2	164.5	130.7	114.8	113.9
1975	252.2	128.4	196.4	142.3	114.7	124.1
1976	271.1	140.9	192.4	153.9	122.2	125.9
1977	295.9	147.3	200.9	167.1	124.7	134.0
1978	313.2	159.2	196.7	181.8	127.3	142.8
Average rate of increase (%) for 1971–1978	+15.3%	+6.0%	+8.8%	+7.8%	+3.1%	+4.6%

Notes:
1. Cost is per manufacturing time
2. Wage cost index is as calculated by authorities from wage index/labor productivity index
Source: Bank of Japan "International comparative statistics," 1980

3. Labor productivity in the Japanese automobile industry

Despite the various limiting factors described above, if we compare the Japanese and US automobile businesses using financial indices, we can confirm the sluggish growth of the latter – indicated by deterioration in international competitiveness and stagnancy in labor productivity – for the ten years leading to 1980, and the contrasting rise in international competitiveness and labor productivity of the Japanese automobile industry. We can also make the assumption that the difference is based not on temporary factors such as the land subsidies in Detroit at the beginning of the 1980s, high interest rates, inflation, the rapid change in the automobile market due to rises in gasoline prices (the rapid shift in demand from large cars to small cars), or recession in

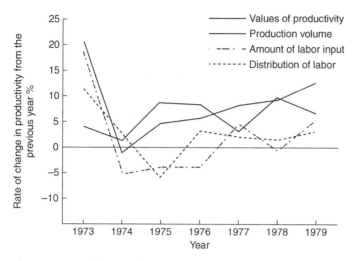

Figure 1.5 Trends in production volume and labor productivity of the Japanese automobile industry; amount of labor input manpower distribution

the automobile business, but on an accumulation of structural factors. There is no question that this is a serious issue that is also related to the strategic responses made in Detroit at that time to introduce technological innovations. But before getting into a discussion about that, let us first use some statistical data to investigate the improvement in labor productivity in the Japanese automobile industry.

In Japan, the Ministry of Labor publishes an annual report called the "Labor Productivity Statistical Survey Report," which shows labor productivity as a function of working hours for various types of industries. This report is not just a computation or analysis of value added but also includes the productivity indices and their rate of increase from the previous year based on the various departments and processes for the different industries.

Making use of these production statistics, if we look at the automobile manufacturing industry (Figure 1.5), the rate of change in productivity shows a slight decline in growth from 1973 to 1974, immediately after the first oil shock. (Production volume in 1973 changed to negative growth from the 20% increase in the previous year; but if the decrease shown in other factors, such as production volume, labor input, and labor distribution, is taken into account, then in actuality the rate of increase does not show a negative growth.) Other than the decrease in

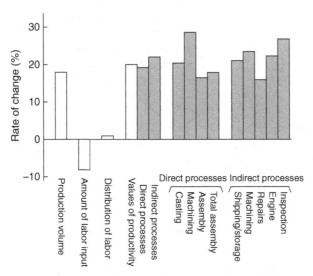

Figure 1.6a Changing standards in productivity, labor input quantity, and process-wise required labor hours of the Japanese automobile industry (1975–1978)

growth rate shown in 1977, which was due to an increase in the amount of labor input, the growth rate shows an upward trend. The most important point is that productivity never showed negative growth, and the fluctuation in growth rate showed a yearly increase of some sort. This constant incremental increase in growth rate continued following the reduction in production volume in 1974. After the deterioration in labor input and distribution of labor in 1974 and 1975, the growth rate increased slightly, but the rate of increase was lower than the production volume and productivity.

Figure 1.6a looks at changes in the values of productivity, distribution of labor, amount of labor input, and production volume during the period 1975–1978. Production volume increased by 18 percent over this period, while labor input showed an 8.5 percent reduction and the distribution of personnel grew by about only 1 percent. As a result, labor productivity increased by almost 20 percent. If we look at this increase in productivity in terms of the various processes, each process shows an increase of over 15 percent. Within this, direct processes such as machining, and indirect processes such as inspection, show increases above 25 percent.

If we take 1975 as the baseline and look at 1978 (see Figure 1.6b), production volume shows 25 percent growth against a decrease in labor

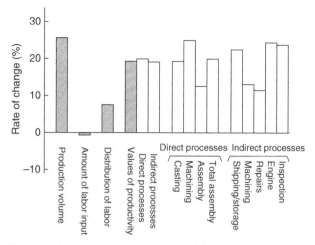

Figure 1.6b Changes in productivity, labor input quantity, distribution of labor, and labor productivity in the Japanese automobile industry (1975–1978)

input of 1 percent, and an increase in distribution of personnel of 6 percent. The result is that the increase in productivity over this period is almost the same at 20 percent.

Looking at productivity by process, there are some noticeable variations during 1973–1977. For instance, the rates of change for assembly (direct process) and repair (indirect process) were below 20 percent, while the rates for machining (direct) and inspection processes were above 25 percent. Adding the shipping and storage to this shows a progress rate of over 20 percent. Figure 1.7 looks at the process-wise growth rate of productivity for the periods of 1973–1975, 1975–1979, and 1973–1979. There are some periodic variations in the growth in machining, in the total assembly from 1973–1975, and in the rough body machining, but over the total period 1973–1979 all the processes show growth at an average rate.

The productivity data shown in Table 1.6 extend to the automobile industry in general, but now we will attempt to analyze the process-wise and shop-wise data for labor time required per vehicle by means of four tables that tabulate the increase in productivity per automobile or per small car against the previous years. First, if we look at the trend in the time required for labor per vehicle as classified by direct and indirect department, we notice that the fluctuation for the direct areas does not

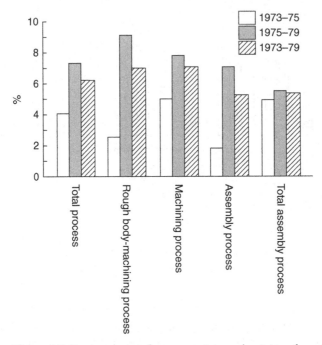

Figure 1.7 Progress rate of process-wise productivity of small passenger car factory (yearly rate)

show much variation compared with the previous fiscal years (see Table 1.7). In other words, if we exclude the 1.6% of 1967 and 1.5% of 1977, from 1966 until 1972 there is an annual increase of more than 10%. While the increase drops to around 3% in 1973 and 1974, it returns to 8–10% thereafter. Compared with this, in the indirect departments there is a great deal of variation, from the highest value of 24.2% to the lowest at –2.4%, and we do not see stability in the values before 1974. However, in these indirect departments, there is some sign of constant growth after 1977.

Next, if we look at the department-related labor time required per small car in Table 1.8, we see a constant increase compared with the previous fiscal year for the engine, which itself includes a lot of variations, and for the chassis unit. In contrast, body cabin and overall assembly show several minus values. After 1973, the few minus values are smaller, and since there is considerable improvement in the previous and following years, they do not have a great deal of influence on the

Table 1.7 *Labor time required per vehicle as per direct and indirect departments*

Year	Direct department		Indirect department		Total	
	Time	Increase from previous year	Time	Increase from previous year	Time	Increase from previous year
1966	59.55	11.9	25.38	16.5	84.93	13.4
1967	58.58	1.6	25.21	0.7	83.79	1.6
1968	52.04	11.2	19.11	24.2	71.15	13.1
1969	44.58	14.3	17.08	10.6	61.66	13.8
1970	40.08	10.1	17.50	−2.4	57.58	6.6
1971	35.45	11.6	14.49	16.6	49.94	13.3
1972	31.87	10.1	14.51	−0.1	46.38	7.1
1973	30.75	3.5	14.41	0.7	45.16	2.6
1974	29.76	3.2	14.26	1.0	44.02	2.5
1975	27.11	8.9	12.84	10.0	39.95	9.2
1976	24.74	8.7	11.93	7.1	36.67	8.2
1977	24.36	1.5	11.20	6.1	35.56	3.0
1978	21.64	11.2	10.43	6.9	32.07	9.8
1979	20.56	5.2	9.82	6.2	30.38	5.5

overall trend. However, there is a significant amount of deterioration between 1967 and 1968, which is thought to be due to the sudden increase in the type of models and the fierce competition in model changes.

Table 1.9 shows the labor time required per small vehicle for casting, machining, and assembly for the period 1966–1979. Die casting and engine machining show a slight variation, but improvement is generally constant, with only the overall assembly process recording negative values in 1972 and 1977 (the values for overall assembly are the same as those of Table 1.8). Die casting growth was negative from 1966–1968, but this is thought to be because of a particular set of circumstances due to new casting technology. Once this period was overcome, the productivity of this process showed steady growth.

Machining shows a consistent increase, although with some unevenness. Nonetheless, the improvement shown in this process overall is the highest. In 1974 and 1977, the rate of improvement in all three processes was low (for assembly it is zero or −5%), but this is reflected in the

Table 1.8 *Labor time required per vehicle as per small car automobile and department (direct departments)*

Year	Engine Time	Engine Increase from previous year	Chassis unit Time	Chassis unit Increase from previous year	Body cabin Time	Body cabin Increase from previous year	Total assembly Time	Total assembly Increase from previous year	Total Time	Total Increase from previous year
1966	11.09	-0.1	12.20	11.7	7.99	-2.0	26.54	20.8	57.82	15.0
1967	9.97	10.1	11.85	2.9	9.10	-13.9	28.02	-5.6	58.94	-1.9
1968	9.66	3.1	10.65	10.1	11.20	-23.1	16.92	39.6	48.43	17.8
1969	7.96	17.6	8.43	20.8	8.77	21.7	16.25	4.0	41.41	14.5
1970	7.72	3.0	6.92	17.9	7.50	14.5	14.98	7.8	37.12	10.4
1971	6.61	14.4	6.16	11.0	6.71	10.5	13.74	8.2	33.22	10.5
1972	6.04	8.4	5.58	9.4	6.08	9.4	12.39	9.8	30.09	9.4
1973	4.45	9.8	4.64	16.8	5.55	8.7	12.48	-0.7	28.12	6.5
1974	5.18	5.0	4.64	0.0	5.66	-2.0	12.31	1.4	27.79	1.2
1975	4.59	11.4	4.60	0.9	5.43	4.1	11.25	8.6	25.88	6.9
1976	4.02	12.4	4.27	7.2	4.90	9.8	10.20	9.8	23.39	9.6
1977	3.92	2.5	4.11	3.7	4.81	1.8	10.41	-2.1	23.25	0.6
1978	3.34	14.8	3.59	12.7	4.28	11.0	9.19	11.7	20.40	12.3
1979	3.16	5.7	3.27	9.8	3.82	12.0	8.89	3.4	19.14	6.6

Table 1.9 *Labor time required per vehicle as per model and production process (direct departments)*

Year	Casting		Machining		Assembly		Total assembly		Total	
	Time	Increase from previous year	Time	Increase from previous year	Time	Increase from previous year	Time	Increase from previous year	Time	Increase from previous year
1966	13.74	-4.9	11.76	4.5	5.78	25.4	26.54	20.8	57.82	15.0
1967	15.52	-13.0	10.69	9.1	4.71	18.1	28.02	-5.6	58.94	-1.9
1968	17.73	-14.2	9.81	8.2	3.97	15.7	16.92	39.6	48.43	17.8
1969	14.14	20.2	7.72	22.3	3.30	16.9	16.25	4.0	41.41	14.5
1970	12.32	12.9	6.58	14.8	3.24	1.8	14.98	7.8	37.12	10.4
1971	10.67	13.4	6.02	8.5	2.79	13.9	13.74	8.3	33.22	10.5
1972	9.65	9.6	5.07	15.8	2.98	-6.8	12.39	7.8	30.09	9.4
1973	8.61	10.8	4.33	12.6	2.70	9.4	12.48	-0.7	28.12	6.5
1974	8.57	0.5	4.21	2.8	2.70	0.0	12.31	1.4	27.79	1.2
1975	8.17	4.7	3.86	8.3	2.60	3.7	11.25	8.6	25.88	6.9
1976	7.35	10.0	3.42	11.4	2.42	6.9	10.20	9.3	23.39	9.6
1977	7.04	4.2	3.26	4.7	2.54	-5.0	10.41	-2.1	23.25	0.6
1978	6.19	12.1	2.78	14.7	2.24	11.8	9.19	11.7	20.40	12.3
1979	5.55	11.5	2.77	0.3	1.93	16.0	8.85	3.8	20.56	-0.7

department data as well. This period reflects the reduced output of 1977 and the peak output of 1977.

Lastly, Table 1.10 shows the labor time required for different indirect processes. The machine tool department shows a steady increase in productivity, as does the engine department. As for shipping, storage, repair, and inspection processes, the values are negative for several years in the aftermath of the first oil shock, up until 1974. After 1975, all of these areas show remarkable improvement, most notably in the engine department. This can be related to the promotion of rationalization following the oil shock in areas such as conservation of energy, shipping and inventory, repairs and inspection, etc., as well as Quality Circle activities extending to the indirect departments. Until that period, not much effort had been put into improvements in the indirect departments, but subsequently they began to systematically increase productivity.

Combining the analyzes above, it is possible to make some general observations. After the first oil shock in 1973, labor productivity as time required per vehicle started to show relatively stable growth compared with during the oil shock, when it showed extreme fluctuations. Some processes or departments, such as engine, chassis unit, and machining, showed a constant improvement in productivity even before the oil shock. Departments or processes that showed large fluctuations before the oil shock began to show trends of stability afterwards. This was especially prominent in body cabin and casting. In addition, indirect departments where fluctuations and variations were large started to show a balanced and stable improvement after the oil shock, indicative of the results of the total rationalization movement within Japanese automobile makers.

4. Changes in productivity gap and investment patterns in the Japanese and US automobile industries

If we could study data similar to that discussed above for the US, we would be able to develop a clear international comparison. However, although the Japanese Ministry of Labor based its labor productivity data collection on what was being done in the US, the US government stopped collecting this kind of data in the 1950s. Thus it is not possible to obtain similar tabulated data. Nonetheless, Table 1.11 shows the overall data concerning labor productivity for transportation

Table 1.10 *Labor time required per small vehicle as per process (indirect departments)*

Year	Shipping/storage		Machining		Repairs		Engine		Inspection		Total	
	Time	Increase from previous year	Time	Increase from previous year	Time	Increase from previous year	Time	Increase from previous year	Time	Increase from previous year	Time	Increase from previous year
1966	5.87	21.5	7.82	8.2	4.09	21.6	1.78	20.2	5.82	16.3	25.38	16.5
1967	6.13	-4.4	7.32	6.4	3.95	3.4	1.80	-1.1	6.01	-3.3	25.21	0.7
1968	4.42	27.9	5.42	26.0	3.49	11.6	1.41	21.7	4.37	27.3	19.11	24.2
1969	3.22	27.1	5.06	6.6	3.81	-9.2	1.37	2.8	3.67	17.2	17.08	10.6
1970	3.64	-13.0	4.98	1.6	3.86	-1.3	1.33	2.9	3.69	-0.5	17.50	-2.5
1971	2.80	23.1	4.09	17.9	3.11	19.4	1.25	6.0	3.24	12.2	14.49	17.2
1972	2.85	-1.8	4.01	2.0	3.15	-1.3	1.17	6.4	3.33	-2.8	14.51	-0.1
1973	2.93	-2.8	3.69	8.0	3.27	-3.8	1.15	1.7	3.37	-1.2	14.41	0.7
1974	2.90	1.0	3.48	5.7	3.88	-3.4	1.17	-1.7	3.33	1.2	14.26	1.0
1975	2.76	4.8	3.09	11.1	2.99	11.5	1.07	8.5	2.93	12.0	12.84	10.0
1976	2.45	11.2	2.92	5.5	2.96	1.0	0.96	10.3	2.64	9.9	11.93	7.1
1977	2.30	6.1	2.81	3.8	2.74	7.4	0.88	10.4	2.46	6.8	11.20	6.1
1978	3.15	6.5	2.64	6.0	2.60	5.1	0.81	5.8	2.23	9.3	10.43	5.9
1979	2.12	1.4	2.35	12.3	2.50	4.0	0.74	9.4	2.10	6.2	9.80	6.2

Table 1.11 *Input, output, productivity ratio, related to transportation equipment (1967 = 100.0)*

Year	Actual yield	Labor inputs	Investment inputs	Total inputs	Overall productivity
1948	31.0	56.3	42.5	52.8	58.8
1949	31.5	54.1	40.3	50.5	62.3
1950	41.4	58.9	42.3	54.6	75.7
1951	45.9	73.7	51.6	68.0	67.5
1952	53.3	91.6	54.5	82.0	65.0
1953	65.0	107.2	58.3	94.5	68.8
1954	59.5	90.6	60.4	82.8	71.9
1955	69.9	95.7	63.6	87.5	80.0
1956	60.6	93.8	68.6	87.3	69.4
1957	65.0	95.3	70.9	89.0	73.0
1958	53.7	81.9	68.5	78.5	68.3
1959	59.6	80.1	69.4	77.4	76.9
1960	61.2	78.4	69.0	76.0	80.6
1961	58.0	73.5	69.2	72.5	80.0
1962	68.7	80.9	71.8	78.6	87.4
1963	77.1	83.7	74.9	81.5	94.6
1964	80.9	82.5	78.4	81.4	99.3
1965	91.6	98.5	82.9	87.8	104.3
1966	99.5	98.4	91.3	96.6	102.9
1967	100.0	100.0	100.0	100.0	100.0
1968	112.8	106.8	106.3	106.7	105.7
1969	108.3	105.0	111.9	106.7	101.5
1970	88.4	88.3	110.0	93.7	94.3
1971	97.9	84.0	108.2	89.9	108.9
1972	105.4	87.3	112.8	93.5	112.7
1973	112.7	94.1	117.8	100.0	112.7
1974	96.3	86.1	120.9	94.7	101.8
1975	91.9	79.1	118.4	88.8	103.6
1976	114.7	84.4	120.0	93.1	123.2
1973 I	114.5	96.8	114.1	101.9	112.3
1973 II	114.9	94.3	115.0	100.3	114.6
1973 III	110.1	91.7	116.7	98.7	111.6
1973 IV	111.2	92.1	117.7	99.2	112.1
1974 I	100.0	85.5	118.5	94.4	106.0
1974 II	103.6	95.8	119.1	94.8	109.3
1974 III	95.2	86.8	120.3	95.8	99.4

Table 1.11 (*cont.*)

Year	Actual yield	Labor inputs	Investment inputs	Total inputs	Overall productivity
1974 IV	86.4	84.6	120.8	94.3	91.6
1975 I	76.8	76.9	118.9	88.0	87.4
1975 II	80.8	78.9	119.5	89.6	90.2
1975 III	104.8	79.7	118.9	90.1	116.3
1975 IV	105.3	79.9	118.3	90.0	116.9
1976 I	110.6	84.3	117.9	93.3	118.6
1976 II	116.6	84.6	118.3	93.7	124.4
1976 III	115.4	84.1	117.4	93.0	124.0
1976 IV	116.4	83.8	117.8	93.0	125.2

Source: J. W. Kendrick and E. S. Grossman, *Productivity in the United States*, Johns Hopkins University Press, 1980, p. 158

equipment in the US from 1948 to 1976, and there are already clear signs of deterioration toward the latter part of the 1960s. If we study the growth in financial indices and investments, we can get a better understanding of the stagnation in labor productivity in the US automobile industry, and the reasons for it.

Looking at the transition in the indices and the content of investments, we notice the lag on the part of US automobile makers to make investments relating to technological innovations and rationalization to improve productivity, or their small-vehicle strategy. The US businesses actually began to tackle this situation after the second oil shock, when they became aware of Detroit's fall in international competitiveness following the recession faced by the US automobile market (see Table 1.1, Table 1.2, Figure 1.3, and Table 1.3).

Strategic investments aimed at downsizing and introducing fuel-efficient small cars had already begun, following the energy conservation law of 1975 and the tightening of fuel efficiency requirements in 1978, but rationalization in conjunction with strategic investment started only after the second oil shock. Figure 1.8 shows the proportion of investment going into short-term equipment, such as metal molds and die tools, and Figure 1.9 shows the ratio of investments in long-term equipment against sales. The proportion of short-term investment for both GM and Ford decreased yearly, while the ratio between long-term

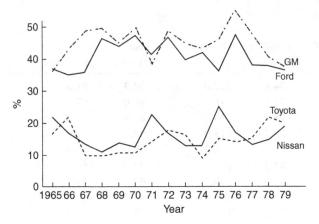

Figure 1.8 Ratio of investment occupied by short-term equipment investment (die, tools)

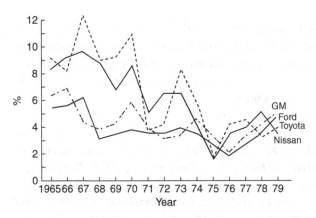

Figure 1.9 Ratio of long-term investment as per sales (equipment investment other than die, tools)

investments and sales increased annually. From the first oil shock until the end of 1976, the proportion of investment in long-term equipment fell for both companies, and investment in short-term equipment increased to its maximum. However, since then the proportion of investment in long-term equipment has increased, while the proportion of investment in short-term equipment has fallen correspondingly. All this clearly reflects the start of strategic investments in response to government regulations. But the proportion of both type of investments in 1977 and 1978 only marked a return to the levels of 1973 and 1974. After 1978, the proportion of short-term investment continued to fall while the proportion of long-term investment continued to increase. The absolute value of the total investments for GM, Ford, and Chrysler increased from $6 billion in 1977 to $9 billion in 1979 and more than $10 billion in 1980.

This indicates the seriousness of the issue for the US automobile industry from 1980 onward. Long-term investment tied to a rationalized investment strategy was emphasized only after the second oil shock, when the gap in productivity and competitiveness with Japan became very noticeable and the extent of the productivity problems influencing the regeneration of Detroit was recognised.

The timing of the change in investment strategy was more than simply a question of decisions related to investment policies for the industry. There were also structural elements, such as energy regulations, and the drastic changes in the Japan–US automobile market that had brought about a rapid change in the profit structure. In order to change from a large-vehicle focus (which largely supported the profit structure of the Detroit automobile makers) toward making small vehicles, the US automobile industry had to adopt an investment strategy that would support changes in profit structure. Detroit had for many years been assured of a market for large vehicles and thus did not compete with the automobiles of either Japan or Europe. It had therefore relied on frequent minor model changes that did not require large-scale design changes involving platform, or an increase in the number of models, so the emphasis had been on short-term investments involving tooling and die cast rather than longer-term investments into low-profit small vehicles. As pointed out earlier, rather than competing in the area of value added per person, the US companies followed the path of less risk by competing on the price of value added per vehicle. In other words, Detroit, with its high profit structure based on a large-vehicle market, tried to make up for its low productivity per person, as compared with Japan, by its high profitability per vehicle. This profit structure kept the Detroit automobile makers relying on short-term investments rather than the long-term investments that are more readily associated with increase in per person productivity.

Improvement in per person productivity is not achieved just by making long-term investments. It is self-evident that this must be accompanied by managerial efficiency in production processes, morale, quality control (QC) circles, and inventory, along with improvements in parts and material supplies, if the expected productivity increases are to be realized. Rationalization policies come to life only when the strategic long-term investment in equipment is clear and well defined. Investment in energy-saving robots and new equipment for improving productivity gained momentum in the US following the second oil shock, suggesting that the US businesses had started to map out a course where they put all their efforts into increasing their low per head productivity. This was imperative if the Detroit companies were to compensate for the low per-vehicle profitability once they moved away from producing large vehicles. The competitive conditions for the US automobile industry shifted toward an increase in productivity competitiveness initiated by innovation and production rationalization. Competition was no longer based on increasing market share but on increasing per head profit per vehicle, market segmentation, and high-level strategic shifts.

5. New aspects of competition and basic factors contributing to the productivity gap

The new competition was based on technological innovations centered on production processes for small and fuel-efficient cars, with high quality, reliability, and endurance.

As W. J. Abernathy noted, when the US automobile industry focussed solely on streamlining production in its pursuit of economy of scale and value added per vehicle for large vehicles, this resulted in a trade-off between production efficiency and innovative flexibility.[6] For example, he cites the case of the US auto industry making a huge investment in automating the manufacturing of cast-iron brake drums, which probably delayed its transition to disc brakes by more than five years. There are several other similar examples. This resulted in segmented markets focussed on large vehicles integrated with marketing that was obsessed with differentiation, based on the tacit assumption that production efficiency and quality improvement are trade-offs. As a result, quality levels deteriorated and process-related technology innovations for domestic vehicle production in the US stagnated.

Technological stagnation and monopoly conditions persisted until the US industry was faced with direct competition from small vehicles made in Europe and Japan. Direct competition emerged in both the

market and price structure, and the challenges of quality and technological innovation became paramount.

Abernathy indicates clearly how the new dimensions of competition
came to the surface and debates how this problem relates to the gap in
automobile productivity between the US and Japan.[7] Besides objectively
reviewing the superiority of Japanese auto manufacturers in production
cost and quality, he emphasizes that this advantage was not brought
about simply by the new market competitiveness arising from changing
from large-vehicle to small-vehicle production, but was largely due to
the micromanagement approach that successfully developed process-
related technological innovations.[8]

Abernathy analyzes the difference in production cost between
Japanese and US. automobile manufacturers in the following manner.
It is known that in 1974 the output per labor hour in the Japanese
auto industry (including parts suppliers) was 88% of the level of that
in the US. In the 1970s, the growth in labor productivity in the
Japanese auto industry averaged 8–9%, whereas the comparable figure for the United States was 3–4%, leading to a difference of 5%,
which gives a productivity of 1.18 for Japanese makers. Abernathy
explains that this reversal in labor productivity is partly due to the
comparative advantage of Japan in the wage rate, but points out that
much of it is due to the differences in productivity and plant management.[9] According to his analysis, in 1974 the hourly compensation
rates in Japan were about 37% of those in the United States, but by
1980 were almost 50%. Dividing the compensation ratio 0.5 by the
productivity ratio 1.18 yields a unit labor cost of 0.424. Since this
figure is the unit labor cost between Japan and the US, using
$1 - 0.424 = 0.575$ to avail of the labor cost per vehicle we arrive at
a Japanese comparative advantage cost of $2911 \times 0.575 = \$1{,}673$
(see Table 1.12). The labor cost per vehicle for the US is calculated
by adding the hourly labor at the level of the makers (original equipment manufacturer (OEM), the salaried wages, the purchased components, and the purchased materials. Subtracting tariff and freight costs
of $400, the $1,673 cost advantage derived in this manner gives us a
landed cost advantage of $1,273 on a 1980 subcompact vehicle that
sells in the US market for $5,500, i.e., a cost advantage of 23%. It is
estimated that, even with carrying out some necessary adjustments to
this, the Japanese makers would still enjoy a cost advantage of
$1,200.[10]

Table 1.12 *Calculation of US and Japanese labor costs for a subcompact vehicle*

	Share in OEM manufacturing costs	Average OEM hours per vehicle	Estimated OEM employee cost per hour	Estimated cost per vehicle (a)	Labor content (b)	Labor cost per vehicle c=a×b	US–Japan difference d= c×0.575
OEM labor hourly	0.24	65	$18	$1,170	100%	$1,170	$673
Salaried	0.08	15	21	315	100	315	181
Purchased components	0.39	NA	NA	1,901	66	1,235	721
Purchased materials	0.14	NA	NA	683	25	171	98
Total	–	–	–	$4,875	NA	$2,911	$1,673

Source: W. J. Abernathy, K. B. Clark, and A. M. Kantrow, "The new industrial competition," *Harvard Business Review*, September–October, 1981, p. 80; *Diamond Harvard Business Review*, February, 1982, p. 25

Table 1.13 *Estimated per-vehicle employee costs for Ford and Toyo Kogyo in 1979*

	Ford	Toyo Kogyo
Domestic car and truck production (in millions)	3.163	0.983
Total domestic employment	3.163	0.983
Automotive	219,599	24,318
Non-automotive	19,876	2,490
Total domestic employee hours		
Automotive in millions	355.75	46.20
Total employee costs		
Automotive in millions	$7,794.50	$482.20
Employee hours per vehicle	112.5	47.9
Employee cost per vehicle	$2,464	$491

Source: Ibid., p. 80; *Diamond*, p. 25

However, the basis of these values does not reflect the differences between the US and Japanese auto makers in their degree of vertical integration, the nature of relationships with parts suppliers or in the difference in product mix and range of vehicles. Abernathy compared the total assembly labor cost per unit (see Table 1.13).

To adjust for product mix, the cost to Ford of producing the Toyo Kogyo (now Mazda) mix was calculated by computing a weighted average to the relative manufacturing cost indices, which was found to be 1.00 for Toyo Kogyo (adjusting the vertical integration of Toyo Kogyo by 15–20%, the assembly labor cost per vehicle is increased from 47 hours to 56 hours). The result is that the gap in administrative expenses for both companies is $1,300, and if we adjust the US advantage in selling and administrative expenses, tariff and freight costs for Japanese imports, and the Japanese productivity advantage, we get a cost advantage for Japanese makers of about $1,400. In other words, Abernathy estimates that the landed cost advantage of Japanese makers calculated on the basis of micro and macro base is $1,400.[11]

Abernathy's calculations of the Japanese advantage have some inaccuracies, such as the fact that even though he uses data from 1980 for total subcompact cars, when comparing Ford with Toyo Kogyo he uses the figures from 1979. Another problem is that in comparing the wage rate between Japan and the US he underestimated it at 50%.

By expressing the 1.18 gap in productivity on the basis of output per labor hours, he also underestimates this. These problems in the basic calculations mean the real difference in wages is smaller while the productivity gap is larger. Due to the lack of sufficient data and difficulty in making quantitative adjustments, it is impossible to debate the validity of the $1,400 comparative advantage. What we can confirm, though, is that despite a high increase in wage percentage, the Japanese auto makers showed an increase in labor productivity, and a landed cost advantage of over $1,000 in the subcompact car class.

Japanese automobiles showed superiority not only in cost advantage but also in quality of assembly and finish, and in reliability and endurance, thus contradicting the conventional wisdom in the US regarding the trade-off between cost and quality. Abernathy presents consumer reports and automobile data to compare US and Japanese automobiles for quality, incidence of repairs, and consumer loyalty (see Tables 1.14a, b, and c). The data in these tables show the superior quality of Japanese automobiles and their high reliability. US customers clearly have a strong preference toward product quality and economic efficiency, as shown in Table 1.14c.[12]

Following his analysis of Japanese cost advantage and quality, Abernathy states that this advantage originates in superior strategic management, i.e., in the meticulous strategic management of people, materials, and equipment. Abernathy analyzed seven factors related to successful strategic management and which affect productivity on the basis of extensive discussions with industry executives, consultants, and engineers, and compared each with the US ones. These seven factors are: (1) process yield (includes the dimension of incorporating quality during the process to increase process productivity as adopted by Japanese auto makers), (2) quality systems, (3) process automation in technology, (4) product design, (5) managing absenteeism in the workforce, (6) job structure, and (7) work pace. He ranked these factors in terms of their relative weights as to their importance in determining their influence on productivity. Amongst these factors, product yield is the highest at 40%, showing a high influence on production, second is job structure at 18%, third is absenteeism at 12%, fourth, process automation at 10%, fifth, quality systems at 9%, sixth, product design at 7%, and finally work pace at 4%, even though the latter has been considered to influence efficiency (see Table 1.15).

Table 1.14a *Quality comparison of US automobiles versus certain imports*

Vehicle category	Condition at delivery Scale 1–10 10 is excellent		Condition after one month of service Number of defects per vehicle shipped
Size	Domestic vehicles	Imports	
Subcompact	6.4	7.9	
Compact	6.2	7.7	
Mid size	6.6	8.1	
Standard	6.8		
Domestic models			
Omni	7.4		4.10
Chevette	7.2		3.00
Pinto	6.5		3.70
Rabbit (US)[1]	7.8		2.13
Horizon	7.5		N/A
Imported vehicles			
Civic Fiesta		8.0	1.23[2] N/A
		7.9	
Colt		7.8	N/A
Corolla		7.8	0.71[3]

Notes:
[1] Average defect of European Rabbit is 1.42 defects per vehicle shipped
[2] Honda average
[3] Toyota average
Source: Rogers National Research, Buyer Profiles, 1979 and other industry sources; ibid., p. 74; *Diamond*, p. 17

What is noteworthy is that the hardware associated with technology – such as new automation and product design – turned out to be rather insignificant in assessing the competitive difficulties faced by the US auto manufacturers, even though their importance in future success continued to grow.[13] Abernathy recognizes the significance of the importance of process yield, which symbolizes process-related technology innovations, and emphasizes that this is the key to the Japanese success. Explaining that since process yield is influenced by management systems involving what is well known as the "just in time" or "kanban" system, it is closely linked to production planning and

Table 1.14b *Ratings of body and mechanical repair*

Average = 10; maximum = 20; minimum = 0		
All models	Body 1980	Mechanical 1980
Domestic		
Buick	9.3	9.4
Chevrolet	8.4	8.9
Dodge	10.0	10.0
Ford	7.2	9.2
Lincoln	8.1	8.4
Oldsmobile	8.4	9.3
Volkswagen	11.3	8.6
Imports		
Datsun	15.3	10.8
Honda	16.0	11.1
Mazda	17.5	12.7
Toyota	16.9	12.4
Volkswagen	11.3	10.0
Volvo	11.9	10.5

Notes: The data cover frequency of repairs of mechanical systems, components, and body. The ratings are given in five categories: average, below average, far below average, above average, and far above average. Zero indicates far below average, 5 is below average, 10 is average, 15 is above average, and 20 is far above average. The total score is indicated by the sum of body and mechanical systems
Source: Consumer reports annual auto issue, April 1981; ibid., p. 75; *Diamond*, p. 18

production control, and he points out that it is this yield category that reflects Japanese superiority in operating processes at high levels of efficiency over long periods of time. Although engineering aspects are significant here, such as machine cycles, plant layouts, etc., the Japanese advantage is more to do with the close interaction of the materials control system, maintenance practices, and employee participation. Consequently, process yield is determined by rated machine speed (expressed as total parts per hour) multiplied by uptime (hours per year), multiplied by 1– defect rate (expressed as good parts/total parts), which gives us the annual output of good parts.[14]

The kanban system typifies process yield centered around process technology, and Abernathy, et al., explain that this system keeps inventory to a minimum as well as helping to expose wastage of time or

Table 1.14c *Customer loyalty – percentage who would buy same model again*

	Domestic	Imports	Total
Subcompact	77.2	91.6	81.2
Compact	74.2	91.4	72.4
Midsize	75.3	94.5	76.9
Standard	81.8	–	–
Luxury	86.9	94.6	87.2
Weighted average	78.7	91.8	–

Source: Rogers national research, Buyer profiles, 1979; ibid., p. 74; *Diamond*, p. 18

materials, use of defective parts, or improper use of equipment. Furthermore, since this system does not work if there are frequent or lengthy breakdowns, it creates an inescapable pressure on maximizing uptime and minimizing defects, which in turn supports an active maintenance program and underpins the relationship between the producers and the parts suppliers. Suppliers work toward providing consistent quality, and line workers, who are equipped with stopping devices, strive to maintain high quality levels, remove wastage, and find defects. It is difficult to separate the effects of the kanban system from, say, job structure or quality system, or to separate them from the benefits of having a loyal workforce with low absenteeism. Abernathy, et al., thus emphasize that the Japanese advantage in production is largely accounted for by workforce management which supports the process yield.[15]

After analyzing the reasons behind Japan's comparative advantage in process-centered productivity, Abernathy, et al., point out that, while this had a significant impact on competition, it was nothing more than a precursor to the arrival of new automobile technology and technological innovations in manufacturing processes. They emphasize that the decisive factor for recovery and rejuvenation of the automobile industry will be management skills that can organize effective production by laying the foundation of strategic technology initiatives. In other words, the fate of the automobile industry will be determined by whether it moves toward technological stability or technological stagnation. The era of relying on modification or expansion of conventional concepts must give way to the development of completely new concepts

Table 1.15 *Seven factors affecting productivity – comparison of technology, management, and organization*

Factor, with ranking and relative weights	Definition	Comparative practice Japan relative to US
Process systems		
Process yield 1 (40%)	Output rate varies in conventional manufacturing lines; good parts per hour from a line, press, work group, or process line. Key determinants are machine cycle times, system uptime and reliability, affected by material control methods, maintenance practices and operating patterns	Production-materials control minimizes inventory, reduces scrap, exposes problems. Line stops highlight problems and help eliminate defects. Operators perform routine maintenance; scheduling of two shifts instead of three leaves time for better maintenance
Quality systems 5 (9%)	Series of controls and inspection plans to ensure that products are built to specifications	Japanese use fewer inspectors. Some authority and responsibility vested in production worker and supervisor; good relationship with suppliers and very high standards lead to less incoming inspection
Technology		
Process automation (10%)	Introduction and adaptation of advanced, state-of-the-art manufacturing equipment	Overall, the state of technology is comparable. Japanese use robots; their stamping facilities appear somewhat more automated than average US facilities

Table 1.15 (*cont.*)

Factor, with ranking and relative weights	Definition	Comparative practice Japan relative to US
Product design 6 (7%)	Differences in the way the car is designed for a given market segment, aspects affecting productivity tolerances, number of parts, fastening methods, etc.	Japanese have more experience in small-car production and have emphasized design for manufacturability (i.e., productivity and equality). Recent US models (such as Escort, J-car by GM) are first models with design manufacturing specifications comparable to the Japanese
Workforce management		
Absenteeism 3 (12%)	All employees' time away from the workplace, including excused, unexcused, medical, personal, contractual, and other reasons	Levels of contractual time off are comparable; unexcused absences are much higher in US
Job structure 2 (18%)	Tasks and responsibilities included in job descriptions	Japanese practice is to create jobs with more breadth (more tasks or skill per job) and depth (more involvement in planning and control operations); labor classifications are broader; regular production workers perform more skilled tasks; management layers are fewer
Work pace 7 (4%)	Speed at which operators perform tasks	Evidence is inconclusive; some lines run faster; some appear to run more slowly

Source: ibid., p. 76; *Diamond*, pp. 20–21

that radically influence the underlying processes. This transition will inevitably be marked by great turmoil in equipment, process, skills, and organization, along with changes in production process from a rigid, continuous, fluid production system (product-process configuration) to a fluid process-product (process-product configuration) prompted by new fuel-efficient technology.[16]

Abernathy, et al., point out that, in order for the US automobile industry to renew itself, there are three important elements. These are: (1) an increased assessment of technological innovations in the market-place, (2) increased diversity in the technology of components and production processes, and (3) an increasingly radical effect of factors (1) and (2) on established configurations in the productive unit as a whole. They point out that this sudden burst of drastic and abrupt changes in product technology and process innovations could provide a competitive basis for new entrants to the field. While the concentration of industries that enjoy the results of the process innovations through innovative products may be temporary, even so, the industry concentration in the long run will become far less stable. Abernathy, et al., conclude that the basis of competition will have changed to reflect the now crucial importance of technology-driven industries.[17]

6. Conclusion

We have thrown light on the productivity gap between US and Japanese auto makers from the perspective of value added per person and production volume, value added per vehicle, labor equipment percentage, etc., and analyzed improvements in labor productivity by looking at the yearly trends for each process and each department in relationship to labor per hour. From these analyzes, it becomes clear that the decisive factor for the gap in cost and productivity between Japanese and US auto makers was not simply due to the differences in wages or purchasing cost of parts, but was influenced significantly by a management system focussed on process technology. As the automobile technology entered the era of change, it became impossible to measure productivity simply by means of the effects of mass production. In other words, concealed in the productivity gap are other aspects, such as scale benefits and manufacturing speed, besides the simple criterion of mass production. These can be expressed by means of creating high quality during the process, eliminating down time, and maximizing effective operating time.

Until this point, automobile production in Japan and US showed two strikingly different competitive patterns: pursuing per-vehicle value added versus pursuing labor productivity per person. These two different competitive approaches established the very special structural problems of the US auto industry, including process design and control that focussed on high-speed and mass-production effects while disregarding long-term investment. This was possible due to the privileged market environment and monopolistic structure, which allowed US auto makers relying on value added per vehicle to focus on large vehicles, and made them leaders in market segmentation and product differentiation.

In the 1980s, Detroit was compelled to change its competitive position from pursuing per vehicle value added to pursuing per person productivity. A new kind of competition began to evolve which focussed on quality and technological innovations. With the appearance of this new competitive dimension, Detroit changed its strategy toward huge amounts of long-term investment. However, the problem is not simply about the amount invested in equipment but whether it is utilized effectively and produces high-quality automobiles. The decisive factor is how to set up the production processes and management so as to reduce wastefulness and defects with a given set of equipment. For this, there is no other means but to break away from the style of management that until then had been inclined toward economies of scale, and to set up a system with a thorough maintenance of the production process, eliminate idle time as much as possible, match quality with productivity, and establish some sort of US style of management system that would organize flexible production where there would be no defective work or defective components. Abernathy suggests that it is wiser for Detroit not to duplicate the Japanese pattern of competition and cautions against blind imitation.[18] He suggests that even more than devoting oneself to technology-initiated strategies based upon changed ideas, it is important to develop a US style of micromanagement that is rooted in the attributes of US work behavior, parts procurement systems, and plant management. Already, starting with GM, several US companies have implemented QC circles or partial "just in time" production systems on the shop floor, but it remains to be seen to what extent this will be effective in motivating the autonomy and the work practices of the workers and managers and in improving productivity.

Turning to the Japanese automobile industry and ignoring whether the Japanese challenge was intentional or not, by breaking the myth of scale benefits and devoting attention to manufacturing practical cars where quality matched productivity, even small-scale makers were able to establish their competitiveness through flexible responses to production technology. The superiority of this type of management at the heart of Japanese process technology is supported by the cohesive relationship between parts and material suppliers, a stable labor and management relationship, and a high work ethic among workers.[19] The low cost of parts procurement and the high quality of components would have been impossible had it not been for careful management of process technology by the parts makers themselves. In line with this, it would not be possible to discuss a flexible system that simultaneously pursued high quality and high productivity but was not caught up with scale merit if it were not for the cooperation of labor unions in developing effective wage policies that supported high productivity. High productivity coexisting with high quality and a flexible production system that is not based on economies of scale cannot be realized without labor cooperation. If we look at it that way, we can see that the success of Japan lies in the social system that supported the style of management, which in turn made continuous technological innovations possible. While automobile technology witnessed drastic changes and progress in every area, Japan was able to carve out a new technological scenario that gave competitive advantage in productivity. However, it was the system of process technology-centered micromanagement that made it possible to cope with flexibility.

We now come to the final question, which is, could the comparative advantage that Japan enjoyed have continued for longer, and if it were to collapse, then what could be the conditions for this to happen? This question relates to the main subject of this book, which is, would Detroit recover, and how? This is a subject connected to political factors, such as the unexpected trade friction of the time, and hence it is not possible to readily pass a verdict. However, there is also the issue of, first, will the Japanese process-centered micromanagement continue or not? And second, what would happen if there was a radical product-related innovation that the micromanagement was unable to cope with?

Regarding the first question, if there is some kind of big friction or stagnancy in the elements that support the success of micromanagement, such as work ethic, stability of labor–management relations, or the relationship of closeness and mutual development between parts makers and parent company, the success of process technology-centered micromanagement would not be sustained. Second, regarding the appearance of a radical, product-related innovation, this itself may invoke radical innovations in process technology (equipment, process, skills, changes in organization), but the problem is that it is unclear in what form such a radical product innovation will appear. Of course, one can argue as to whether, despite a radical innovation in product technology, the macromanagement would be flexible enough to cope.

There have been serious problems connected to environmental issues and global warming, and Japanese auto makers are developing hybrid and battery-operated cars. No one can answer to what extent micromanagement or process technology will be able to cope with the necessary innovations in product technology. If we take our clues from the specialists who think that, for the time being, the only changes will be gradual, it is difficult to know at this stage whether a radical product technology might materialize that would undermine the foundation of the Japanese management system. Consequently, preserving Japan's comparative advantage in productivity will be influenced above all by such factors as work ethic, labor–management relations, and the relationship between auto makers and parts suppliers. When looking at it long term, the key lies in technology-initiated strategies.

Addendum

The great change in industrial competitiveness explained in this chapter – from a full commitment to the pursuance of added valued per car to the pursuance of labor productivity per worker – which is attributed to the reverse phenomenon of international competitiveness from 1979 to the early 1980s, is influential even today. This means a paradigm shift from a full commitment to pursuing volume efficiency to a flexible production system where there is, for example, a quick response to high-mix production or model changes.

As is well known, this paradigm shift has had a huge impact on the manufacturing industry. It was later named the lean production revolution by MIT's International Motor Vehicle Program team. It brought a major change to the production systems for auto and auto parts industries around the world. The lesson was reflected in the revival of the US automobile industry in various ways.

Since then, the industrial competitiveness of the Japan–US automobile industry has evolved dynamically along with political and economic trends, including the high yen after the G5 summit of 1985. Moreover, extremely large differences in productivity and quality between Japan and the US, which existed at the beginning of the 1980s, vanished. This happened especially because the Big Three paid attention to micromanagement in factories and put every effort into responsibility and the checking of quality in production processes.

There is almost no quality difference between Japanese and US autos, and there is no difference in quality in the early stage after production, but there are differences in quality after a certain period has passed since production. This is because the Big Three could not complete a set-up and guarantee of perfect quality in the production process and improve QC circle or other reform activities overnight. This is symbolized in the production system of factories, where the tradition of a work structure with a single-job worker, based on the old paradigm of mass and high-volume production, remains. Of course, the Big Three have shown some progress in developing a lean factory system, but they have not managed to include all factories. Total reform requires a reform of labor practice, and thus a change in generation of workers is necessary. The Big Three are also significantly different in their model line-up in comparison with Japanese auto makers. The profit structure of the Big Three is basically supported by light trucks (mini-vans, SUVs, pickups), while Japanese makers mainly produce passenger cars. Light trucks have a long cycle and high standardization of chassis and components, in contrast with passenger cars with a short model-change cycle. Production of passenger cars certainly requires a lean production system, but the production of light trucks requires a small number of man-hours per truck and easily fits into the traditional mass and high-volume system of the Big Three.

Thus the Big Three emphasize light trucks, which have high volume efficiency and added valued per car. They especially emphasize added value per car, and this is proved by their stress on increasing production of luxury, large SUVs, which have a high added value per car.

Though the Big Three pay attention to the importance of process engineering and high quality and productivity per head, their profit source is still light trucks with high-scale benefits. This means that US auto makers face a major dilemma, in that they will postpone reform of process engineering and moving toward lean factories if they assume that productivity per head and quality guarantee in the process are the focal points for international industrial competition. According to an

Assembly Plant Study conducted by J. P. MacDuffy and others, though the quality and processes of US auto assembly plants are improving, Japan is still ahead in international competitiveness in productivity and quality at the process level.

Comparing international competitiveness based on process engineering renovation, which was pointed out by Abernathy, no longer represents all of the elements that explain international industrial competitiveness in the automobile industry. The current high-profit structure of the Big Three is attributed to their bold and precisely calculated strategic ideas and drastic reduction of parts procurement costs, as well as improvement in white-collar productivity due to reform of engineering at headquarters and indirect departments. The strategic and systematic ideas aimed at converting a huge loss due to a business system exclusively committed to benefits of scale were improved further by the aggressive usage of information technology at the beginning of the 1990s, and this is a future theme for Japanese auto makers, which are based on a full commitment to the importance of field sites.

Notes

1. D. H. Ginsbung and W. J. Abernathy (eds.) *Government, Technology and the Future of the Automobile*, McGraw-Hill, 1980. R. H. Hayes and W. J. Abernathy, "Managing our way to economic decline," *Harvard Business Review*, July–August, 1980.
2. K. Shimokawa, "Beikoku JIdoshasangyo Keieishi Kenkyu" (*A Business History of the U.S. Automobile Industry*), Toyo Keizai Shimposha, 1977, pp. 265–394.
3. "Anteiseichoki ni Okeru Jidoshasangyo no tenbo," Kikai Shinkyokai Keizai Kenkyusho, 1977, p. 19.
4. L. J. White, *The Automobile Industry Since 1945*, Harvard University Press, 1971, p. 203.
5. For example, the financial data of the two American companies was announced on the basis of connections, but the numerical value in foreign countries is divided in the case of Japan. In addition, a gap between the settlement of accounts time and difference in depreciation method and a difference in the estimation of personnel expenses with numerical value could not be used because adjustment was difficult.
6. R. H. Hayes and W. J. Abernathy, "Managing our way to economic decline," *Harvard Business Review*, July–August, 1980, p. 73.
7. W. J. Abernathy, K. B. Clark, and A. M. Kantrow, "The new industrial competition," *Harvard Business Review*, September–October, 1981.

8. Ibid., p. 72.
9. Ibid., p. 71.
10. Ibid., pp. 72–73.
11. Ibid., p. 73.
12. Ibid., p. 73.
13. Ibid., p. 74.
14. Ibid., p. 77.
15. Ibid., pp. 75–76.
16. Ibid., pp. 77–78.
17. Ibid., pp. 78–79.
18. Ibid., p. 79.
19. Shimokawa, K., 'Shakaikankyo no Henka to Nichibeijidoshasangyo,' Nihonkeieigakai, "80 Nendai no Kigyokeiei," 1981, pp. 48–49.

2 | The internationalization of the Japanese automotive industry and local production overseas

1. The "new" global imperative for the Japanese automobile industry

The Japanese automobile industry has reached a major strategic turning point. Following the collapse of the bubble economy in 1991, the Japanese domestic automobile market experienced a protracted three-year sales slump and underwent major structural changes. This forced the industry to come up with a new strategic response through restructuring and rationalization. Hard hit by the so-called Heisei recession that followed the collapse of the bubble economy, each of the major Japanese auto makers saw a dramatic worsening of its financial results, to the extent that one wonders what has happened to the competitive strength of the world's most powerful global competitors.

The contrast is striking: during the peak years of the 1980s through to 1991, when the companies' operating results were substantially stronger, the eleven auto manufacturers generated profits in a single year of around ¥1.1 trillion, but within a few years profits had fallen to less than half that, at about ¥500 billion, with three of the eleven firms reporting a loss and several others only borderline profitable.

Until this recession, the Japanese industry had generally experienced nearly constant growth, showing a rising curve of sales, volume, and profits. The only times when the industry experienced a decline in production was in 1973, as a result of the first oil crisis, and again in 1981, as a result of the second oil shock and the imposition of voluntary export restraints to the United States. In each case, the decline lasted only for about a year, with production increases restored by the following year. In the current Heisei recession, however, the industry has experienced an unprecedented two years of straight declines in output. On the two previous occasions, sharply weaker domestic demand had a similarly severe impact, but production cuts were necessary for only one year, in part because of the boost provided by strong external demand.

Shortly after the first oil crisis, both the US and Middle East markets showed strong growth; and while exports to the US market after the second oil shock were hampered by the imposition of the VER and the increase in import duties on light trucks, exports to European countries grew sharply, helping raise overall export levels.

During the Heisei recession, domestic weakness has been com-pounded by the fact that it has become increasingly unlikely that a similar export spurt will offset the weakness in the home market, which declined for two straight years, from a peak of 7.8 million vehicles sold in 1990 to 6.94 million units in 1992. The reason for the poor export outlook stems from simultaneous recessions in Japan's main export markets in the US and Europe, and heightened trade friction over automobile exports. Furthermore, since starting basically from scratch twelve years ago, Japanese auto makers have progressively expanded production volumes at their overseas production plants, which has supplanted substantial export volume. For example, while exports to the United States total about 1.65 million cars per year, local production already supplies 1.60 million cars, and it seems almost certain that locally produced cars will for the first time outnumber those imported from Japan in the current year (2010). The strengthen-ing of the yen, which has led to a deterioration in export earnings, has a significant impact on the worsening performance of the Japanese auto industry.

Today, the industry is suffering the consequences of the non-lean practices it acquired during the "fat" years of the bubble economy. In the space of only three years, from 1987 to 1990, the domestic auto market in Japan expanded by a total of about 2 million vehicles, with a dramatic proliferation in the number of individual vehicle variations and the shift to the high-end, luxury segments of the market. According to statistics in the White Paper on Labour, the number of basic model types that were produced in Japan essentially doubled from about 200 in 1984 to 400 in 1991.[1] Naturally, this growth also led to a sharp expansion in the number of different parts used, and, coupled with the increase in model types, represents a major reason for the sharp rise in fixed costs for the industry. And while a highly efficient new-model-development system and rapid response times to new model changes are seen as characteristic of the Japanese auto industry, the reduction in the model-change cycle (which arose as a response to the speed-up in new car replacement during the surging bubble years, but eventually came to exceed the real needs of most consumers) led to a sharp rise in research and development (R&D)-related expenses as well.

Today, the most telling evidence of the industry's urgent need to correct the many non-lean practices acquired during this period and to redefine its business strategies can be found in the current efforts at rationalization and reorganization. Key elements in this restructuring process will be a reduction by 20–30 percent in model types, a similar reduction in the number of different parts and components, along with greater sharing, or communization, of such parts, as well as revision of the pace of model changes. These efforts are already well under way, and have been accompanied by efforts to shut down the least efficient facilities and concentrate production in the newest, most productive plants.[2] The industry is vigorously pursuing such efforts to eliminate non-lean practices, and it is likely that the results will become apparent through lowering of industry break-even levels within two to three years.

In parallel with these rationalization efforts at home, accelerating the industry's global diversification assumes an increasing strategic significance. It is fair to say that, while domestic rationalization may pose the greater urgency in the near term, in the longer term the key to the industry's future lies in the direction in which the diversification drive evolves.

Broadly speaking, this globalization effort can be divided into two main regional components. One is the further expansion of local production capacity in the industrialized countries of North America and Europe; the other is the extension of local production arrangements and cooperative division of labor to serve the fast-growing China and South-east Asian markets.[3] The immediate focus is likely to be on the pace at which localization of management, parts procurement, and R&D proceed in North America, where the number of locally produced Japanese vehicles is rapidly overtaking that of cars imported from Japan.

The logic of localization in Japan's largest overseas automotive market, the United States, is no longer simply an issue of supplementing exports. Rather, localization is now the industry's principal strategic objective in North America, where the ability to produce all strategically important model types locally is fast becoming a reality. With an estimated investment of $8.6 billion in local production facilities in North America, the Japanese auto makers have expanded local production capacity to a total of 2.5 million vehicles per year.[4] The sheer scale of this investment suggests the importance which the success of these operations holds for Japan's automotive globalization efforts.

In its initial stages, the effort focussed mainly on transplanting Japanese production systems, training practices, and parts procurement procedures to US soil. This effort was initially managed for the most part by Japanese specialists in cooperation with the locally hired labor force. Today, however, the process has entered another phase, which centers on transferring key administrative responsibilities to local employees. Moreover, in line with the bilateral agreement to sharply increase procurement of US-made parts by Japanese auto makers signed last year, collaboration between Japanese auto makers and local parts and components suppliers at the "design-in" phase of development has also begun to gather momentum. This chapter will focus on case material drawn from the experiences of Toyota, Nissan, and Honda in these areas, as well as local field research, in an effort to gauge how effectively this process of localization is actually taking place along the lines described.

2. Putting strategy into practice through localization of management

The degree to which the Japanese auto makers succeed in localizing their operations in North America represents the linchpin in their ongoing globalization strategy. The process, broadly speaking, can be divided into three major elements. One is the localization of management at factory level, particularly those aspects involved directly with human resource development, especially personnel administration, training, evaluation, and quality control activities. The second is further expanding procurement to widen relationships with local suppliers in order to raise the level of local content. The third is the localization of R&D-related activities to embrace the entire spectrum of design and development, starting at the "design-in" phase of development.

Naturally, all three of these elements are closely inter-related, and reflect the fact that US employees are assuming an increasingly central role in these areas as production at the Japanese transplant operations moves into full gear. At Honda, which has the longest experience of local production in North America, the focus has been to reduce the number of Japanese nationals on site, from a peak level of 400. With a view to eventually replacing most of these with local employees, Honda has set up a program to send more than fifty US employees to Japan for postings at headquarters lasting up to two years.[5] The emphasis has thus shifted from sending Japanese employees to assist in setting up local production and administrative systems to bringing US employees on-site at Japanese facilities, with the assumption that they will return and play a key role in the localization of management at home. This shift marks a change in the prevailing view that they are becoming self-reliant (though not independent) entities largely managed by local employees of Honda. The basis for instilling such an attitude of self-reliance is the full involvement of US managers and workers in major strategic issues, such as decisions regarding model changes and new model introductions.[6] Needless to say, having a local R&D capacity is a basic condition for establishing self-reliance, but setting up such an operation is itself a function of the degree to which the localization of management and procurement has advanced.

The degree of progress in these efforts differs to some extent among the three major auto makers, Toyota, Nissan, and Honda. Significant progress has certainly been made in improving the effectiveness of work habits as local production has been ramped up, with the focus on increasing familiarity with practices such as team-based production, simplification of work procedures to allow more flexible rotation, multi-skilled employees, and so on. In this sense, a form of technology transfer has been accomplished in the successful adaptation by local employees and engineers of the relevant practices developed at the Japanese "mother plants." It is clear that the Japanese transplants focussed their initial efforts and substantial investment on achieving these objectives.

While Japanese companies are generally known for their enthusiasm for in-house training, Toyota had to invest several times more to develop a highly organized training system at its Kentucky plant than it would have in Japan. Initially, Toyota's managers in charge of training inexperienced local workers saw training in technical skills as their principal focus, but soon recognized that, in order to foster the kind of teamwork needed, they also needed to emphasize inter-personal skills such as speaking and listening, as well as team-based problem solving, and so on. These aspects of the training program were well received by local workers.

From these activities over the past five years, the company has accumulated substantial expertise in all the various hardware and software facets of worker training and education at its local training center, and will continue to place major emphasis on these activities.[7] Yet for all the focus on training, these activities do not preclude the emergence of a variety of problems which is not easily resolved, such as problems related to maintenance of the production line by local workers. In some instances, mechanical problems which might take only ten minutes to clear up at a Japanese plant might take more than an hour to fix in Kentucky. Gradual elimination of such problems, however, is likely to be mainly a matter of time, as the relevant skills and experiences are gained through on-the-job training.

The situation is somewhat different at Honda, which has had longer experience with training-related activities. In one example (cited by a Rover employee who happened to be working in Ohio), the response to a problem that arose on the assembly line was for the group leaders in charge of areas such as painting and welding to gather at the problem location and quickly delegate responsibility for determining what impact the stoppage might have on the flow of cars into and out of the line, as well as the flow of parts, and so on. Through their joint efforts, the problem was solved in fifteen minutes. One training-related factor, however, is that in the initial start-up phases when many of the activities are new to all workers, and high levels of motivation and interest tend to be shared by all individuals, differences in ability are not generally very pronounced. Yet as time goes by, personal skills and motivations are likely to emerge that set some workers apart from others. How the auto makers will evaluate (and reward) such differences remains a potentially problematic issue still to be fully addressed.

While pay differentials in Japan tend to be based mainly on length of service, it remains to be seen how the transplants will resolve potential conflicts over pay between those hourly workers who acquired a broad range of flexible skills in the initial start-up phases compared with those who joined later on. For the time being, such problems are being handled mainly by applying a teamwork approach, and evaluating only those employees ranked as team leaders or higher in terms of their individual performance. Yet by the same token, even hourly workers who want their work to be individually evaluated at Honda may elect to do so, and by fulfilling the necessary qualifications can be promoted up the ranks from team leader to coordinator, and so on. There are some employees at Honda, for example, who began as hourly workers but eventually rose to the position of manager, indeed even to director level, demonstrating the diversity in individual career opportunities that is available. Even without graduating from college, employees have a path to becoming engineers.[8]

The North American factories of Toyota, Nissan, and Honda are essentially non-unionized, in contrast to the factories set up by Japanese companies as joint ventures or collaborative efforts with US auto makers, which have had to accept UAW representation. Though they may be union-free, the Japanese transplants nonetheless face the issue of how to resolve disputes and handle complaints from local employees. Though these plants have been in operation for only about 5–6 years, at most 10 or so years, they have generally accepted the UAW seniority rule with regards to eligibility for job rotations and other workplace changes.[9]

In order to improve communications with employees, Toyota conducts a major survey annually, and three smaller surveys, in order to identify potential sources of dissatisfaction. The company also runs a hotline through which employees can register their complaints and opinions anonymously by phone, and the company has pledged to respond to all of them. In addition, Toyota has instituted a "round-table" discussion series, at which the president and other top-level US managers, such as the head of personnel, meet informally with groups of 20–25 employees selected at random. These meetings are held four times a year for each of the three shifts, for a total of twelve meetings, and as a rule the workers selected come well prepared to discuss issues of concern to their particular work groups. A fourth effort involves members of the company's labor relations department, known as "representators," who go out to different groups in the plant to listen, and suggest solutions, to a host of everyday problems. By making full use of these communication channels, the company hopes to bring into the open any problems that might otherwise be allowed to fester. For really major issues affecting the livelihood of the entire plant, such as announcements relating to major increases or reductions in production levels, or other events that might impact working hours, the companies try to address the workers more directly – Honda, for example, using plant-wide voting by employees, and Toyota holding assemblies for all employees.[10]

Other practices, such as participation by local employees in suggestion systems and QC activity, have also made substantial progress as the plants have now been in operation for some time. In the case of

Toyota, for example, the suggestions received in the early stages tended to focus on matters related to reducing costs through energy savings and reduced waste. More recently, however, suggestions tend to focus on identifying potential defects or mechanical problems along with suggestions for rectifying them, or simplifying work routines, and so on.

At Honda, a range of activities, including suggestions, safety, and participation in QC activities, is incorporated into a comprehensive effort called "VIP" (voluntary improvement program) to serve as the vehicle for promoting individual participation by employees. Honda's experiences have shown that the effectiveness of such activities depends on the degree to which it fosters self-initiative by the employees themselves. While progress has been achieved, Honda's management has to continue to seek ways to encourage further participation. Ultimately, the success of QC activities seems to be a function of how effectively the basic training efforts have taken root. Another way of putting it is that QC activities are likely to fail if they are introduced too quickly, before the basic level of training has been achieved.

The real objective of QC activity is to understand why certain kinds of problems occur, and to find ways to resolve them, but to do so effectively requires a high degree of discipline and a strong foundation. If full-scale QC activity is initiated without the involvement of the appropriate core personnel and an appropriate level of training, only problem identification is likely to occur, but this is not really sufficient. Without adequate preparation, QC does not automatically lead to the most important objective, namely a disciplined discussion of ways to actually solve those problems. The Japanese auto makers have recognized that to gain the full benefits of QC circles, they cannot rush into this activity or try to impose Japanese methods in a mechanical way. Rather, they need to develop a group of US leaders who will lead the process of adapting and expanding such activities, and to create the kind of environment in which QC becomes a natural, and consistent, element of the corporate culture.[11]

Thus, as we have noted, the Japanese auto makers are making significant progress in the area of localizing management. It is expressed in a range of activities centered on production and labor management practices, in practical training programs, in personnel evaluation and promotion, in complaint resolution and efforts to facilitate labor-to-management communication, and finally, in the form of voluntary participation in QC activities and suggestion systems. Yet issues remain to be worked out, particularly in the degree to which local employees, including senior managers in key staff functions such as personnel, general affairs, and finance, are promoted to strategically important positions, as well as raising the absolute numbers of QC leaders, and introducing individual evaluations at the production-worker level.

3. Beyond local contact to supplier support and "design-in" activities

The expansion of local parts procurement is a pivotal issue in the evolving globalization strategy of Japanese auto makers. From an initial local content ratio of perhaps 50 percent at best, the transplant factories have progressively raised the level of local procurement, including critical engine and drive-train components, to the extent that it is not unrealistic to aim for 75–80 percent local content. The 1992 bilateral agreement between the US and Japanese governments that aimed to dramatically expand purchase of US components has added an impetus for accelerating efforts to expand relationships with local suppliers. Yet the main obstacles to wider collaboration with local suppliers continue to be found in the difference between Japanese and US parts-supply and purchasing practices. A number of problems in this area still have to be worked out in order for full localization to be achieved.[12]

There is evidence, on the one hand, that the Japanese transplants are developing long-term relationships with local suppliers, and that these suppliers for their part are showing real interest in raising quality levels, shortening lead-times, and raising their overall technical capabilities. On the other hand, there are still problems in their ability to supply small lots, to make rapid and flexible design changes, and to provide the transplants with adequate quality assurance. Perhaps the biggest problem derives from the relatively small number of local suppliers (with the exception of the largest US system component makers) that have a fully fledged in-house design and development capability. The vast majority of suppliers tend to build and deliver parts on the basis of highly detailed blueprints and specifications provided by the auto makers themselves. By and large, Japanese transplants have not found many suppliers with the ability to respond quickly and flexibly to the needs of their own development system, in the sense of pushing along the development of automotive electronics and new materials not yet in widespread use in the US.

Honda in particular found local suppliers generally uninterested in supplying parts in the relatively small lot sizes which its factory required during the initial start-up phases when production was being ramped up to about 150,000 vehicles per year. On top of that, many of the parts which Honda requested were compact, lightweight pieces requiring high precision tooling that could be made only by special order, which raised their unit cost substantially. Under these conditions, and with the small lot size that prevailed at the time, Honda found it hard to make real progress on localization of procurement, but as production volumes rose to 300,000 vehicles, it began to be seen as more commercially viable by local suppliers, who started to express interest in Honda's orders.

Local suppliers initially found Honda's specifications for materials, quality, finish, cost, and delivery time so severe that just getting prototypes from local suppliers cost twice as much, and took double the time it would have taken Japanese suppliers. Moreover, problems cropped up as local suppliers found it difficult to ramp up from engineering samples to volume production, so that even if Honda was satisfied with the prototypes it was shown, problems emerged as soon as suppliers shifted to volume production. This forced Honda to approach its suppliers and investigate the way products moved from engineering to production, and to offer suggestions as to how to solve the problems. Honda initially found suppliers reluctant to engage in this practice, since they feared it would lead to a leakage of trade secrets or technical know-how. More recently, however, local suppliers have recognized the advantages of working with Honda at this level of detail in terms of winning new business on the basis of what they have learned.

Yet the transplants are still finding it difficult to achieve the necessary levels of quality assurance from local suppliers, and Honda, for example, has found it necessary to conduct strict incoming inspections since suppliers cannot guarantee the necessary level of quality. Honda as a rule makes an effort to work with suppliers whenever problems are found to locate and correct the problems at the source in the supplier's production system. Production in Ohio in the early 1990s was up to 1,500 vehicles per day, but the inventory of finished vehicles kept at the plant was generally no more than 500 units. For this reason, any problem that halted the assembly line would quickly deplete the inventory on hand, and force an immediate and rapid response. In order for local suppliers to understand the gravity of the situation, Honda invited local vendors to observe the production process and understand first hand the risk which defective components pose to the operation.[13]

Nissan experienced similar problems at its plant in Tennessee. The company's procurement activities were raised to a new level of significance as production expanded from the initial Sentra subcompact to include the mid-sized Altima model, as well as the start of engine production at the site. The US vice-president in charge of purchasing at Smyrna, Tennessee, made the following comment:

"Procurement is entering a new phase as local content will be expanded to serve the production of engines. Our basic philosophy with respect to procurement is to promote long-term relationships on the basis of mutual trust with those suppliers that meet our strict qualifications and rules for single-supplier vendors. Yet the way we operate has changed over time and will continue to evolve. Originally we purchased various parts and materials on the basis of competitive bidding, and it is true that we experienced some problems with our suppliers. Yet by evaluating them in terms of quality, cost, and delivery time, we have seen substantial improvement in reducing defects, and more recently have begun to focus on evaluating potential suppliers on the basis of their technical capacity.

"We've found it particularly important to stress technical abilities for suppliers who will be involved in production of new models, and as a result the old competitive bidding approach has largely disappeared. It is not just a model change, as we are adding an entirely new model (the Altima) and have chosen to work with our suppliers to help raise the level of their technology and to collaborate in bringing about a long-term reduction in costs.

"We have decided to introduce the target-pricing approach, moreover, as we want to avoid the kinds of misunderstandings that can arise between suppliers' cost estimates and the carmaker's future price levels. We began, in the case of the Altima, to test various suppliers, and later set up a new parts procurement group, introduced cost-planning and supplier training, as well as VE-and VA-based contracts."[14]

With respect to the issue of quality assurance, he notes: "We have a system for rewarding those suppliers who achieve significant quality improvements, but at the same time don't expect that all quality issues have to be handled entirely by the suppliers. Rather, on the basis of the trust that we've established, we work together to raise quality by exchanging information and know-how. We try to determine what kind of assistance they might require, and what we can do to help, and run our quality standards committee on an open basis to make the information available. GM and other US carmakers are also moving to introduce similar practices, such as long-term relationships, quality assessment, target pricing, and so on, but this is a relatively new trend for them. At Smyrna, we have done these things from the very beginning, and suppliers are judged on the basis of what they can accomplish by working with us. In this respect, suppliers are competing to be qualified with us.

"We have also entered a new phase in terms of the degree to which suppliers assume responsibility for quality, as we shift from incoming inspection to getting suppliers involved by sending their engineers to Smyrna to investigate and fix whatever is causing the problem. Naturally, to be successful, this requires a high level of openness in providing information to suppliers, and for their part, constant efforts to strengthen their quality assurance standards."

In parallel with efforts to strengthen quality standards, Nissan is moving to strengthen its local R&D capability through collaborative development efforts with suppliers with which it has established ties. As Nissan's Detroit-based technical center, NDR, becomes involved in the development of finished cars and components, the proportion of parts designed locally will have the effect of strengthening the development capacity of local suppliers over the next several years, as in the past the factory issued orders only for components that had been designed in Japan.

Securing reliable suppliers also becomes more important as Smyrna starts production of engines, and raises the ratio of locally procured components in addition to simpler parts and materials. To do so requires finding the kind of systems supplier who can develop and deliver more complex modules, along the lines of the approach used in Japan.

Regarding issues which remain in the area of procurement localization: "While we don't want to go to the extreme of making suppliers completely responsible for a certain component, we want to get local suppliers involved at the initial stages of development. While the objective of procurement localization is obviously to raise the level of local content as high as possible, simply farming out production is likely to weaken the suppliers' technical skills and quality evaluation skills. Depending on the type of component, some degree of in-house production will have to be maintained in order to achieve the most efficient procurement system. Moreover, in order to expand our procurement activities to include engines, we will have to search out and train other suppliers. This is why we have focused on setting up a vendor association which will be open to any vendors that meet certain minimal requirements."[15]

This description of Nissan's local procurement activities may sound somewhat idealistic, since in reality the effort has only just got under way and will take considerable time, especially in terms of making progress on quality assurance and VE/VA-related activities with local suppliers. With respect to "design-in," with reference to the earlier comment that a high degree of simultaneous engineering would be difficult to achieve, this has only just entered the trial-and-error phase.

Design-in will become necessary in order to accomplish the goal agreed to in 1992 of substantially expanding local procurement. The design-in process covers a fairly broad range of different approaches by Japanese auto makers, so it is hard to make any hard and fast generalizations. In broad terms one can distinguish two main approaches. One is to make a concerted effort to include local suppliers in the design-in process as local R&D gets under way; the second is to take a more deliberate approach to move to design-in only after carefully nurturing relationships with local suppliers in areas such as purchasing practices, quality assurance, price negotiations, and technical assessment. Again, it is hard to generalize as to which factors may make the design-in process easy or difficult, since it depends on a range of factors, such as differences in types of components, the technical skills of various suppliers, and so on. However, the degree to which Toyota succeeds in localizing procurement through design-in with local suppliers may come to be seen as a test case, since the company has achieved outstanding results in Japan in working with suppliers to raise their technological capabilities.

The starting point for the evolution of Toyota's parts procurement policies began with the company's effort to gather information on local suppliers as part of its joint venture with GM at Nummi in Fremant, California. At the start of the Nummi joint venture in 1984, Toyota established a parts depot in Chicago, where the objective was to conduct exhaustive surveys of the cost, quality, and technical levels of the local supplier industry, including GM's own Midwestern parts division. Toyota then tried to determine which components would have a significant impact on the overall quality and performance of its cars, and to strictly distinguish those standards on which it was willing to compromise, and those on which it was not. The know-how which Toyota accumulated during this phase will be increasingly applied at the Kentucky plant. Gradually, the company hopes to shift from relying on blueprints in which all quality, costs, and technical details are specified, toward the Japanese system of "approval description" of blueprints, in which Toyota's general requirements are indicated, but vendors are allowed to substitute materials and make other compromises as the situation demands. Such "Toyota blueprints" frequently have the effect of enticing suppliers to find the cheapest possible way to meet the indicated requirements.

For the time being, since quality assurance has not been fully achieved by individual vendors, Toyota insists on strict incoming inspection of all parts. The fact that all parts have to be inspected in the US therefore represents a major competitive handicap in comparison with production in Japan. The company also wants to shift to a three-year target pricing approach from the current style of holding annual price negotiations with vendors, yet to do so all at once would be impossible. Price and quality levels are based on standards set in Japan. Yet among US suppliers, some companies may try to tender cost estimates that are too low to win the initial bidding, but then demand price increases later on. In this regard, Toyota has to ensure that vendors actually can supply the parts at the prices they have quoted. Another factor is that, while defect ratios tend to be expressed in terms of parts per million in Japan, in the US they are still often quoted in terms of percent, that is parts per hundred, and so Japanese makers have to continue in their efforts to raise the tolerance levels of their US suppliers.

At present, the efforts of Toyota's local procurement office focus on the following areas: (1) to ensure that the national vendors' association which Toyota launched in 1990 becomes an effective arena for discussing specific issues related to quality improvement and technical standards, rather then simply letting the twice-yearly meetings become a social event; (2) to develop a core staff of US purchasing managers who are knowledgeable in the company's procurement policies and technical specs and blueprints, in order to more effectively coordinate relationships with local parts vendors; (3) to use the opportunity provided by the establishment of Toyota's US-based R&D program to integrate all of the various activities, such as testing, parts design, offer evaluation, order placement, and so on, into a single, effective vehicle; and (4) to narrow the selection of suppliers to those companies which meet its criteria and long-term requirements.

Design-in naturally assumes increasing importance in raising local content, but it is also important to change the attitudes and interests of the local suppliers themselves. This aspect has improved significantly over the past ten years, to the extent that some US components suppliers have opened liaison offices in Japan to facilitate the design-in process. Yet the auto makers, if they want to prevent misunderstanding, must also make efforts to help local suppliers understand the benefits that they can get from taking part in the design-in process. There have been cases in which suppliers who have been admitted to the design-in process for certain components then suddenly turn round and raise their prices by 50 percent. Nonetheless, the attitude seems to be positive, and the auto makers should take the next step of setting up value-engineering (VE) assessment meetings in order to suggest ways in which suppliers can address problems, for example, to suggest how a supplier might switch to using lighter materials after the engineering prototypes have been completed. The goal is to get them to recognize that the design-in can be profitable for suppliers as well.[16]

In addition to Toyota's efforts to improve relations with local parts suppliers, the company launched its supplier support center in September 1992, which has the objective of providing additional support to local suppliers. The center provides practical training in design-in and advice on such subjects as Toyota's quality assurance philosophy and ways in which it can be systematically applied. Use of the facility is not limited solely to existing Toyota suppliers, but is open to any company that wants to study the Toyota production system. For the time being, the center will work with existing suppliers to develop model practices which can then be passed on to other suppliers with whom it does not yet do business.

It appears that, as a result of these efforts to transfer knowledge of the Toyota production system, many local suppliers have become more positive about studying its features, yet, perhaps due to a lack of familiarity, still seem to regard the Toyota system as a kind of magic. For this reason, the goal of the center is to conduct a thorough investigation of a supplier's operations and to point out all the problems that have been found within two weeks, and then ensure that the suppliers themselves start to address their problems within a month. This effort to train the companies to recognize problems and find potential solutions of their own is intended to wean them from relying on Toyota's support as quickly as possible. At the time of writing, the center has a staff of about thirty. It should be recognized that its activities represent a voluntary effort by Toyota to support US suppliers, indeed US manufacturing industry in general, to become more efficient through rationalizing their operations. Another way of stating it is that the objective is to find ways to make more productive use of the personnel who would otherwise become redundant through such rationalization efforts. The staff at the center include some US employees who have had experience at Toyota headquarters in Japan, as well as local employees from Toyota's three North American plants who have asked to work at the center. It may be a long drawn-out process, but one can assume that the day will come when they will be able to apply the knowledge they have gained from helping local manufacturers improve their operations to help make Toyota's design-in and "Kyosei" collaboration with local suppliers a reality.[17]

Toyota will continue to pursue these two parallel approaches, one through a broad range of purchasing-related activities aimed at encouraging existing suppliers to become more familiar with Toyota practices and to move in the direction of design-in, the other through promoting understanding of the Toyota production system to a wider range of companies, including those it does not do business with.

Efforts to train local suppliers are not limited to the US, but are also highly regarded in other countries where Toyota has production facilities. For example, in Taiwan, where Toyota has set up production most recently, the government raised the issue of training local suppliers as one of the key elements in its policy for nationalizing its automotive industry in 1986.[18] In line with the Taiwan government's strategy of developing the country into a leading production platform, of parts and components rather than finished automobiles, Toyota has already made progress in training local suppliers, working with some of its major Japanese components suppliers. The result has been to improve the quality and technical standards of Taiwanese parts suppliers, whom Toyota regards as important elements in the international division of labor and as a bridge to the ASEAN and Chinese markets.

4. Obstacles and opportunities in localizing R&D activities

Efforts by Japanese transplants to raise their local content include not only design-in but also R&D. Local R&D facilities play an increasingly important role, not only in terms of facilitating design-in with the design centers but also, crucially, in providing the original ideas and input for new car development. Local R&D first emerged in the context of raising the quality and technical standards of local parts, but gained impetus from the need to develop parts locally. More broadly speaking, the need for an integrated approach to local design and development, leading to the ability to design entire new models locally, arose from the recognition that such a capability was needed in order to satisfy the diverse needs of the US market, and to develop products which would satisfy the needs of local consumers.[19]

While each of the major Japanese auto makers has established design centers and R&D facilities in the US, Nissan and Honda have perhaps made the most progress toward design localization. Nissan's efforts in this area focus on the activities of the San Diego design center, NDI, and the Detroit-based technical center, NDR. The heads of both organizations are Japanese, but one gets the impression that a US employee could quite easily be appointed head of NDI, which is now in its thirteenth year, whereas NDR, which is only six years old, is unlikely to see such an appointment very soon. From the outset, NDI was set up to draw on the creative talents of its US chief designers, to whom the entire design process was effectively delegated, whereas the R&D center almost inevitably requires a Japanese president, at least for the time being, to accommodate the differences in Japanese and US development systems and administrative matters.

NDI's chief designer, Gerald Hirschberg, who moved to Nissan from GM thirteen years ago, relates his experiences prior to his arrival at Nissan and his basic philosophy of design as follows: "The reason I moved from GM to NDI was that, even though I was allowed to do a lot of advanced design at GM, I never felt this contributed very much to the design of real cars. I always felt frustrated by the fact that our work never came to realization. I was pretty fed up with advanced design, and wanted to try my hand at design that actually had something to do with making cars. Instead of pursuing a lot of unrealistic designs, I believe the design process should begin with a solid conceptual basis, more directly tied to production, from which the ideas are gradually refined. In automotive design, there are cultural factors as well. The emergence of Japan's small cars opened a new path of learning in the design world, which led me to choose Nissan.

"The nature of design work is shaped by the stringent conditions placed on it, and we can only achieve satisfactory results through the challenge of coming up with something new that can pass scrutiny through a series of contests. At NDI, the designers compete with each other, and while we cooperate to the extent necessary with our colleagues at the Nissan Technical center in Sagamihara, we also compete to see how these fresh designs can be translated into actual designs. I have told my staff not just to look at things in terms of design, but rather to consider the role engineering and technology can play as a source of inspiration and originality."

In terms of the issues confronting NDI today, Hirschberg adds the following: "NDI's role is to serve as a conceptual center, to provide stimulus to NTC in Japan, and to aim for the highest level of automotive design in the world. In order to achieve the best results, both centers pursue parallel projects simultaneously, and by dividing project responsibilities, try to determine what works and what doesn't. There are constant tensions between the two organizations, and both are run in a dynamic way to permit as much creative freedom as possible. In terms of priorities, it is important for both of us to recognize our mutual differences, and to work on a basis of mutual trust. It is also necessary at the planning stage to think in terms of strategic styling and design. For this to work, it is essential to get timely feedback from Nissan's top management on how our design work fits with the company's strategic plans. Even more than in the past, we have to develop an effective partnership between US and Japanese designers.

"Another issue is to study how cultural values are changing, and in order to bring fresh design concepts into the process, we have to have our designers follow cultural and market trends. We make a constant effort at NDI to sharpen our cultural sensitivities by encouraging the staff to go out and have a look at art exhibitions, collections, musical events and concerts. A third point that would be raised in the long-term perspective is to look at the design and development effort as a creative team, for which we have to develop a design process that always maintains a pioneering attitude. Over the long run, the real meaning of localization at NDI is to serve as a key member of the Nissan family that can incorporate the cultural values of both countries and combine market needs with our dreams in a systematic way."[20]

The key to Nissan's success in localizing its development process is the collaboration between its design studios at NDI and the NDR development center in Farmington Hills on the outskirts of Detroit. Former NDR president Tanuma, who was the overall director of

R&D localization, noted the following: "The first obstacle we ran into in promoting localization of R&D was the marked difference in the US and Japanese approaches to the management of the development process. They may appear superficially similar, particularly with regards to adopting a more top-down approach or giving priority to a more consensus-based approach, but we will need more time to learn from each other.

"There are also differences in how the design process is moved along, step by step, whether to take the US approach in which authority and responsibility are clearly defined and the work proceeds in a sequential fashion, or the more Japanese approach, in which responsibility is more ambiguous, and the work moved along with the necessary adjustments made at the end.

"Another problem stems from the fact that, with the exception of some functional components, local parts suppliers do not generally do their own development work, and responsibilities thus differ. So for the time being at NDR, no matter how much time it takes, we still have to do the design work ourselves. But US suppliers have changed their attitudes and have become more positive about doing such development. But in order to make it possible for everyone to work together at the same time, we have to develop a technical support system in which key information contained in CAD-CAM drawings can be used by everyone, rather than becoming fragmented and isolated in the hands of only those engineers working on one or another specific aspect.

"The characteristic Japanese approach to overlapping development by a number of teams working in parallel has become well known internationally for its effectiveness in reducing overall development time. But at NDR we can't jump into this overlapping approach all at once and instead have adopted a step-wise approach which is based on clear confirmation of how far the work has progressed at each stage. Having done some development work locally, we've found that, unless we modify the designs, we can't use US-made parts, and we can't simply bring in Japanese parts either. It's not just the design of parts, however, but the broader picture. I'm constantly reminded of how difficult it is for someone who has grown up in a typical small Japanese home to fully understand the needs and preferences of the US consumer.

"There are some areas in which US technology is more advanced, and the fact that some materials such as engineering plastics are much cheaper here, and there are many parts and components for the body and chassis, as well as electronics such as part circuit designs, that can be incorporated in the development process. But in the area of engines and major drive-train components, the level of innovation in Japan is definitely more advanced. The same is true for complex components using engineering plastics, aluminium and castings, in which Japanese products tend to be superior, and of course for tools and dies we're likely to depend on supply from Japan."

Even as it grappled with these problems, NDR played a central role in the joint development of the Quest minivan with Ford, all the way up to the development of the pre-production prototypes, signing off on blueprints and even tapping the resources of the NTC design center for certain aspects of the development work. Having successfully completed this trial run on the minivan project, NDR was also responsible for the remodelled Terrano sports utility vehicle, as well as a third model which was in progress at the time of writing. Indeed, NDR is not only involved in development of automotive prototypes but is also engaged in more basic research and safety-related work, the results of which are transmitted back to Japan. Following an initial three-year start-up phase, the next three-to-four-year period for NDR focussed on developing a suitable supplier network to strengthen the organizational structure needed for developing cars in the United States. In the third phase, which will last until the end of the present decade, the center will take on the role of a fully localized independent engineering firm with US management capable of challenging headquarters with new ideas. In terms of staffing, Tanuma says that he wants to promote younger members, as well as creating career opportunities for mechanical engineers. Priority issues in the near term are three-fold: to gather a network of local suppliers with the required R&D capability; to simplify the extremely complex development and engineering process; and finally, to transfer control of critical development responsibilities to the right kind of talented local staff.[21]

Mr. Narita, who succeeded Mr. Tanuma as president of NDR, makes the following comment: "Of course NDR's role is to serve as the development center for Nissan in North America, but with a staff of only about 500, it does not yet have all the resources needed to handle the entire development process and will therefore have to coordinate on division of responsibilities with Nissan's main development center in Japan. For the time being at least, the division of labor is likely to be as follows: Japan will remain in charge of the design and development of major power train components, chassis, and under-the-floor aspects, while NDR will handle body components, interior, panels, glass, doors, and so on.

"A key issue for NDR will be to strengthen local design-in capabilities, and from 1993 onwards, the development of components for Smyrna. We learned a great deal from our joint development project of the minivan with Ford, in areas such as their positive management system, for example their inside auditing for safety issue, and by making clear the division of authority and responsibility within the framework of the co-production description, we were able to resolve the problems that arose. I would say that Ford was also able to learn about the design-in procedures at Nissan, and our approach to teamwork in the development process. But while both sides benefited from the collaboration, this was still 'round one' as it were, and it would be an exaggeration to say that everything went without a hitch. Moreover, as design-in was limited to only a few areas, it would be inaccurate to say that we really took advantage of true simultaneous engineering. We will need to make further efforts to reduce development lead times and lower overall development costs."[22]

Toyota and Honda have generally encountered the same kind of difficulties as Nissan in their efforts to localize design and development. In Honda's case, the main function of Honda Research & Development of the US (HRA), with only 200 employees, has been to serve a supporting role in efforts to raise local content, but more recently the center has taken on some development-related work as well. Starting essentially as an effort to replace parts made in Japan through local procurement, the remit has grown to include the procurement of parts for simultaneous development and is evolving into a total systematic approach aimed at ensuring uniform quality standards. For design-in activities, a number of US companies, including TRW, visited Honda's Tochigi Research center and took part in joint development efforts, starting with the 1990 Accord model. Since then, the number of parts makers involved with the 1994 Civic has increased substantially. However, it will take until 1995 to install the large-scale equipment needed for local development of power-trains and other major components. From the 1994 model year, the company intends to draw up plans in accordance with local production levels.

Honda will be able to draw upon previous experience with motorcycles and general-purpose engines, but it will not compromise by having to use local parts that do not meet its standards, or which might detract from the overall quality of Honda cars. To illustrate this, in one case the company found that a locally made oil heater had a design problem that caused it to leak. Honda advised the local supplier that it would use the part if the supplier was willing to make the necessary modifications to prevent the leakage. Some suppliers have certainly benefitted from allowing Honda's quality control specialists into their plants to examine their procedures, and by understanding the Honda approach not only raised their quality standards but also lowered their costs. But the choice of adopting such Japanese-style practices remains that of the suppliers themselves. When selecting local suppliers, Honda tries to look beyond the immediate price issue to try to determine whether the management is willing to accept new challenges and delivery schedules.[23]

Thus, while there are individual differences in the way the Japanese auto makers have approached the issue of R&D localization, they generally face a similar set of obstacles. A major difference, however, is suggested by the divergent approaches taken by Nissan, to work in conjunction with a US company like Ford on some projects while also pushing ahead quite aggressively on R&D localization, and that adopted by Honda, which takes a more stringent view of ensuring that suppliers measure up to the company's standards and image, and thus is pursuing localization and design-in with this outlook. In Toyota's case, the company set up its California design center in the early 1980s, and established its Ann Arbor development center to serve as the focal point for its efforts to support local suppliers for three production facilities, at Nummi, Georgetown, and in Canada.

In general terms, each of the major Japanese auto makers is moving ahead to localize development of new body styles, interiors, and so on, but not as a rule the major platforms and drive-train components. In terms of model types, the companies have moved first to develop sportier niche models locally, such as the Toyota Supra, and the Nissan Exa and Terrano models. In addition, they have pushed the local development of models that are basically offshoots of major model types, such as the Camry and Accord Wagons, and are gradually increasing the local component sourcing and design-in process, as well as design work, for models such as the Altima, and the new Camry and Accord models.

5. Conclusion

We have examined the current situation and major issues facing the leading Japanese auto makers in their globalization strategies, with a specific focus on their efforts to localize production networks in the United States. In their home market, these companies are having to restructure their operations in the wake of the collapse of the bubble economy. The principal objective of this restructuring process is to eliminate non-lean practices that had sharply raised break-even levels. The industry is making serious efforts to retreat from the excesses which emerged during the boom period of the bubble, which can be expressed as the degree to which processes diverged from the industry's original lean practices.

In the near term, the focus of restructuring and rationalization will be on lowering costs, through such measures as reducing model and parts variations, more sharing of parts, reducing the costs involved in model changes, and so on. To some extent, positive results for the automotive industry will not end with such short-term cost-control measures. Rather, the critical issue will be to what extent the industry can reorganize itself in order to strengthen its ability to cope with down trends in the business cycle and the overall lower growth that is expected, and how to develop a structure that is recession-resistant. It will have to find a way to evolve, from the lean production system that proved highly advantageous during the period of high-volume growth, to a system that has the necessary degree of resilience to respond to economic fluctuations and recessions, in other words how to implement what might instead be called "lean optimization." This system of lean optimization is not something that will occur only in Japan. There is no doubt that the pace of the industry's globalization will increase dramatically, given the fact that in 1993 local production was to exceed exports from Japan for the first time.

As we have noted in this chapter, the localization of management, and of production and personnel in the Japanese transplants, has already made substantial progress, but will shift to another level as the industry deals with such remaining issues as developing local leaders, and promoting them to top positions, as well as introducing systems for evaluating the abilities of individual employees. Parts procurement is still at the stage of trial and error, but progress is being made in areas such as the expansion of design-in, VE and VA activities with local suppliers, and a gradual shift to single sourcing and long-term supply contracts.

A range of problems remains unresolved, notably expanding participation of local suppliers in simultaneous projects, strengthening the suppliers' in-house technological capabilities, and their ability to provide sufficient total quality assurance. To achieve progress on these issues will require a further strengthening of cooperative relationships between each of the Japanese auto makers and their local suppliers, but the need for overall improvement in the standards of local suppliers and their production systems also gives efforts such as Toyota's supplier support center an important role to play. Attempts by all the Japanese auto makers to strengthen their relationships with local suppliers, and to help them improve through cooperative efforts, are not just an issue for the Japanese firms themselves but will also indirectly benefit US auto makers.

Moreover, while the importance of localizing R&D will continue to grow in significance for the Japanese auto makers, the evolution of design-in and the localization of R&D are inseparable, and further progress on both is an important key. Localizing design-in can help Japanese auto makers learn from the creativity of US designers. An important indication of how successful the Japanese auto makers are in localizing R&D is likely to be found in how effectively they manage the significant cultural differences between Japanese and US organizational behavior, and whether they make effective use of the individuality and creativity of US designers. This will have to be achieved within the broader context of managing R&D organizations through promoting practices such as simultaneous engineering and teamwork between development groups, as well as effectively coordinating overlapping development by different sections.

As we have seen, the focus in the near term is on how well the Japanese auto makers achieve "lean optimization" through restructuring and rationalization. From a medium-term perspective, the success or failure of the industry's globalization strategy will have an enormous impact on its future. The decisive element in this strategy will be the degree to which the industry succeeds in localizing operations in the US market, which represents its biggest overseas investment, and in developing a global network. In the immediate future, it is readily apparent that there are limits to the number of vehicles which will be exported from Japan, and thus the problem arises of how the industry can make a soft landing by replacing those reduced exports with local production. In the medium term, further consolidation of domestic production capacity will become necessary, as a result of the structural shortage of younger workers in Japan, with the result that global production will also have to expand to offset the expected reduction in Japan. In a sense, the process now visible in the overseas operations of Japanese auto makers can be regarded as a shift to what might be called "lean hybridization," which is occurring as Japanese companies accommodate local cultures and habits.

An experiment is under way to see which elements of the Japanese lean production system are really universal and adaptable to local cultures and their people. There may well be important lessons to be learned from this process of "lean optimization," and from Japan's experiences in establishing a system that avoids the excesses that emerged during the boom period of the bubble, such as excessive overtime and multiple model variations.

Finally, strengthening the globalization strategy of the Japanese automotive industry, in which all of the Japanese car makers have some degree of experience already, will also have an impact on expanding cooperative relationships with the US Big Three auto makers. It is likely that the kind of collaborative relationship which Nissan pioneered with Ford will continue to expand, in terms of joint development, joint production, mutual supply of components, OEM supply of cars, and so on. There is thus little doubt that the industry's global strategy will contribute to both the promotion of healthy competition and the development of cooperative relationships with foreign auto makers.

Notes

1. The fuel-efficiency requirement of the US government, which began in 1978, increased fuel efficiency gradually until 1985, and 27.5 MPG (a 27.5 mile drive per gallon) was required. Some US makers were paying a fine, while most Japanese cars satisfied the requirement in the 1980s.
2. The increase in price was covered by an extension of the installment period, which was prolonged from an average forty-eight months to sixty months.
3. K. Shimokawa, "The globalization and strategy of the Japanese automobile industry," MIT International Motor Vehicle Program Meeting Research Paper, October, 1992, p. 3.
4. Refer to Table 5.1.

5. From an interview (September 1991) with H. Yoshino, president of US Honda Manufacturing (later, president of Honda).

6. From an interview (September 1991) with T. Amino, then vice-president of US Honda Manufacturing.

7. From an interview (September 1991) with F. Cho, president of US Toyota Manufacturing (at the time of writing, later president of Toyota).

8. Ibid.

9. M. Kenney, and R. Florida, *Beyond Mass Production: The Japanese System and Its Transfer to the US*, Oxford University Press, 1993, p. 104.

10. Ibid., from an interview with F. Cho.

11. Ibid., from an interview with T. Amino.

12. Kenney and Florida, pp. 130–131.

13. Ibid., from an interview with H. Yoshino.

14. K. Shimokawa, "Nissann no genchika senryaku: Sono jittai to kadai," *Jidosha Journal*, January, 1991, pp. 8–9 (Localization strategy of Nissan).

15. Ibid., pp. 9–10.

16. From an interview with Mr. Sato (a resident assistant chief of staff of Toyota, Detroit, at that time).

17. K. Shimokawa, "Toyota supplier support center institute," Nikkan jidosha shinbun, January 27, 1993.

18. K. Shimokawa, "The internationalization of the Japanese automobile industry," in G. D. Hook and M. A. Weiner (eds.), *The Internationalization of Japan*, Routledge, 1992, p. 138.

19. Ibid., K. Shimokawa, 1991, pp. 12–13.

20. Ibid., pp. 13–14.

21. Ibid., pp. 15–16.

22. From an interview with Narita, a president of Nissan R&D, September 1992.

23. From an interview with N. Hashimoto, a vice-president of Honda R&D, September 1991.

3 | The recovery of European and US auto makers, and relocating and changing lean production

1. Introduction

As we have witnessed, the competitive relationship between the Japanese and Western automobile industries has experienced a dramatic transformation in the age of globalization and worldwide restructuring. In the 1980s, the Japanese automobile industry led the world with its lean production system, which was implemented at local plants in Europe as well as in the United States. All three major differentiating factors – just-in-time production systems and total quality control (TQC) activities, the *keiretsu* supplier system, and a product development system based on simultaneous engineering with a short lead time – functioned together to create the Japanese automobile industry's competitive strength. While Japanese companies introduced these systems in their overseas plants, Western auto manufacturers applied themselves to learning the system. This chapter investigates the transformation that took place, and considers the lessons to be learned in the context of a new management paradigm for the automobile industry in a global era.

2. Rapid learning of lean production by European and US automobile makers

The basic Japanese production system

European and US automobile makers recovered their competitiveness and learned the Japanese production system extremely quickly, partly because they conducted a thorough systematic analysis of the Japanese systems and shared information. Though some of the reforms to their factories were not satisfactory, various, more successful reforms were conducted in other areas.[1]

The US auto makers were already looking at the structural factors for Japan's competitiveness in the mid 1980s, and began working toward improvement at the public and private levels. This was not limited to the automobile industry – the Reagan government established the Industrial Competitiveness Enhancement Act[2] and created a system in which industrial sectors could create industrial standards together and conduct cooperative research without breaking antitrust acts. The Marcom Boldrige Award was awarded to groups or individuals who successfully contributed to quality improvement. The Automotive Industry Action Group (AIAG) was established, and consisted of the Big Three and the leading auto parts makers. This group began setting common standards in the automobile industry in order to reform the US's automobile parts trade and its logistics. This reduced business waste and the information gap existing in the parts trade, and provided a framework for moving to a JIT-style parts-supply system. These AIAG activities also accelerated IT reform in the automobile industry. The US and the Big Three's renewal is described below.

Establishing strategic management and rivalry from new model strategies

US automobile makers were already studying or introducing partial lean production systems as early as the first half of the 1980s. For example, they introduced workers' QC circles or organization-and-method under an agreement with the UAW, they narrowed down the number of parts makers, and organized cooperation groups among parts makers. But the Big Three realized that this was not enough to catch up with Japan, and thus began establishing strategic management.

However, the Big Three were not slavishly copying Japanese automobile makers; instead they combined and adapted model strategies, lean production, IT, and other advanced technologies.[3] The model strategies of the Big Three, especially Ford and Chrysler, focussed on new market segments in light trucks, while Japanese automobile makers focussed on passenger cars. Ford concentrated efforts on pickup trucks, Chrysler minivans and SUVs. The market for light trucks gradually expanded to become larger than that for passenger cars, growing from 20 percent to 50 percent of the market. Since a frame chassis was used for these US models, the model-change cycle was longer than that for passenger cars, and this fitted well because the factories of the Big Three were built for mass production. Moreover, many vehicles could be manufactured using one type of chassis and the cost per vehicle was cheap; thus a relatively low price could be set in comparison with passenger cars.[4]

This model strategy helped to build a concrete revenue basis and create conditions that assured cash flow for global business. Ford set up eight plants for manufacturing light trucks before 1985 by switching passenger car plants over to pickups or by building new plants, which helped to expand the production of pickup trucks and improved their profitability.

Strategic introduction of lean production and reforming the supplier system

Originally, US automobile makers tried to copy the Japanese lean production system, but eventually adapted those parts of lean production which they could use promptly and creatively. US automobile makers focussed on changing the supplier system and reforming product development. The level of QCDE was thoroughly analyzed by benchmarking, the number of outsourcing suppliers was reduced, and there was an attempt to focus on business with suppliers who supplied a system or a unit. As a result, the structure of the parts trade became close to a pyramid shape, and contracts with suppliers became mainly long term. Suppliers' participation in design and development at an early stage also became possible. The ratio of in-house production became lower by spinning out the parts divisions of companies, and competitive ability was increased by changing suppliers into megasuppliers who carried out their business with their own strategies.[5]

However, reforming the supplier system was not easy. Parts divisions for in-house production were still acting rigidly in a traditional high-volume manner, and the development abilities of the divisions were not equal.

Recognizing that reforms could be managed only by narrowing down the number of suppliers, it was promoted under a thorough benchmarking system. Only system suppliers and module suppliers were selected,[6] and business was focussed on them. The suppliers themselves also underwent mergers and acquisitions, they supplied parts in cooperation with other companies, and emphasized the design divisions. Gradually, data on Japanese and other suppliers around the world were collected into a global base, and suppliers were marked and selected according to a total balance of QCDE. Relations with them were also strengthened.

In short, this was a supplier strategy that aimed to integrate the suppliers and to promote a total development of their abilities.

Reforming the product development system

US automobile makers also reformed product development by removing barriers to development sections and carrying out parallel development, so that a speedy development system which was close to market needs could be developed. This development system was called concurrent engineering, and the development lead-time was close to that of Japanese makers, so that the previously typical development time of sixty months for one model was reduced by half.[7]

Reforming plants with difficulties

Reforming production systems had been postponed for two reasons – first, because of the difficulties in carrying out all the necessary changes in one go, and second, because the type of process designs based on all-round workers used by Japanese companies was impossible to conduct in traditional high-volume plants. In a completely new plant, such as GM's Saturn plant, all-round working or teamwork had been introduced, but this was an exception.[8]

Efforts have been made to reduce and control stock at production sites, but quality guarantees and the setting up of quality in a perfect process are at too early a stage to give the responsibility to work sites, so many QC personnel have been allocated. Delaying reform of production has become a major preoccupation for the Big Three. The break-even point of old plants with one-job workers is high, and losses result even with a slight decrease in production. Changes in demand structure and market needs are accelerated in automobile markets in advanced countries, and demands for shortening the model-change cycle and for responding to flexible production are getting stronger, even in the fields of SUVs and pickup trucks. Reforms in plants are thus urgently needed in order to respond to these demands.

Introducing IT and its strategic use

When we talk about the recovery of the Big Three, their swift introduction of IT should not be forgotten. Japanese companies fell behind in the strategic use of IT. During the 1990–1991 recession after the Gulf War, the Big Three tried to continue the restructuring that had started at the beginning of the 1980s. They used IT to review their control systems, to simplify white-collar jobs, and to flatten management layers. The introduction of IT also helped the companies develop database structures for benchmarking, and to improve and communicate digital-design data in concurrent engineering. This prompt use of IT greatly contributed to a change in corporate culture and the structure of strategic management because the US automobile makers used IT as a strategic tool, synchronizing the world of implicit knowledge created by Japanese-style experientialism with the production process by using manuals, flow charts, and systems analysis.[9]

At the beginning of the 1990s, it was thought that it might be another ten years before European and US automobile makers had learned and incorporated Japanese production systems. It was assumed that, by then, the Japanese automobile makers would have refined their systems and would continue to dominate. But US companies were quicker than expected because they analyzed information about the systems thoroughly, and then systematized what they needed, while at the same time using IT to create a database and establish evaluation systems for benchmarks.

3. Learning from the adoption of the lean production system by Western automobile manufacturers

Western automobile manufacturers were quick to understand Japanese production systems and then integrate and use this knowledge, developing concurrent engineering and benchmarking systems that met their own needs. The concept of supply chain management came from the ideas of JIT, expanding it beyond plants and suppliers to include logistics and distribution, *and manage all waste in the system or hidden in business practices (for instance, duplication).* This type of conceptualizing ability is not well developed in Japan.

As the automobile industry continues to internationalize, there is a movement to establish a comprehensive logistics system and this concept also seems to be based on JIT ideas. Lean management and business systems are being built utilizing the full capacity of IT. As management systems get leaner, a system for making strategic decisions quickly is also evolving, suggesting the emergence of a dynamic organizational preference for lean management.

Strategies and conceptualization of deployment, from TQC to TQM

Japanese QC circle activities are different from the typical, old-style US type of statistical quality management that involved only those who understood complex statistical analysis and probability theory. Rather, the Japanese QC circle activities are designed to be understandable to workers at the plants, resulting in "QC 7 tools." Workers make their own data charts according to their own sites, and can then identify their own problems for consideration. This eventually leads to a solid TQC activity across the entire company, resulting in improved quality overall. Western manufacturers are using TQC activities at a higher level by expanding the idea into a form of total quality management (TQM) not only at the plants but also in the areas of distribution, supplies, related sections, and departments, and even outside their own company to promote quality improvement. This shows the strategic and conceptualizing ability of these companies. Recently, Japanese companies have begun to change in name from TQC to TQM, but it is not clear that they really understand the true difference between the two.

Restructuring the elitism for site management

When US focus was on mass and high-volume production using single-skilled workers, it was believed that plant workers should not be expected to learn complicated processes and procedures; they were expected to do simple tasks exactly in accordance with the manual. Production management was conducted by specialists, who analyzed processes, created charts, schedules, flow charts and manuals, and finally managed the operation and progress of each single-skilled worker.

Japanese companies expected their site managers to understand QC circles and JIT production methods rather than simply managing reported data. Western manufacturers learned that management needed to go to the sites and see operations for themselves in order to lead strategically. More managers in US companies now visit production sites and understand the data that are coming from the sites. Not surprisingly, IT is playing an important role, and various data are reported online to the plant managers in real time.

This means, rather than buried with the idea of site realism = site primacy, they request improvement from the workers working at the line, instructing them to discover problems, although they cannot totally rely on them. Thus, the background idea is that they need to lead more strategically.

4. Conclusion

European and US automobile makers adopted a Japanese-style production system much more quickly than was expected, but their renewed international competitiveness and the establishment of hegemony via globalization cannot be attributed only to this. The strategic ability of European and US automobile makers – something which was absent among Japanese automobile makers – was a major contributor to their success, as was rapid adoption and strategic deployment of new information technologies and a systematic approach to switching from experiential knowledge to systematic knowledge. Product development, supplier, and other systems that urgently needed upgrading were also reformed.

The Big Three responded quickly to competition from Japanese automobile makers in the first half of the 1980s and to the establishment of transplants by Japanese makers in the US and in the UK in the latter half of the 1980s. Each of the Big Three companies also tied up with Japanese automobile makers in various ways. In Europe, Japanese transplants began to be established in the latter half of the 1980s, but this did not become a significant threat to European companies. The fact that the French and Italian automobile markets were not completely liberalized for Japanese cars led to European companies delaying their response. Adoption of Japanese production systems began mainly among mass-production automobile makers in Europe. For example, GM's affiliate, Opel, built a new plant in Eisenach, Germany, using lessons learned from GM's experiences establishing Nummi in the US, a joint venture with Toyota. European car makers also reduced the number of supplier systems. Renault established a new technical development center that introduced concurrent engineering, VW established a flexible production line for the new Polo, and PSA Citroën planned a plant based on the Toyota production system.

Notes

1. K. Shimokawa, "FORD Chicago koujyo houmonki" (My visiting impression of Ford Chicago plant), Nikkan jidousha shinbun, June 3, 1988.
2. K. Harada, "Beikoku jidousha sanyou yakushin no senryaku" (The strategy of great advance of the US auto industry), Kougyou chosakai, 1995, p. 29. The Reagan government established the National Cooperative Research Act in 1984, and cooperative researches were approved for areas which would not prevent free competition among companies.
3. K. Shimokawa, "Kigyo no kaigaisenryaku to kaigai chokusetutoushi/ beikoku jidousha kigyou no jirei: 1980 nendai no fushinnkara 90nenndai no saisei e," (The overseas strategies and direct investment – the example of US automobile companies), *Journal of Investment*, July 2002, p. 26.
4. Originally, small-size pickup trucks did not exist in the US. They appeared in the US automobile markets in the 1970s when Japanese automobile makers exported Datsun trucks, the Toyota Hilux, and others. However, as the US revenue authority introduced a cab-chassis tax, which increased the tax on trucks from 3 percent to 30 percent, exports of pickup trucks from Japan decreased dramatically. After 1985, the price of Japan-made small cars of the Corolla class increased from US$6,000 to $9,000 in 5–6 years because of Japan's voluntary export restraints and the hike of the yen, in contrast to the price of US-made pickup trucks, which were around US$7,000.
5. Ibid., K. Shimokawa, 2002, p. 27. The representative cases for spin-off were Delphi, which spun off from GM, Visteon from Ford, and Faurecia from the French PSA. Delphi and Visteon, which have more than 100,000 employees, became numbers one and two in the world sales ranking.
6. System suppliers means that the suppliers do not produce and supply individual parts but rather supply, for example, fuel-injection pumps or radiators, which are themselves a system with a function. Many Japanese *keiretsu* suppliers are system suppliers. Module suppliers means suppliers that supply parts, segments, functions, or materials in a total and integrated style. For example, the plastic frame of an instrument panel to which all gauges and air-conditioning devices are loaded is called an instrument-panel module. Whether module suppliers are used or not depends on the decision of each automobile maker.
7. A typical case is the Neon, the small-size car from Chrysler. According to the analysis of international comparative data in *Product Development Performance*, by T. Fujimoto and K.B. Clark (Diamond-sha, 1993, p. 105), US makers' average development period was more than 61.9 months, in contrast to Japanese makers' 26 months in the latter half of the

1980s. But the development period of the Neon was about 32 months when it appeared in 1993 – the period was reduced by almost half, and this surprised Japanese automobile makers.

8. K. Shimokawa, "GM Saturn koujyo houmonnki" (My visiting impression of the GM Saturn plant), Nikkan jidousha shinnbun, January 6, 1996.

9. Ibid., K. Shimokawa, 2002, p. 28.

4 | Early 1990s – the Japanese automotive industry loses international competitiveness, and the development of restructuring strategies

1. Demise of the bubble economy and factors relating to deterioration in competitiveness

As recently as fifteen years ago, the Japanese automobile industry was said to be the most efficient and internationally competitive, having eleven major automobile makers, including truck manufacturers, to the US and Europe's two or three. However, toward the end of the bubble economy, figures from the Japanese auto makers began to deteriorate rapidly. The profits of the eleven auto makers, which reached ¥1.1 trillion between the 1980s and 1991, had fallen to less than half that, ¥400 billion, by early 1993. Three out of the eleven companies went into deficit, and people began to question what had happened to Japan's competitive power.

Until the economic bubble burst, signaling the start of the Heisei recession, Japanese auto makers had shown steady growth every year, even during periods of reduced production following the 1973 and 1981 oil shocks. Yet in both cases this was only for a year before production increased once more. So four consecutive years of reduced production following the collapse of the bubble economy was unprecedented.

Reduced production on each occasion was greatly influenced by a reduction in domestic demand, but after the two oil shocks, an increase in exports led to greater production. Immediately following the first oil shock, exports to the US and the Middle East increased, and after the second oil shock, exports to Europe grew. However, in the depression of the early 1990s, domestic demand fell for three consecutive years, from a peak of 7.8 million in 1990 down to 6.5 million in 1993, and exports failed to increase to balance this fall; Western auto markets went into recession at around the same time and trade friction intensified. In addition, Japanese domestic auto makers began to focus increasingly on indigenous production rather than exports. Japan exported 1.54 million cars to the US in 1994, while local production was over 1.78 million.

The second devaluation of the yen ($1 = ¥130 to ¥85) added to the domestic market doldrums and the drop in exports. Calls for adjusting production capability were not just for a temporary reduction, as seen in the weaving, shipping, and iron and steel industries in the past, but for a reduction in production capacity via restructuring.

As we have seen, the Japanese auto industry was internationally competitive due to its system of high-quality parts makers and the short lead times for product development, which was built around a flexible and effective production system. But the Japanese auto industry changed greatly during the economic bubble (1987–1990), thanks to an expanding domestic market and the popularity of luxury models. Although the profit structure for the main Japanese auto makers in the early 1980s was export, and most profits came from exports to the US after 1985, the depreciation of the yen meant that profits from exports fell, and the profit structure had to change to one of market expansion.

Curiously, production during the recession was still 1 million vehicles higher than in the year before the bubble economy collapsed. In 1986, the domestic auto market was around 5.8 million units (including small cars); from 1987, there was a sudden expansion in this market, reaching 7.8 million vehicles in 1990, an increase of almost 2 million. This figure fell by 0.86 million in 1992, to 6.94 million. Compared with seven years before, that was still 1 million more vehicles, so it is difficult to understand why/how the Japanese auto makers faced such a bad recession all of a sudden. Why, then, despite production being around 1 million vehicles higher than seven years before, did profits fall to such a degree? The overall profits of the Japanese auto industry were actually quite low, despite the industry being internationally competitive. Low profit rates per vehicle of 2–4 percent were offset by the growth in volume, so that when the growth in volume faltered, the fall in profit was quickly apparent.

The rise in break-even point is usually due to expansion of fixed asset costs, such as equipment investment or investment in R&D. Japanese auto makers, instead of investing for speculative profits, were directing their businesses the wrong way. Their investment strategies made one-sided growth a prerequisite, and huge amounts were invested in diversification to produce luxury models.

Japanese auto makers moved away from the processes that had served them well in the past. There was a strong tendency to invest in high-tech information technology to automate plants and computer integrated manufacturing (CIM), instead of the kaizen activities that supported the Japanese production system. Japanese makers placed too much confidence in the ability of their flexible processes, short lead times, and high efficiency to adapt to increasing numbers of models and parts. The stance was to maintain short model-change cycles compared with overseas makers even if it cost them to do this, whereas in the past, Japanese auto makers had tried to achieve an effective operation rate with limited equipment, space, and resources, hence JIT. The trend toward greater numbers of models and parts eventually reached a limit, in the sense that it got the manufacturers into the vicious cycle of high cost.

In the early 1990s, after four consecutive years of recession and large reductions in profits, can it really be said that the Japanese automobile industry had lost its competitive edge? The situation faced by each auto manufacturer was different and it remained to be seen what would be the effect of the restructuring in progress. A lot also depended on the overseas production and global strategy adopted by the Japanese auto makers.

If the various attempts at restructuring – reduction in model numbers, part sharing, reviewing the model-change cycle, consolidating unprofitable factories, collaboration between parts makers, advance and devaluation of break-even point, responses to economic fluctuations – could withstand the ups and downs in the economy of a matured market, then a fall in competitive power would be temporary. The potential of Japan's international competitiveness was not yet lost in spite of the recession; the flexible and effective production and parts supply systems, and product development, still functioned.

The Japanese production system of the time can be interpreted as a one-sided diversification of consumer needs while pursuing appropriate quantity production. The large number of models required to follow this strategy places a burden on development and on the plant, and can lead to a fall in the ability to adapt to quantitative changes, so production might not match up to consumer needs. Therefore, it was important to adapt so that production was sufficiently diversified to match market needs, and at the same time have a system that was flexible enough to produce suitable models in variable quantities.

Table 4.1 is a compilation from newspaper reports in 1993 showing what kind of restructuring the main Japanese car manufacturers carried out. Table 4.2 shows the effects of restructuring on profits after 1992, when restructuring began. As Table 4.2 indicates, the most effective ways to increase profits were parts sharing, model reduction and VA, VE (value analysis and value engineering) with the parts makers.

The greatest focus of the restructuring was undoubtedly on rationalization of production plants, but the method of product development was also important. The Japanese auto industry had an effective and respected product development system, so why was it the focus of the first restructuring? It was quite clear that product development by itself was not sufficient – it needed to take into consideration the market and industry environment and the needs of consumers. Much doubt was expressed over the effectiveness of this product development during the initial phase of restructuring.

Product development had not always been effective. In the post-war period, many Japanese auto makers produced under European license, so product development was similar to that of Western auto makers. However, Japanese car makers concentrated on building small cars from the very beginning and were under pressure to make these cars with minimum costs. This was not limited only to product development, and Japan, which was a late developer, had to contain costs in production equipment, factory space, manpower, purchase of parts, etc. In other words, this was exactly what came to be called the "lean production system."

Product development as pioneered by Toyota, for example, gave product development managers a lot of power, and established a system of a select group of experts who could accelerate product development. Generally, in automotive design and development, development is promoted by assigning responsibilities to each section, the chassis (nowadays referred to as the "platform"), body, engine drive parts, interiors, and so forth; however, the automotive companies of the West carefully divide development into sections and each section sequentially pursues design and development in stages.

Many of Japan's auto makers copied this style at first, but they eventually linked the individual development sections to one another horizontally under the authority of a single chief developer, and adopted an overlapping structure of design and development that

Table 4.1 *Restructuring of five Japanese auto makers (1993–1996)*

Nissan	
Reduction of clerical employees (no.)	4,000
Reduction of factory workers (no.)	1,000
Parts sharing	
Reduction in models	40%
Reduction in no. of parts	40%
Rate of operation of plant	85%
Total amount of cost reduction (¥1 billion)	200
Breakdown:	
Parts cost	100
Manpower cost	25
Parts sharing	30
Production efficiency	10
Other	35
Honda	
Reduction of clerical employees (no.)	900
Reduction of factory workers (no.)	0
Parts sharing	
Reduction in models	50%
Reduction in no. of parts	50%
Total amount of cost reduction (¥1 billion)	60
Breakdown:	
Parts cost	30
Manpower cost	10
Parts sharing	10
Production efficiency	5
Other	5
Mazda	
Reduction of clerical employees (no.)	5,500
Reduction of factory workers (no.)	1,000
Parts sharing	
Reduction in models	40%
Reduction in no. of parts	40%
Total amount of cost reduction (¥1 billion)	60
Breakdown:	
Parts cost	30
Manpower cost	10

Table 4.1 (*cont.*)

Mazda	
Parts sharing	10
Production efficiency	5
Other	5

Toyota	
Reduction of clerical employees (no.)	2,000
Reduction of factory workers (no.)	0
Parts sharing	
Reduction in models	20%
Reduction in no. of parts	30%
Total amount of cost reduction (¥1 billion)	260
Breakdown:	
Parts cost	200
Manpower cost	20
Parts sharing	20
Production efficiency	10
Other	10

Mitsubishi Motors	
Parts sharing	
Reduction in models	30%
Reduction in no. of parts	30%
Total amount of cost reduction (¥1 billion)	40
Breakdown:	
Parts cost	20
Manpower cost	0
Parts sharing	10
Production efficiency	5
Other	5

Source: Morgan Stanley Report

allowed for as much simultaneous parallel work as possible. They also pushed a design-in process that brought parts suppliers with formidable development strengths into development at an early stage.

Like their counterparts in the West, Japanese auto makers originally handled the detailed designs of each specific part, prototyping, and

Table 4.2 *Factors for increase and decrease in profits for Japanese auto makers in fiscal year 1993*

	Reason for increased profits				Reason for decreased profits				
	Total	*Parts sharing *Reduced models VA,VE	Reduced depreciation cost	Reduced expenses, etc.	Total	Loss from exchange rate	Reduced sales	Increased personnel expenses	Increase and decrease in business profits
Toyota	1,600	1,000	340	260	1,812	1,200	300	312	−212
Nissan	600	300	30	270	800	500	300		−200
Honda	382	190	192		525	275	250		−143
Mitsubishi	236	116	120		280	180	100		−44
Mazda	530	100	430		750	300	450		−220
Suzuki	111	76	7	28	128	76	0	52	−17
Fuji heavy industries	100	74	0	26	290	160	70	60	−190
Daihatsu	121	19	14	88	72	53	19	0	49
Hino	73	36	37		86	21	48	17	−13
Isuzu	400	100	0	300	312	130	160	22	88
Total	4,153	2,011	2,142		5,055	2,895	2,160		−902

Source: Based on Mitsubishi Research Institute documents on automobiles

testing themselves, and then outsourced the actual manufacture based on shop drawings. But as parts suppliers enhanced their technical capabilities and development strengths, they began partaking in the development processes via design-in work.

Coupled with this, the level of production engineering at the plants operated by Japanese auto makers rose even higher, so the time from prototyping to test-production and actual production launch was greatly shortened, to less than half of that required by Western automotive manufacturers. Because the production response on the plant side was so quick, the trial production runs that used to be so troublesome became extremely fast. By making development efficient, with a minimum number of processes and a quicker lead-time, the product development systems of Japan's auto makers became known as the most efficient amongst automotive manufacturers worldwide.

What took the Western automotive manufacturers a minimum of six to eight years of development, and as much as ten years for a luxury vehicle, was accomplished in half that time and, at times, in just three years by Japan's auto makers. Nevertheless, this parts development efficiency went virtually unnoticed up until the early 1980s, while Japan's auto makers were devoted to just compact cars. Though the low cost, high quality that reflected the production engineering level of Japanese cars drew attention, production engineering and development efficiency also improved and contributed to the low cost.

The high development efficiency of Japan's auto makers was internationally compared in detail against product development strengths elsewhere in *Product Development Performance*, co-authored by University of Tokyo Professor Takahiro Fujimoto and Harvard Business School President Kim Clark and published by Harvard Business School Press in 1991 (translated by Akehi Tamura, Diamond, Inc., 1993). This analysis had a tremendous impact on the US's Big Three and European automotive manufacturers alike.

By the 1980s, Japan's high product development efficiency had moved Japan's auto makers away from the basic concept of low-cost, high-quality compact cars and drove their transition to cars of high added-value, resulting in a shift to larger luxury vehicles. This led in particular to higher performance, such as the DOHC engine and the development of car electronics. The ability to launch new vehicle after new vehicle with minimal lead-time made Japanese cars that much more interesting and stirred new demand, despite the slightly higher price tags.

In the US market in particular, while the price of cars imported from Japan unavoidably rose because of the start of voluntary restraints on passenger cars in 1981 and a rising yen following the G5 summit of 1985, the fact that Japanese auto makers were able to launch high-grade vehicle after vehicle spurred new demand and helped to diversify market needs, which brought a certain degree of success.

The short lead-time and efficient product development system caused the Japanese market to expand rapidly and shift toward a higher cost structure, particularly during the days of the bubble economy. Gradually, the emphasis on cost reduction and basic performance that had served as the starting points of product development became forgotten and the tendency turned to making the next-generation car.

The sharp rise in domestic demand from 1987 onward rapidly expanded the automobile market, started a trend toward higher costs, and greatly influenced how manufacturers went about product development. Volume not only increased but luxury versions of most makes also sold well. The highly competitive automotive companies not only continued to launch new car after new car but also increased the numbers of models and versions they competed with.

Figures 4.1 and 4.2 show that, in less than ten years, the number of base models alone grew from 200 to 400. Under the pretence of diversifying consumer needs, manufacturers pursued models that were basically unnecessary, which greatly increased the number of parts and greatly drove up costs. Not only did they increase the number of models and parts but, because the lead-time in new car development was short, they also ran it into the ground by tending to launch more new cars than were necessary.

Model-change cycles for Japanese cars are a short four years on average, but the pressure of additional new car launches suggested that too much faith was placed on the high efficiency of the development system, to the point that product development was like firing rapid shots from a gun in hope of hitting the target. But no matter how efficient development might be, if it is done with no concern for effectiveness, the cost of development and model changes on the whole goes up.

Alongside this trend came the increased adoption of electronics technology in automobiles. Cars were fitted with mechanisms equipped

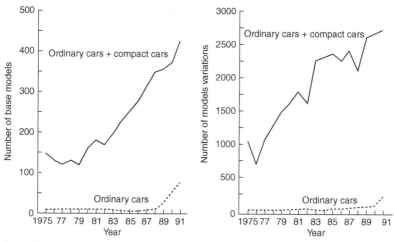

Source: "Automotive Specification Sheet," Society of Automotive Engineers of Japan

Figure 4.1 Number of base models and variations of domestically produced vehicles

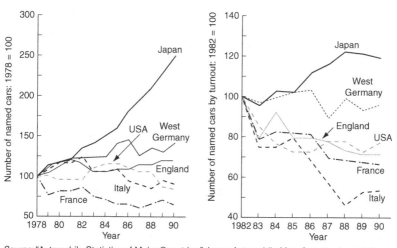

Source: "Automobile Statistics of Major Countries," Japan Automobile Manufactures Association

Figure 4.2 Number of named cars by country

with every new technology and a variety of new functions, to the extent that some had functions that their owners would never use.

Japanese automotive manufacturers clearly placed too much value on the Consumer Satisfaction Index (CSI). In each case, the outcome of the increase in base models, the relatively short model-change cycle, and the emergence of multifunctional vehicles toted as hi-tech cars was over-confidence. The CSI results failed to capture the truest and most essential needs of consumers and offered no reflection whatsoever, while consumers reportedly bowed to the manufacturers' product policies and bought luxury cars and high-end versions under the auspices of the economic bubble.

In short, the product development system had forgotten the origins of Japan's success in the automotive industry – the lean production system. While it was still enjoying the limelight of worldwide acclaim, the automotive product development system had gone from high efficiency and lean to a considerably high-cost structure.

From one perspective, this change in product development strategy cannot be looked at as wrong, if we consider that shifting to higher-grade and higher-added-value cars helped the industry survive the worsening export environment of the late 1980s. Nevertheless, befuddled by the economic bubble and fooled into thinking that growth would continue, this development strategy was forced to change when the recession hit and the age of restructuring was ushered in.

The decline in export profits caused by the sudden recession of the Heisei era and a rising yen marked a new beginning for Japan's auto makers. Thrown into an age of restructuring, big changes were made across the board, including product development. The first action most manufacturers took was to slash new model increases by 20–30 percent. Alongside this, they greatly reduced the number of parts via parts standardization.

2. Development of restructuring strategies by Japan's auto makers

Parts standardization saw some significant changes. For example, Honda successfully standardized 60 percent of the parts of its Domani. Its first-generation minivan, the Odyssey, which led the RV boom, used the same platform as its Accord passenger car. Similar examples were seen with Toyota, Nissan, and Mazda. Using the same platform not only cuts design costs significantly but also makes effective use of existing production lines and, hence, saves on equipment investment. For compacts of low added value and large trucks that were heavily impacted by the recession, parts standardization was viewed at an industry level, beyond the differences between manufacturers.

Moves were made to re-examine model-change cycles with some models, because these had become relatively short and seemed to invite cost increases. Though it was not uniform amongst all manufacturers, some attempted to reduce model-change costs without shortening cycle time by standardizing platforms across two or three generations.

Under the restructuring of the 1990s, Japan's auto makers started to correct the various excesses in product development that had emerged during the economic bubble. Efforts were made to take product development back to its origins and especially to find new directions in development that focussed on cost reduction and the core parts that determine true vehicle performance.

Even development systems that made high efficiency a sellable item were re-examined right down to the organization. For example, Toyota Motors, which fathered the development chief engineer system, took the scalpel to its development organization of 12,000 employees. It reshaped the development structure, which had been horizontally organized by function into design, body, engine, and so forth, and assigned discretionary authority to four development centers: FR (rear-wheel drive), FF (front-wheel drive), multipurpose RV, and elemental technologies. This was done because the products tended to look alike, which the company believed stemmed from the fact that, in its former system, a lot of energy was spent coordinating between departments and the organization itself had grown fat. So even Toyota, the self-declared number one in development efficiency, had neglected its development roots while pursuing a luxury vehicle strategy, and was faced with the problem of an obese development organization.

The key point here was development with a long-term perspective rather than a mad rush for immediate profits, such as developing components and platforms that could be used over as many generations as possible. Manufacturers reconfirmed that the starting point for low cost and high quality was sound basic functions and performance without any bells and whistles. Honda decisively channeled efforts into developing elemental technologies that could be used for a long time, as other manufacturers were thinking, such as high-horsepower engines with low emissions.

This tendency to emphasize elemental technologies connects with the promotion of environmental measures, being particularly important in efforts to reduce CO_2 emissions from evolved engines and provide an answer to global warming.

Challenging Japanese automobile makers through restructuring

In June 1995, the Automotive Consultative Group between the Japanese and US governments was launched and Japan's auto makers hammered out global plans. Japan's auto makers had decided to do something concrete about eliminating the friction over automobile exports, which was due to the fact that automobiles accounted for more than half of the trade deficit with the US.

Had the automobile trade deficit with the US been left as it stood, the Japanese yen would have continued to appreciate, which would have worsened export profits and the so-called "downward spiral" would never have stopped. At the time, creating a global system of production and supply that would be unaffected by exchange rates was seen as an urgent issue.

The reason for this was that the value of the yen rose for a second time while Japan's auto makers were busy restructuring in response to the Heisei recession; the yen went from ¥138 to the dollar to ¥80 from 1992–1995. Not only that, but this came at a time when the domestic market flipped from growth to decline, forcing manufacturers to cut back on production by 10 percent or more and, in many cases, by almost 30 percent. The earnings potential of all Japanese auto makers, and particularly those with a high share of exports to the US, suddenly dropped.

Later, the exchange rate settled on a depreciating yen and the export profitability of Japan's automotive industry improved greatly. The international competitiveness that had been momentarily lost when the yen broke the ¥80 = $1 mark recovered considerably, to the point that the US's Big Three again began showing concern over a possible resurgence in automobile exports from Japan if the yen depreciated any further. Later, there was talk of trade friction surrounding automobile exports, but it never came to a head. This was because the situation up until Japan's auto makers came out with global business plans in June 1995 changed greatly. In 1997, exports from Japan to the US fell to less than half the peak of 1.1 million units achieved during the years of the yen's appreciation. Once again, exports began to increase, reaching a solid 1.6 million, but more importantly, the increase in local production was marked.

This trend continued for a while, but eventually the exchange rate turned toward a weaker yen and fluctuated from there. Opinion overseas suggested that Japan's auto makers had recovered their competitive strength because of the weaker yen, but it could not be entirely attributed to that. Japan's auto makers brutally restructured themselves during the four-year recession, and the new tactics, which greatly reduced prices, cannot be ignored as contributors to this recovery of competitiveness.

In the past, when forced to cut back production immediately after the first oil crisis, Japan's auto makers set targets to meet profitability while operating at 70 percent capacity and, by thoroughly eliminating waste via JIT production methods, promoted a Japanese style of streamlining and produced good results. The approach used during the restructuring of the 1990s was a more systematic form of rationalization that went beyond the scope of merely repeating past approaches and returned to the source – design and development. This new approach was also characterized by the fact that parts suppliers were brought in and told to greatly lower their costs.

The new approach was closely tied to efforts to reduce the excessive number of parts and standardize platforms and components across models and generations. It is fair to say that Japanese auto makers cut up the original stream of design and development, and rebuilt the system with the pieces that were left over. To make significant cost reductions, they conducted a thorough review of design and development from the source and, to reduce the number of prototypes, they slashed the number of development steps where overlapping costs were found, and started to effectively utilize digital computer-aided design and manufacturing (CAD CAM).

Prototyping starts by making an actual car from a clay model, then making a second prototype from this first prototype. Then, a production prototype that is easy to mass produce is fabricated. Because of the repeated quality, performance, safety, parts matching, and ease-of-production testing that is done at each prototype stage, they say it is necessary to make between seventy and eighty prototypes to the tune of about ¥50 million per car. If this could be reduced by one third, costs could be cut by as much as 20–30 percent. For this reason, Japan's auto makers run simulations using a computer-aided engineering (CAE) system prior to the first prototype, to identify and eliminate problems in advance and transition directly from the first prototype to a production prototype. In other words, they have greatly reduced the number of prototypes by either grouping the first and second prototypes into one or skipping the second prototype entirely.

However, to reduce the number of prototypes, not only must design and development be efficient, but also design quality must be top-notch from the outset, and the quality and performance of parts in the production stage must match this. When many prototypes are made, quality, performance, safety, and so forth can be tested repeatedly, but when working with fewer prototypes, design and production must be closely linked and integrated. The Japanese auto makers which saw this focussed their efforts in this direction and produced good results.

First steps toward streamlining the "sacred land" of design and development

A great amount of effort went into minimizing the number of design changes in the prototype stage, which had been accepted as routine in the past. Reducing the number of design changes drastically changed the design practices of Japan's auto makers, which until then typically launched production of a designed prototype and dealt with any problems that arose there via design changes because of the excellence of their production engineering.

These highly frequent design changes were even attempted manually at times, after mass-produced cars were already being sold on the market. This practice aimed at shortening the overall period of design and production, and enabling an appropriate response to the situation as dictated by market needs and available technologies. However, frequent design changes place an unnecessary burden on production floors because they easily drive up costs via jig and tool modifications and also saddle parts suppliers with heavy burdens. For a parts supplier, unreasonably numerous design changes are not only a cost burden but also divert efforts away from their most important task of improving engineering and development strengths.

Because of this, Japanese auto makers introduced a concept engineering stage prior to design to pinpoint new product design concepts and necessary conditions. As part of this, they strongly requested parts suppliers to join in from the early stages of design through a thorough process of simultaneous engineering (SE). For example, it became a widespread practice to simultaneously develop molds, pressed parts,

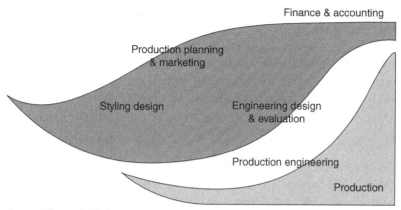

Source: "Toyota R&D System," Toyota Motors

Figure 4.3 Simultaneous engineering

engine parts, transmission and gear boxes, and so forth at the same time that the auto maker was designing and developing the platform, body, and dynamic parts (see Figure 4.3).

Development was said to cost somewhere between ¥50 billion and ¥100 billion per car, but the auto makers and parts suppliers joined together to greatly reduce costs by cutting back the number of development steps all the way back to the source, and by innovating the development process.

Simultaneous engineering with parts suppliers already existed, but these activities were augmented and participation in design and development was established at an earlier point. Efforts included proposing advanced technologies, joint VE, and reducing the number of development steps. As a result, parts suppliers proposed even more new technologies than before, noting in particular system design techniques that reduced the number of parts affected by part design changes, and single-body molding in processing, as well as decisively less processing and shorter lead-times via total production that included mold making, pressing, molding, and assembly. The cooperative relations between auto makers and parts suppliers in design and development were taken to greater depths and, by re-examining design and development right back to the source of the auto maker, it became easier for the parts supplier to streamline design and made tremendous cost reductions possible.

In addition to this trend, new car launch time was shortened by going back to the source and integrating production and design via SE activities. This shortened production lead-time quickened launches after model changes. Before, it took time to run tests on a prototype after design and development, and then, once tests were completed, prepare the production system for a production prototype. By re-examining design at the source, it became possible to prepare for production at the same time that tests were being run.

Improved competitiveness via on-site development engineers

Development engineers were stationed on the production floor, care was taken to ensure it would be easy to build the line and eliminate unnecessary steps, and design was pushed toward facilitating automation in processes. Development engineers also visited plant production engineers regularly to hear their requests and proposals as to how to integrate production and design via SE. At the same time, SE activities also involved parts suppliers, and these were carefully selected down to the second and third tiers, resulting in cost reductions of as much as 30 percent in just three years.

These activities greatly minimized design changes, which cost unnecessary manpower, and drastically minimized the number of production prototypes needed, hence greatly reducing the lead-time to launch. This created a system that swiftly and flexibly adapted to changes in, for example, the RV boom and the demand structure of passenger cars. The shorter lead-time that resulted from the integration of development and production reduced product development from 36–40 months to 20 or fewer months per vehicle. By the early 1990s, Toyota reported eighteen months to develop the RAV 4 and Mazda reported fifteen months for its Demio. Ten or twelve months to develop a model on a common platform were no longer far-fetched dreams.

3. Contrasts in strategy-building ability and management reorganization among Japanese auto makers undergoing global restructuring

Foreshadows of global restructuring

Around the mid 1990s, differences in strategy-building ability and management skills among Japan's auto makers became obvious, dividing them basically into winners and losers.

As we have seen, the heyday of the economic bubble caused Japan's auto makers to be misled by multiple interlocking strategies that drove up development costs, burdened them with overinvestment in state-of-the-art plant automation, increased parts procurement costs, etc. They also misjudged the expansion potential of the light truck market in the US, which was the highest revenue-producing market for them, and made wrong strategy decisions that caused them to lose out on commercial vehicles. These strategy mistakes were, generally speaking, common to all Japanese auto makers. The results of these mistakes began to show in the mid 1990s, particularly around 1993 when the economic bubble burst and the yen started rising for a second time. In response to this, all Japan's auto makers should have reformulated their strategies, restructured, and started producing results by 1995 or 1996. But, for some reason, they became clearly divided into a winners' camp of Toyota, Honda, and Suzuki, and a group consisting of Nissan, Mitsubishi, Mazda, and Isuzu, whose performance remained in a slump. This is where a contrast in strategy-building ability and general management skills can be seen amongst Japan's auto makers, foreshadowing the global restructuring that was to come.

Nissan's strategy mistakes and the Ghosn revolution

The most notable strategy mistakes were probably those of Nissan Motors, which eventually saw the company facing more than ¥2 trillion in accumulated interest-loaded debt in 1999 and risking bankruptcy. As a result, Nissan formed an alliance with Renault of France, welcomed Carlos Ghosn as CEO, and began rebuilding and recovered its footing one year ahead of schedule. In comparison, Honda, which, like Nissan, had seen annual profits dwindle, in this case to one-fifth of their peak at just ¥30 billion in 1993 and ¥14.3 billion in 1994, rebuilt its strategy from the top down and climbed out of its hole by introducing TQM. These two examples show how decisively important this problem was for Japan's auto makers.

What must first be pointed out here is that, in 1993, while Nissan was in the red, Toyota and Honda had greatly diminished returns but were not in debt. As was already mentioned, Honda's profits fell to one-fifth in 1993 and its operations in Japan, Europe, and Asia were completely in the red. At Toyota, too, domestic sales fell into the red on a monthly basis. In 1993, under the direction of then CEO Yoshifumi Tsuji, Nissan restructured and saw some improvement that put the company momentarily in the black by announcing the closure of its Zama Plant, cutting the workforce, reducing procurement costs, and slashing bloated expenses. But its debt-ridden structure surfaced again later and it eventually had to turn to an alliance with Renault in an attempt to recover. Nissan clearly did not have the necessary strategy-rebuilding and management ability inherent in the company.

Historically, Nissan has always had all-round, world-class technological strength, from design and development to production, to rival that of Toyota. Even people from Renault have admitted that the quality and productivity of Nissan's plants are far better than anything at Renault.[1] Yet, despite these accolades, Nissan has always played second fiddle to Toyota when it comes to sales power, marketing, and brand strength. That being said, from time to time it has had a hit, but those successes were sporadic and lacked comprehensive product strength. In addition, Nissan made several mistakes in the overall direction of its product strategies. For example, in the early half of the 1980s, Nissan tried to bounce back in the domestic economy car market (1200–1500cc class; Toyota: Corolla; Nissan: Sunny) where it had an inferior position compared with Toyota, and launched a number of new cars in this segment. But the primary markets in both Japan and North America shifted from economy cars to compacts (1600–2000cc; Toyota: Corona and Camry; Nissan: Bluebird and Silvia; Honda: Accord) and, as Toyota focussed its efforts on this market, Nissan lost share in a market where it was originally strong. Furthermore, as export profits began to worsen from 1985 onward, while the company did well to follow the trend toward higher-end cars and launch the Cima, Skyline, and Silvia as luxury cars, its mistake of putting too much energy into economy cars hung over it and its capacity was for the most part operating at the limits dealing with just the domestic market. The company was forced to pull back from the North American market, which was its lifeblood, and forego new car launches for the time being, so struggled with sales in North America. Though it was second after Honda in building a plant in North America, its Tennessee plant, like those of Honda and Toyota, made small pickup trucks, not passenger cars.

Nissan's small pickup truck was known to users in North America as Datsun. Until the 1970s, the pickup truck segment barely existed in North America, so Nissan was one of the pioneers of this segment. In 1981, the pickup truck had 4 percent lower tariffs than passenger cars because of the cab chassis, but all of sudden, duties of 25 percent or more were levied, making it impractical to export pickup trucks from Japan. Looking at later performance, the pickup truck market expanded rapidly in North America and, since Japanese pickup trucks were not being imported, the Big Three, especially Ford, took advantage of their absence. The growth of the light pickup truck segment would become the lifeline of the product strategies of the Big Three.

In 1981, after the Japanese government imposed voluntary restraints on automobile exports to the US, the price of Japanese compacts gradually rose and an appreciating yen exacerbated this. As a result, the price of entry-level subcompacts rose to almost $2,000 more than pickup trucks. When that happened, the number of users who used pickup trucks as passenger cars increased sharply.[2] Despite this tailwind behind the pickup truck, Nissan made the strategy mistake of not increasing pickup production, which it had started at a local plant, and switched production over to passenger cars. This poor decision was probably spurred by the fact that Toyota and other rival Japanese auto makers started producing passenger cars locally and the world's top manufacturer, GM, under the stewardship of Roger Smith, stubbornly continued to make passenger cars up until almost the mid 1980s. Incidentally, in 1983 Ford made the bold strategy call of converting twelve of its twenty-two North American plants from passenger cars to pickup trucks and, as a result, established a solid source of revenue.[3]

So, despite the excellence of its development and production technology, Nissan sent its product strategies in the wrong direction in 1980 and, because of that, lost market share. Even the occasional hit product failed to boost the overall product strength, and synergy, and the company became caught in a downward spiral that would make it poorer and poorer. As market share dwindled in Japan and North America, the situation solidified and expanded to a high-cost structure.

In the mid 1980s, Nissan's president, Yutaka Kume, and the rest of the company, recognized the strategy mistake. Though widespread cost-reduction plans were initiated and helped to some degree,[4] the collapse of the bubble economy hindered reform.

The biggest reason for Nissan's decline was that there was universal approval for the high-cost structure. Behind this was a long history of a cosy corporate milieu, an elitist group, and a corporate culture that allowed it, as well as rampant problems with labor–management relations. It was quite well known how preliminary meetings, held under the guise of labor–management coordination with labor unions mediating the business decision-making process, prevented management from taking the business reins and from making responsible decisions. This practice seriously affected the management structure at Nissan.[5] During the years of strong growth, this "labor–management coordination" produced something, but it got in the way of attempts to reform the high-cost structure. These abnormal labor–management relations were done away with in form, but they undeniably lingered as a structural factor that prevented the company from sharing a common sense of danger.

It has already been pointed out that the economic bubble encouraged high-cost structures, but how these were manifested varied. During the economic bubble, Nissan pumped up its production capacity both in Japan and abroad, and accelerated the high-cost structure with its excessive production capacity. In particular, it built state-of-the-art automated plants in Kyushu and Iwaki, and serially invested in capacity increases at its overseas plants in North America, Mexico, and England. This investment in state-of-the-art automation was in itself promoting equipment modernization and the use of information, and influenced the investment behavior of rival auto makers, most notably Toyota, but in Nissan's case, it was a mistake to leave plants with inefficient equipment in a state of excess production capacity. Though this problem did not surface during the bubble years because the work factor for this equipment momentarily rose, when the bubble burst, this equipment suddenly became fixed assets and overwhelmed the Nissan management. With the economic bubble over and the company locked into a downward spiral without a hit car, Nissan's visible debt came to a head. Compounding the problem, Nissan's existing plants were, for historical reasons, dispersed across urban areas, which made physical distribution and other operations inefficient.

Nissan's management at the time was aware of the high-cost structure of their excessive production capacity and took a certain degree of action after the collapse of the economic bubble, for instance, stopping automobile production at the Zama plant in 1995, but this was not enough to solve the problem. Plant restructuring obviously meant deep and painful personnel cuts, and it is hard to imagine just how difficult this was. In fact, the soft-landing approach that management came up with as a way to solve this dilemma was most likely chosen at the time for that very reason. There was, for example, a rush in demand just prior to the consumption tax hike. For a moment, there were signs of a recovery in performance and both Japanese business people and governmental leaders believed the reactionary recession after the collapse of the economic bubble to be temporary. They placed their faith whole-heartedly in the possibilities of an economic recovery and so Nissan, which desperately needed to reform the hard way, once again side-stepped reform.

While a major problem with the high-cost structure was excessive production capacity, another big factor was the high cost of parts procurement. Generally speaking, because of their string of affiliations forged during the years of growth, Japan's auto makers should have had a certain advantage in terms of cost, quality, and delivery over Western automobile manufacturers, which operated under a different business structure and system. However, Nissan was not good at managing purchase costs (though this depends on the actual part), and it notoriously paid more than Toyota and the others. This can be easily surmised from the reported ¥290.3 billion decrease in procurement costs achieved in just two years under its revival plan.[6] Since procured parts account for 60 percent or more of the overall cost of a car, this is not small change. With the boom over, the volume of parts transactions decreasing, and needing to reduce the number of parts suppliers as a result, Nissan failed to hammer out an effective plan of action. In particular, while the parts procurement world was globalizing and taking business transactions online, and automobile manufacturers in Japan and abroad were modifying their parts business structure, Nissan did not come up with effective measures. This is because, in contrast to Toyota, Nissan insisted on doing business with affiliated suppliers, yet the truth behind this business with affiliates was that it was greatly influenced by the preservation of a collusive attitude among a certain group that was not associated with strict cost management. The real problem in Nissan's case was not that it depended on affiliated business but that there were problems in the very practice of affiliated business.

In addition to the problems of excessive production capacity and parts procurement costs, Nissan was faced with high distribution costs for sales in Japan and the US. In particular, Nissan had developed a multiple channel network of numerous dealers to compete with Toyota in Japan, but compared with Toyota, Nissan had fewer dealers that were stable businesses managed with local capital, and many were directly operated by an auto maker in the red.[7] Consequently, sales costs such as rebates, incentives, and dealer support costs became an increasing burden year after year.

Domestic auto sales were a fierce war fought between franchises of just eight passenger car manufacturers. Naturally, it was based on fair competition, therefore all the manufacturers were heavily burdened with sales costs. But in Nissan's case, the company had lost market share because it did not produce a hit product and had too many dealers, so when the economy depressed, the number of dealers in the red increased. It was not rare that, at any one time, more than half of its dealers were operating in the red. It was also pointed out both inside and outside the company that the directly operated dealerships and head-quarters were excessively cosy with one another and vague about distribution costs. Many of the presidents and executives at the directly operated dealerships were sent from or retired from headquarters, so there was no way to eradicate this interdependence. Of course, Nissan was fully aware of this and stopped redeploying and rotating from within. It integrated its multichannel dealers[8] and either merged or shut down excess sales outlets, but these efforts did not have an immediate effect.

Nissan was in a brutal battle not just in Japan but in the US market as well, and sales costs escalated, sending the company into the red to the tune of several tens of billions of yen. One of the main causes was that the new models launched during the economic bubble bogged the company down because they were focussed solely on the Japanese market, and the company did not come up with a hit product for the North American market. The situation was also affected by the change-over to lease sales in the early 1990s, which were popular at the time because Nissan cars did not offer favorable prospects. The move to lease sales was carried out to keep the local plants in Tennessee and Mexico up and running. It is common practice for the Big Three to keep plants running by reducing inventory through lease sales and sales to car-rental companies. When a lease runs out, the manufacturer must take back the vehicle. When taking into account vehicle-recovery expenses and interest burdens, back-end costs can escalate if lease sales increase excessively.

There was another element that amplified the business risks at Nissan, and this problem was not limited to Nissan alone. The main banking system that supported Nissan's growth went bust. As the Heisei recession endured through the 1990s, Japan's financial system was being pressured by deregulation, a financial "Big Bang," and big changes within the context of ongoing globalization. At the core, the most marked change was the failure of the main banking system, which was so obvious that anyone could see it. Long-term growth and the economic bubble combined to make finance more accessible, as the value of loan collateral, such as land and stocks, went up, the more borrowers could borrow and refinance. An astronomical sum of more than ¥2 trillion yen in accumulated interest-loaded debt accrued because the banking system allowed it. When collateral rises in value, latent profits are earned, therefore, as long as a strong economy and growth persevere, one can continue to borrow and refinance. Nissan was using the Industrial Bank of Japan and Fuji Bank as its primary banks, and the president and many of the executives hailed from these primary banks, so Nissan could borrow money whenever it wanted.[9] However, during the prolonged deflationary recession, the value of collateral fell and, when banks could no longer rely on hidden assets and latent profits, the main banking system went belly up. As a result, Nissan was stuck with a mountain of accumulated debt.[10]

In May 1998, Nissan announced the "Global Business Revolution," in which it hinted at possible tie-ups with foreign companies. In March 1999, the Nissan–Renault alliance was announced and, in response to a strong request from Nissan, Carlos Ghosn of Renault transferred to Nissan and assumed control, with full power to rebuild the company. It is well known that Ghosn had rebuilt the business at French tire manufacturer Michelin, and he had joined Renault based on those credentials, soon acquiring the nickname of "Cost Cutter." Ghosn set about restructuring Nissan's business with equal vigor, yet he was operating in a country with a very different culture and tackling a company that had a significant reputation within the Japanese business community.

Before touching upon the business restructuring that Ghosn instituted, it is necessary to describe the characteristics of the Nissan–Renault alliance. People from Nissan and Renault have openly stated that the alliance was triggered by the cross-Atlantic merger of Daimler–Chrysler.[11] It must be emphasized that Nissan's alliance was different in character from the mergers that abounded at the time.[12] Unlike a unilateral takeover, in which a merger takes place under a single corporate culture, the biggest features of this alliance were mutual respect for both corporate cultures, mutual respect for separate brand identities, and a pretext of self-responsibility. Another major feature was that both parties would collaborate and boldly promote the project in a way that would create a synergetic effect that both parties could benefit from. Accordingly, the collaboration was broad ranging, extending into diverse areas such as parts standardization and joint purchasing, joint development, and use of platforms for low-cost production models, joint utilization of plant capacities, joint use of advanced technological development, human resource exchange, and open access to sales networks in specific markets. What was important to this form of collaboration was that responsibilities were clearly spelled out so that feelings of mutual trust would be preserved. The general rule throughout the deal was to share the real profits of collaboration fairly, according to the efforts and contributions each side had made.[13]

With broad support for the alliance, Ghosn set out to restructure Nissan. He set a target to identify problems and hammer out a clear strategic vision as quickly as possible, have everyone concerned determine what was best to do in line with that vision, and create a model where everyone's vectors would meet.[14] Ghosn did not stop with a one-dimensional restructuring that merely cut costs; he established a cross-functional team that would be active across departmental boundaries and would help him to understand the problems related to the overall management structure and push cost reduction and restructuring forward. This gave Nissan the chance to eradicate the abusive practices of "departmental optimization," where individual departments pursued business for themselves and had lost sight of the company as a whole.

While building a clear strategic vision, Ghosn set unmistakable targets to share a sense of risk with all Nissan employees and attempt to eliminate that risk. That strategy was presented both inside and outside the company as the Nissan Revival Plan (NRP), and put Nissan on course for the first major revitalization in its history. Yoshikazu Hanawa (then chairman) noted that there was a restructuring plan from the days of the previous executive department, but Ghosn did not include any part of it in his NRP.[15] Ghosn personally confirmed the trouble spots at Nissan before writing the NRP. When it was announced, his senior managers swore that they would be responsible for ensuring the plan was put into action in its entirety, the so-called "Commitment" promise, and that they shared the same sense of risk as the Nissan employees. The ambitious target of the NRP was to reduce costs by ¥1 trillion,

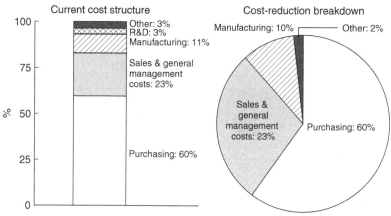

Source: Nissan Press Information, October 18, 1999

Figure 4.4 Nissan revival plan – cost-reduction effect: ¥1 trillion

as shown in Figure 4.4, and to amortize the company's interest-loaded debts within three years. The ¥1 trillion cost reduction breaks down into ¥600 billion in procurement costs for parts, supplies, and tools (effectively the primary cause of the high-cost structure), ¥280 billion in general sales management costs, ¥100 billion in direct manufacturing, and ¥20 billion from other areas. The cost curtailments in manufacturing came from the closure of three assembly plants, including the Murayama plant, and two power train plants,[16] in order to reduce domestic production capacity. The remaining capacity was integrated into four leading plants, where the work factor would be raised from 53 percent to 82 percent, and the number of platforms reduced from twenty-four to fifteen and eventually twelve by 2004. The NRP also called for painful personnel cuts of 21,000 employees, which would take the workforce from 148,000 to 127,000, but in order to gain acceptance by the labor unions, the plan included retirement benefits and job-transfer support. In anticipation, Nissan posted losses of ¥680 billion, including miscellaneous restructuring costs, for two years straight.

Nissan also spent two years selling off dead assets, raising a total of $530 billion over the two years selling real estate and securities such as stocks of affiliated suppliers and bank shares held reciprocally against its own stocks. As it disassociated itself from affiliations, it also distanced itself from primary banks, secured-loan financing, and latent

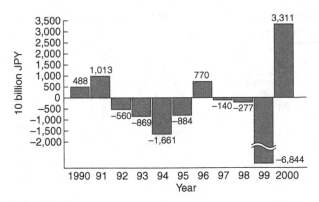

Figure 4.5 NPR recap: consolidated profits

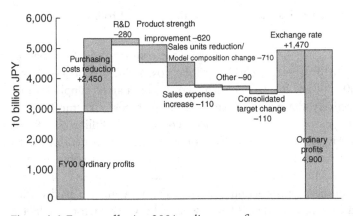

Figure 4.6 Factors affecting 2001 ordinary profits

asset business, which effectively converted its financial strategy over to a cash-flow base.

Under Ghosn's leadership, and with the support of the workforce, Nissan set out on the major restructuring efforts spelled out in the NRP, attaining the targets a full year ahead of the original three-year schedule (see Figures 4.5, 4.6, and 4.7). Contributing to this were a ¥650 billion injection from Renault, the ¥530 billion that was quickly recuperated from asset sales, a quicker-than-expected reduction in purchasing costs, which had been the biggest long-standing issue, more than the targeted 2,000 retirements, an increase in work factor from 51 percent to 75 percent (see Figure 4.8) through closing plants and integrating

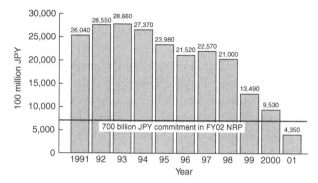

Figure 4.7 NPR recap: consolidated real interest-loaded liabilities of automotive operations

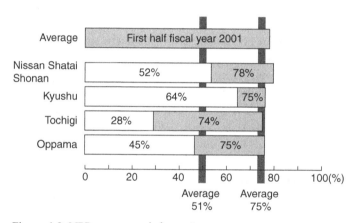

Figure 4.8 NPR recap: work factor improvement

operations into four high-efficiency plants, a reduction in platforms from twenty-four to fifteen, and the tremendous production cost reductions associated with that, the integration of domestic sales channels, including the closure of eighteen inefficient sales companies and 355 unprofitable dealerships, improved sales efficiency, and a reduction in distribution costs. The synergetic effect of a strategy packed with clear reduction targets and systematic management leadership was highly significant.

Overseas operations contributed to the business restructuring in Japan spearheaded by the NRP. This included a hit with the new Altima, which was launched as a domestically produced model, an improvement in work factor at the Mexico plant, which had been in a slump because of local economic turmoil, healthy exports to North America, and a strong Canadian market. In one fell swoop, Nissan's North American operations, which had suffered from accumulating debt for years, found success. They put a stop to the excessive lease sales and incentives that had been long-standing issues, and lowered distribution costs in North America. So, while restructuring was under way in Japan, Nissan was blessed overseas, particularly by windfall ordinary profits of ¥159 billion in 2001 from the North American market. This accelerated results and in May 2002, Nissan announced that it had attained the NRP targets ahead of schedule. In 2004, the company announced the next growth scenario in its "Nissan 180" plan (production increase of 1 million cars worldwide, 8 percent increase in sales and earnings, and zero interest-loaded debt).

The sharp recovery under the NRP was dramatic and Ghosn's leadership provided many lessons for Japanese businesses in strategy-building capabilities. In an interview I conducted with Ghosn and then-chairman Hanawa, he touched upon several key points of the Nissan–Renault alliance and its future development.[17]

To begin with, my questions to chairman Hanawa focussed on "Why, after surviving all these years against erstwhile rival Toyota, did Nissan slip and fall into a pit of risks? Why couldn't the leaders at Nissan prevent the decline? Why did previous attempts to reform the company fail?" He said, very straightforwardly, "The cosy relationships of a company run by salaried employees and backed by the main banking system were not built in a day, so even though management knew about the problems, they didn't want to put the restructuring scalpel to the internal workings at Nissan." In around 1986, during the days of president Kume, and in the 1990s, when president Tsuji was at the helm, the scalpel was wielded in major restructuring, which included internal reforms and even the closure of the Zama plant, but in the end, efforts stopped and the restructuring was never completed. The overall attitude was that, even when the company was in a dangerous situation, the danger was never conveyed at the general employee level. Nissan's management created a rebuilding scenario when faced with danger, and the results it targeted were similar to those in Ghosn's NRP, but these scenarios were never converted into action. What is very interesting here is that Hanawa declared that "Ghosn did not carry over even a single piece" of the scenario, although there were many similarities. Ghosn committed fully to personally identifying the true nature of the risks and clearly spelled out his action policy. He made Nissan employees aware of the dangers and got each and every one of them to think about what he or she should do to address these problems.

As Hanawa noted, Ghosn laid out a clear policy, made managers fully responsible, presented coherent explanations that anyone could have understood, and spoke very persuasively when making requests to Nissan people. To put it simply, management at Nissan was amazed by the professional strategy-building skill Ghosn displayed and the stalwart leadership he showed in promptly putting those skills into action.

Some points from the interview deserve highlighting. First, while Ghosn had taken part in TQM activities at Renault when the company was internally restructuring, he stated that the TQM at Renault and the NRP at Nissan were not directly related. The French manage things from the top down in a logical, reasoned manner, but at Nissan it is a question of how focussed one is, how much purpose and meaning one has, and how effectively one executes duties that demonstrate the effectiveness of management; it is not a logic issue. In this, Ghosn quickly detected that Nissan was lacking the ability to act promptly and needed more than anything else the ability to act with a sense of purpose and meaning from the bottom up under strong leadership.

Second, on Nissan's management potential as the grounds for rebuilding the company and the synergy between Renault and Nissan, Ghosn said: "There are things that cannot be described in numerical figures; trying to express everything numerically is meaningless." Especially for what regards potential, it is only after one attempts to do something that results are known, therefore, even though estimates can be made, the truth is not known until you try. He said the same about synergy. "Supplementing each other's sales areas and jointly using plants can make up shortfalls in a visible way, but platform standardization and parts procurement present many unknowns, and, though expectations are high, you never know until you try." This comment reflects Ghosn's basic principle that grasping the situation, the ability to put ideas into practice, and the ability to act come first, and logic comes later.

The third point – and one that made an impression on me – was how Ghosn was in complete agreement with what top management from Renault had said concerning the inter-relationships of the alliance between Nissan and Renault: "The bottom line is mutual respect and respect for each other's corporate identity." In particular, talking about disagreements between parties and themes that even the Alliance Board could not agree upon, he said, "You can always say 'no' and put a stop to everything," but the prominent feature of this alliance was to recognize that there were merits on both sides and that synergy can be created without pushing one another.

The fourth point came while Ghosn was talking about the parts procurement system, which was the most important theme of the NRP. He said, "I didn't just erase the idea of doing business with affiliates – *keiretsu* transactions – from my head. I merely chose not to use it because there were problems in managing it." It takes time to rebuild business with affiliates, but more importantly, if good management principles can be translated into action, top suppliers from around the world will come. Ghosn respected long-term partnerships, but at the same time he introduced a more competitive dynamism.

Other things that left an impression on my mind from what Ghosn said about Nissan's future were that the company particularly needed to establish its brand identity, but that would require time, so the entire company would have to have coordinated, long-term common targets. He denied outright any possibility of a merger between Renault and Nissan. There were no special meetings or discussions among the executives sent from Renault; each operated in his own department at Nissan.

All in all, I was left with a strong impression of Ghosn as a businessman with a winning ability to act and resolute in his decisions. In particular, he knew the meanings and limitations of various theories, methods, and formulas, and thought like a realist in easy-to-understand terms. My opinion of him as a businessman who skillfully balances strategic vision and swift decisions will never change.

Honda's strategy conversion and TQM revolution at the start of the 1990s

Honda has a notoriously unique corporate culture among Japan's auto makers. It should be pointed out that, of the eleven Japanese auto makers (including truck manufacturers), Honda was the last to start making four-wheel vehicles; previously it made only motorcycles. Amidst global restructuring, this latecomer to the automotive market continues along its own course today, like Toyota, without being burdened by ties to foreign capital. Nevertheless, Honda, faced with a serious fall in performance after the collapse of the economic bubble, had to convert its strategy and revolutionize its business. This section

covers how Honda used TQM to revolutionize the business and ultimately attempts to compare Honda with Nissan. In Honda's case,
rather than making strategic mistakes, like Nissan, the company
found its unusual corporate culture and the associated strategy-building
process no longer matched the harsh changes in the business
environment.

Needless to say, Honda carries on the spirit of its founder, Soichiro
Honda. It relentlessly seeks youth, creativity, and dreams, and refuses
to copy anyone. Its drive goes back to the root of all things and its
corporate culture demands that each employee demonstrates personal-
ity and constantly and knowingly takes challenges. Today it is the
number one manufacturer of motorcycles and probably the second
most well-known Japanese auto maker, despite being the last one to
start making cars. The reason for this unique corporate culture is that
the company did away with the stark hierarchical organization of
preconceived ideas and built its corporate structure around an engineer-
led group that respects free thought and refuses to blithely accept
precedence. The Soichiro generation also had a management genius in
the background in Takeo Fujisawa, and there were many leaders in the
engineering group who kept the founding spirit alive and promoted the
Honda Way as an original corporate culture.[18]

Honda's manufacturing (especially its engine technology), production engineering, and international business development reflect its
experience as the world's number one manufacturer of motorcycles.
One example is seen in its production engineering, where small engine
design skill and flexible production enable quick model changeovers.
Using its history with knockdown plants, which were built in various
countries as part of its international motorcycle business development,
Honda started local production of four-wheel vehicles with a small
plant and production line. It expanded the plant as the market
expanded, and put its experience with motorcycles to use in developing
local suppliers. What is characteristic about its products is the simple
design, shown ever since the first-generation Civic, and awareness of
younger generations. The company pursued a sporty look and
mechanics typical of Honda, and built niche markets of fans who
appreciated these special mechanisms.

Honda's production engineering had qualities not seen with other
Japanese manufacturers, such as production flexibility, mixed production, and production line design. It is not like Toyota's JIT system,

which systematically produces one vehicle at a time; instead, Honda prepares what is necessary for one week's worth of production and changes production whenever needed. Moreover, Honda has separate organizations in Honda R&D to handle product development, and Honda Engineering, which is in charge of developing production hardware and software. Its promotion of unrestricted creative product and production engineering development for both hardware and software is not seen in other manufacturers. Furthermore, in its product development work, though opinions on product planning are exchanged with headquarters, Honda R&D has the leadership over design and development. The chief engineer assigned to a project has absolute authority and, though he organizes a cross-functional team, it is often the case that people who demonstrate creativity are chosen regardless of their age or experience. Thus Honda has a dynamic structure that is very changeable according to the latest development concepts and development processes, so it has a tremendous amount of originality and a system that balances that with development efficiency.

Honda's unique strategy worked well, especially in exporting to the US during the late 1970s and the early 1980s, and the smooth progression made into local production in the US to back up that success. However, come the 1990s, immediately after Nobuhiko Kawamoto assumed the position of president, performance worsened drastically and trouble set in. What's more, the problems were not caused by the collapse of the economic bubble in Japan or the large exchange rate margin losses following the second rise in value of the yen against the dollar, but instead were down to Honda's original strategy and ways of management.

Honda devoted its major efforts to the North American market and sales in Japan, but no matter what it did, it always seemed to be playing second fiddle to Toyota, Nissan, Mitsubishi, and the others.[19] Consequently, it earned most of its consolidated profits in North America and, except for the luxury models that sold during the heyday of the economic bubble, did not produce large profits in Japan.

In the first half of the 1980s, Honda continued its attack in and around the North American market and consolidated profits reached ¥150 billion in 1985, but profits decreased when the yen strengthened after the G5 summit of 1985. Furthermore, even though consolidated sales rose from ¥3 trillion to ¥4.3 trillion, consolidated profits fell year after year (see Figure 4.9 and Table 4.3). In 1993, consolidated sales topped

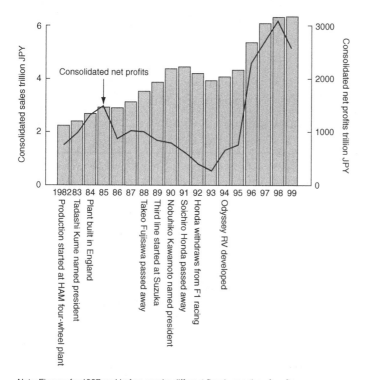

Note: Figures for 1987 and before used a different fiscal year, therefore figures were converted to an annual base
Original data: Nikkei Financial
Source: "Nekkei Business," August 23, 1999

Figure 4.9 Consolidated sales and consolidated net profits for Honda

¥4 trillion, while consolidated profits dropped to ¥30 billion, just one-fifth of the peak level. At this point, Honda was passed by Mitsubishi in profits and lost the third spot behind Toyota and Nissan. The sensationalist media of the times circulated stories of a Mitsubishi–Honda merger.

Up until that time, Honda had translated its inherent youth and free and unrestrained nature into a sellable product and the company was proud of its mechanics, but it neglected the basic rules of organization and did not manage the organization carefully as it grew in size. Unity fell apart and individuals began to act on their own. In particular, Honda R&D was made a holy sanctuary, developing unusual products and technologies without any concern for efficiency. They were interested only in Honda mechanisms and came out with products that were

Table 4.3 *Major business indicators of Honda*

Fiscal year	Production (number of vehicles)			Exports (number of vehicles, sets)	Sales (1 mil JPY)	Net profits (1 mil JPY)	Employees (100 persons)
	Passenger cars	Finished cars	KD sets				
1976.6	430,260	351,289	214,582		563,805	11,954	185
1981.3	977,995	859,237	690,176	7,400	1,344,892	30,137	229
1986.3	1,160,821	986,708	677,195	241,980	2,245,743	45,232	281
1991.3	1,375,236	1,199,888	678,574	–	2,800,199	46,667	316
1992.3	1,330,648	1,195,623	664,875	–	2,911,044	32,566	315
1993.3	1,196,885	1,067,717	589,660	–	2,694,836	30,075	311
1994.3	1,126,572	995,355	541,477	–	2,505,258	14,319	310

Note: Production and finished cars for export in 1976 and before include KD sets
Source: Automotive Industry Handbook, Nikkan Jidosha Shimbun, 1995

not considered products in the consumer's eye. Under their "Waigaya" practice, many people, including directors, could say what they wanted, but all they did was talk; no one took responsibility for decisions. Any corporate culture, no matter how unique and first-rate, can die if not properly supported by management.

In 1990, Nobuhiko Kawamoto from Honda R&D was made president. He was very conscious of the serious dangers the company faced. He clarified responsibilities and authority within the Honda organization, defined decision-making processes, and drastically altered the personnel structure to create a top-down system. In his words, "Forget what we did before; Honda must become an ordinary automobile manufacturer." He also said, "We will keep that which is worth keeping, but we cannot go ahead without changing the way we act. Right now, let us consolidate real proof that supports our dreams. We will, however, maintain our spiritual youth as an asset."[20]

At the same time as it was promoting product development that was in line with market needs, Honda needed to cure its "corporate woes," and the company revised its articles of association for the first time since it was founded. The "Honda Philosophy" was revised into a new system of values and diffused throughout the company; what previously spoke

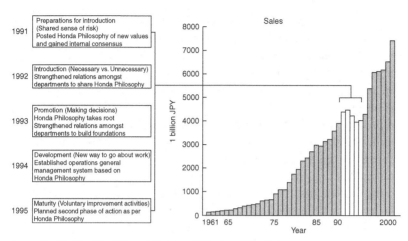

Source: Report by Hiroshi Ito of Research Workshop of Asian Automobile Industry

Figure 4.10 Honda's TQM development

of supplying good-performance products at moderate prices within a global perspective changed to providing high-quality products at appropriate prices in order to satisfy customers around the world. Shoichiro Irimajiri, who had transferred from the US production company HAM, introduced the TQM that he had learned in the US. TQM activities were promoted in stages until a system of values that reflected customer needs was diffused and strongly rooted throughout the organization (see Figure 4.10).[21] From an introductory stage, Honda transitioned to a promotional stage aimed at establishing the new philosophy, then to a developmental stage, in which action based on the new philosophy was promoted and a general management system was created, and finally to a mature stage, in which the new method of production in an entirely new corporate structure had been established.

A big feature of the TQM introduced at Honda was to change the thinking of top management. The responsibility that executives and managers would have to take for the decisions they made was clearly spelled out so that they had to ask themselves whether the decisions they made were implemented and effective or not. Honda already had plenty of QC circle activities and had held annual world QC conferences for many years.[22] Thus there was already a company-wide quality control movement similar to TQC, but it was mainly focussed on departmental coordination in a variety of production and design fields, and there were no activities that questioned the decision-making responsibility and quality of senior management. That itself testifies to the free and unrestrained corporate culture that Honda had evolved, boldly making it the responsibility of top management to evaluate the quality of their own management within a grading system.

In promoting TQM, the company surveyed real market demands and, using this information, pursued ways to eliminate corrections in production, shorten delivery time in sales, and enable model changes simultaneously all over the world. What was particularly emphasized within all of this was a marriage between development and production. Product planning and production planning were interlinked. Molds and production lines were built according to this concept, and the evaluation level was improved throughout, from the planning stage to the development and production set-up stages.

To promote these TQM activities, cross-functional CS teams that brought together managers from sales, production, development, quality control, and parts procurement were formed (until that time, cross-functional activities were limited to engineering sections at Honda R&D). When development lead-time was shortened, Honda supplemented this with conceptualization skills, stressing shorter production set-up lead-times in particular. The new TQM activities made it necessary to change from production tailored to niche markets to production for open markets, shrink the mismatch between vehicle performance and feeling, reduce design changes and start production set-up sooner, introduce evaluation-free steps and omit a number of evaluation events, and reduce the number of trial molds and trial productions.

Honda's TQM completely changed the system of development and production, making it a market-linked structure that could quickly and reliably produce inexpensive products that customers would like (see Figure 4.11). This made it possible for Honda to establish a world-standard production system in an age of global competition. For Honda, this world-standard production system meant building the means that would enable the company to supply attractive cars all over the world in a short amount of time and simultaneously produce the exact same car anywhere in the world. Put simply, it meant building a system capable of simultaneously launching a new car around the world in nine months.[23] By making this possible, Honda became capable of globally standardizing platforms and components, localizing development, and swiftly responding to market changes.

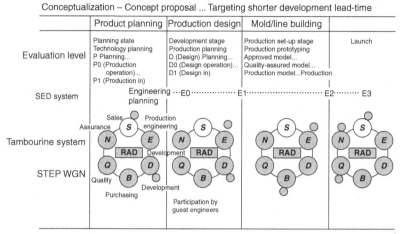

Conceptualization – Concept proposal ... Targeting shorter development lead-time

Source: Reported by Hiroshi Ito of Research Workshop of Asian Automobile Industry

Figure 4.11 Integrated development and production at Honda

The TQM innovations revolutionized the way top management thought, and brought clear direction and synergy to the linkage between development and production, and to cross-functional activities such as sales and parts procurement. Honda successfully synchronized the tambourine system and activities of all departments in the company (see Figure 4.11). Compared with the disastrous situation of 1993, Honda's performance had visibly recovered a few years later. It met with success both in launching new vehicles, such as the Odyssey, Step Wagon, CRV, and Fit, and in maintaining and developing the brand values of global models, the Accord and the Civic. Consolidated profits for 2003 were confirmed to have exceeded ¥400 billion. The painful restructuring and corporate culture revolution spawned from Honda's introduction of TQM led to steady results over a ten-year period.

4. Conclusions: the 1990s acted as the prelude and trigger to global strategy rebuilding among Japan's auto makers

Nissan and Honda are examples of contrasting strategy and restructuring abilities demonstrated by Japan's auto makers in the 1990s. If the two are compared, the following assertions can be made. For starters, Japan's auto makers in the early 1990s needed to address their strategy-building ability and higher-level management skills, and required dynamic organizational skills to implement these improvements. Nissan restructured by closing its Zama plant and making personnel cuts, but efforts to introduce TQM to enhance strategy-building ability and top management skills came late and, consequently, did not go as far as revolutionizing the corporate culture. Addressing the culture problems was put off until the Ghosn revolution that resulted from Nissan's alliance with Renault. In contrast, Honda introduced TQM when faced with a dangerous situation and went about changing its corporate culture into a configuration that matched the changing times. Working with its characteristic speed, Honda quickly produced results. While maintaining the good points of its corporate culture, Honda never forgot to adopt a realistic approach. In comparison, Nissan did not start its rebuilding quickly, but once Ghosn came on board, results were rapid and dramatic. What is interesting here is that Ghosn, during his years with Renault, was one of the key promoters of a top-down format of TQM that employed the efforts of the entire company. In a certain sense, the revolution imparted by Ghosn can be said to have transformed Nissan's corporate culture via TQM on a level that previous efforts by Nissan never reached.[24]

Another interesting point here is that, in the first half of the 1990s, not only Honda but also Toyota introduced TQM. Toyota originally employed the entire company in a quality control campaign and established TQC that even involved its suppliers. In particular, the TQC activities spearheaded by former general manager Masao Nemoto and practised together with the Toyota production system under Taichi Ono greatly helped to improve overall quality beyond the Toyota plant level. Before his death, Nemoto described TQM as the systematic intellectualization of what was done in TQC into a Western style, which Toyota had already done. In his mind, TQM and TQC were synonymous. However, setting aside the interpretations of whether these two sciences are synonyms or not, the fact is that the TQC implemented by Toyota did not go as far as evaluating the decision making and skills of senior management. It was not until after the collapse of the economic bubble that then vice-president Takahashi and president Okuda together undertook the major initiative to implement TQM. The TQC activities conducted previously by Toyota were important for coordination between departments under a single policy to enhance total quality in design, production, and procurement. When Toyota fell momentarily into the red during the Heisei recession, the company was quick to use

TQM to innovate the way management thought across the company as well.

According to then-Denso vice-chairman Takahashi, who played a pivotal role in promoting TQM activities at Toyota, Toyota had a long history of TQC and promoted restructuring in white-collar operations by flattening the organization of managerial departments and promoting a "3-Step Approval Process," but it lacked a perspective for institutionalizing an organizational performance measure that would prompt management to inspect how they thought and acted. Consequently, even the great Toyota fell into the traps of the bubble economy and forgot about how to get the product out and stay customer-oriented. Toyota introduced TQM to steer the company toward the innovative thinking necessary to cope with globalization and a drastically changing competitive environment, and particularly to find ways to enhance creativity and independence so that the company would be managed in a way that focussed on the customer. As a result, activities to develop human resources for cross-functional activities and enable organizational skills permeated through the corporate structure. Management personnel had to get away from a mindset that relied on following procedure in determining what needed to be done and how, and develop a new autonomous and creative mindset in which they determined what to do and acted independently. Self-evaluations were institutionalized within management and the spirit of self-evaluation filtered down from the top all the way to the workplace.[25]

By not contenting themselves with previous TQC results and by being highly aware of risks, identifying risky situations early on, and responding nimbly with TQM activities, Toyota was able to successfully develop new vehicle after new vehicle, produce astonishing results with environmental technologies, and quickly recover its performance in overseas operations, especially in North America.

There is an interesting contrast in corporate behavior after the collapse of the economic bubble in the first half of the 1990s between the Honda and Toyota groups, which quickly set out to revolutionize how management thought via TQM and restructure, and Nissan and Mitsubishi, which were slow to apply TQM-style efforts to improving management and strategy-building abilities, and eventually had to resort to a foreign president to rebuild themselves. Nissan and Mitsubishi were also both heavily dependent on the financial systems of the main banks. However, they were also alike in that they were both staging a hopeful comeback based on technical developments in production engineering, engines, and so forth through their partnerships with Renault and Daimler–Chrysler, respectively, and the potential of business in Asia.

However, Mitsubishi Motors has been violently shaken by recall problems and Mitsubishi Fuso Truck & Bus has been separated and placed under Daimler–Chrysler. Mitsubishi Motors itself has ceased receiving assistance from Daimler–Chrysler and is attempting to rebuild under the leadership of the Mitsubishi Group, but there is a long, rough road ahead. A successful recovery will more than likely be based on whether it can utilize what potential is left and demonstrate its strategy-building ability, previously lacking because of its dependence on Daimler–Chrysler.

Notes

These global business plans were plans for localization and local parts procurement submitted and announced by Japanese auto companies as a result of the hard-line measures pushed by the Clinton administration, and particularly US Trade Representative Mickey Kantor, in 1995 after a favorable agreement on the procurement of American-made automotive parts could not be reached between Japan and the US during a 1992 visit by former President Bush Senior. Because the US was pressuring Japan with high tariffs on Japanese luxury cars, Japan auto makers announced these global business plans. In response to this, the US withdrew its hard-line measures. After that, because American automotive manufacturers made record-breaking profits and Japan's auto makers advanced their internationalization, the situation quieted down, which is where we are today.

1. In an explanation at a press conference, Nissan CEO Ghosn stressed the high quality level of Nissan's major plants in England and Japan when making reference to a survey conducted by an external organization. At the time, he added that, notwithstanding the quality, they had to think about why the brand value of Nissan cars was not rising.

2. At the beginning of the 1980s, US survey agency Harbridge House pointed out the possibility of this trend becoming stronger. Things then began moving when a Japanese think-tank caught wind of this and suggested the need to weigh its importance. Not just Nissan but all Japanese auto makers ignored them. On a personal note, I attended a public symposium on the internationalization of the automotive industry at Hosei University in 1984, where Ichiro Shioji, president of the Confederation of Japan Automobile Workers' Unions, criticized Nissan's Tennessee Plant that

had just started making pickup trucks and claimed that Nissan would fail unless it produced passenger cars.

3. *The North American Automotive Industry*, Fourin, 1988.
4. Interview with Nissan Motors chairman Hanawa, December 24, 2002.
5. This point is colorfully described in detail by David Halberstam in his *Reckoning* (translated by Hakuo Takahashi, Shichosha Publishing, 1990).
6. From Nissan Motors press information, October 28, 2002.
7. K. Shimokawa, "Global automotive business history," Yuhikaku, 2004.
8. Nissan has integrated five channels into two large directly operated channels and continues to close and consolidate inefficient sales outlets even today.
9. In a May 2000 interview with vice-president Kusumi at the Nissan head-quarters, he said that Nissan has not even once had trouble borrowing money.
10. When the main banking system crashed, Nissan relied heavily on the government-operated Development Bank of Japan for its asset management. Here, the government, and particularly the Ministry of Economy and Industry, worked with the strong intention of not letting Japan's second largest auto maker go bankrupt. Later, through the alliance with Renault, Nissan received a capital injection of upwards of ¥600 billion, but a large portion of this came from the French government, which shines light on the fact that the governments of both Japan and France backed the alliance between the two companies.
11. From the previously mentioned interview with Nissan Motors chairman Hanawa, December 24, 2002.
12. It was not just Daimler–Chrysler since Ford commanded Jaguar, Range Rover, Aston Martin, and Volvo's parts supplier of Europe as subcontractors through mergers. Also, GM made Saab of Sweden and Daewoo of Korea subsidiaries.
13. From an interview with executive vice president Duane at Renault head-quarters in March 2001. Excerpted from "Renault's development strategy: talking with executive Vice President George Duane," Nikkan Jidosha Shimbun, June 30, 2001.
14. From the previously mentioned interview with Nissan Motors chairman Hanawa, December 24, 2002.
15. Ibid.
16. From Nissan Motors, "Nissan revival plan" press information.
17. K. Shimokawa, "The truth about Nissan and Renault: talking with Carlos Ghosn," Nikkan Jidosha Shimbun, October 4, 2003.
18. O. Yamamoto, "Honda's origins," Jidosha Journal Publishing, 1976.
19. Around the time Honda sold only compacts and its first-generation Civic, its sales network in Japan was dependent on small dealers which

diffused their motorcycles. This is a recognized handicap of Honda as the last to arrive of the four-wheel manufacturers. After 1975, as the company increased its line-up with models such as the Accord, Honda decided to develop full-scale dealers in the same way as Toyota and Nissan. It opened a new channel with a store in Berno at mostly its own expense. However, it retained its sales channel of small dealerships, now called "Primo," though, despite the significant number of locations, sales efficiency is said not to be good in all cases.

20. *Nikkei Business*, August 23, 1999.
21. Excerpted from "Honda's TQM revolution," Nikkan Jidosha Shimbun, January 8, 2002.
22. Excerpted from "Honda's HN circle world conference," Nikkan Jidosha Shimbun, November 19, 1986.
23. H. Ito, "Honda's TQM revolution," Research Workshop of Asian Automobile Industry.
24. Ghosn said in an interview with me that Renault's TQM was not directly applied to Nissan. But his experience with TQM at Renault certainly contributed toward innovating thinking at Nissan.
25. Interview with Chairman Takahashi at Denso headquarters in November 2001.

5 | The restructuring of the global automotive and auto-parts industries

1. Introduction

The end of the Cold War, the rapid spread of information technology, and international economic globalization have revolutionized many industries, starting with the financial and securities industries and then spreading to the fast-growing information and communication industries. The automobile industry is no exception.

Prior to the global shake-up, the automobile industry, especially in advanced countries, was primarily a national industry, no matter how international its business. Trade disputes, for example, related to the correct way to handle automobile trade, the balance of trade, and job security for a country's labor force. The automobile industry also impacted a wide range of related industries, such as components and materials, on a national level. Because of this background, automobile manufacturers in advanced nations constructed management strategies that centered on their own country. Their overseas strategies were tightly connected to the domestic strategy and had a strong tendency to complement them, no matter how important overseas business and exports were to the company. Therefore car manufacturers' competitiveness was closely related to how competitive they were in their domestic markets and, up until the massive globalization boom of the 1990s, automobile industries competed with each other at a nation-to-nation level. At the same time, the Japanese automobile industry had grown rapidly by introducing lean production methods, which sparked reform in Western companies to remain competitive and led to the globalization of the automobile industry in the 1990s.

Economic globalization infers a free and rapid flow of management resources (people, goods, money, and information) beyond national borders, thus moving automobile companies away from a national perspective by default. Business activities expand beyond the framework of one nation and dynamically develop everywhere in the world, wherever markets exist. We can observe this trend in sections of the automobile industry such as (a) product development, (b) supply systems including factory locations, (c) purchasing systems for parts, components, intermediary material, and raw material, (d) production systems at factories, and (e) automobile sales and distribution systems, although they may be different region by region. All of these are not contained within the framework of a country, but have been developed into a global base and integrated under a global management strategy. This globalization of the automobile industry not only enables the business procedures listed above to take place but also makes them necessary conditions for the automobile manufacturers to survive in the international arena.

Against this background, the global automobile industry is reorganizing, but not always along the same lines. Some reorganization strategies focus on economies of scale at a global level and have attracted public attention, such as Daimler–Chrysler and Nissan–Renault. Other companies, such as Honda, are developing their own global strategies. There is an argument that eventually there will be only about five automobile manufacturers in the world, because manufacturers which are not members of the so-called "4 million unit club" (makers that produce 4 million units or more annually) will probably not survive alone. This raises the fundamental question as to whether scale is the only measure that can decide whether you are big enough or smart enough to compete in the automobile industry in this age of globalization.

Before studying the scale argument, I would like to clarify why global reorganization took place in the automobile industry in the first place. Then I will suggest that there is an alternative to mergers and amalgamation, which single-mindedly pursue scale merit. This alternative could be a network among manufacturers where they maintain their own corporate identities. I will also discuss structural changes in the automobile component industry that are directly influenced by the automobile industry's global reorganization and new environmental strategies.

2. Global reorganization in the automobile industry and the direction of global strategies

In discussing the globalization of the automobile industry, it is necessary to focus on two incidents that have had a decisive impact on globalization strategy at the corporate level. One is the 1998 merger between Daimler and Chrysler, powerful automobile makers representing Germany and the US, respectively. The other is Ford's global strategy aimed at the twenty-first century, Ford 2000, which was announced in 1993.

Let us take a look at the mega-merger between Daimler and Chrysler. The impact of the merger on automobile industries around the world was huge, and triggered a series of tie-ups beyond national borders. For example, the alliance between Nissan and Renault, which was announced in 1999, was directly triggered by the Daimler–Chrysler mega-merger, as revealed in an interview I had with the leaders of Nissan. After this merger, Ford snapped up the passenger car department of Volvo. We also witnessed the start of negotiations between Fiat and GM (which resulted in partial cooperation for joint production using the partners' factories). Even among manufacturers that already had joint relationships, like Toyota–Hino, Daihatsu, and GM–Suzuki, stock-holding ratios increased as part of their corporate groups' global strategies.

What was the background behind the Daimler–Chrysler mega-merger? Ten years ago it was unthinkable that any major automobile manufacturers would merge beyond national borders. True, there had been buy-ups of automobile makers across national boundaries in the past, for example, Renault in France once bought up the number four US manufacturer American Motors (although it was sold to Chrysler in 1987). Germany's BMW bought Rover, the only nationalized manufacturer in the UK, and Ford bought Jaguar, a UK manufacturer of luxury cars, in 1989. However, these mergers involved niche makers producing 300,000 cars per year at the most. The Daimler–Chrysler merger was the first one that involved two huge players producing from 1.2 million to 3 million cars annually.

So how could a previously unthinkable merger take place? Many research organizations expected that automobile manufacturers would reorganize. In fact, France's ministry of economy and industry stated in 1982 that the almost thirty automobile makers in the world at that time would have converged into six companies within ten years.[1] However, this was proven wrong because new aspects of competition in the automobile industry that could not be judged by simple scale merit emerged in the 1980s. First of all, the Japanese automobile industry began to push its international competitiveness using the lean production revolution, which postponed reorganization among the existing eleven automobile manufacturers in Japan. At the same time, European and US automobile companies were trying to learn from the lean production revolution and also restructure themselves, so conditions were not right for any of the companies to begin to think about mergers or amalgamations.

The nature of competition changed in the 1980s. Up to then, international competition among automobile industries was based on their own nation or region. However, swift progress in economic globalization meant that these companies had to develop globalization strategies. Under these strategies, the automobile industry pursued product development, component purchases, factory locations, and supply systems on a global scale. In addition, several other factors underlined the necessity of global strategies toward the end of the twentieth century, including (a) expansion of Middle and Eastern European automobile markets due to the end of the Cold War, (b) Asian population superpowers China and India joining in the global market economy, and (c) emerging automobile markets in such regions as Asia, and Central and South America.[2]

New global strategies to cover emerging markets such as Asia have drastically changed existing approaches, which emphasized markets in advanced nations and were more concerned about the regions and countries where automobile manufacturers were located. While the Asian automobile market is temporarily suffering from a dramatic plunge in demand due to the economic crisis that started in 1997, it is potentially very large, making it essential for automobile makers thinking globally to come up with a strategy for Asia.

The critical point is that automobile makers will not survive if they function only within one country, acting regionally. A manufacturer can maintain stability when it grows from a regional maker into a global one only when it establishes a comprehensive global strategy that covers all markets. Since supply and demand trends in automobile markets differ from region to region, they offset each other and companies can balance the profits across markets, thus compensating for losses and fluctuating exchange rates. Figure 5.1 compares the world's major regions by production capacity and utilization per region.

Against this background, Daimler and Chrysler aimed not at a global strategy of making themselves into global automobile manufacturers but instead at entering into a mutually beneficial alliance that would make the best use of each company's strengths. Both companies realized that being an independent global manufacturer included a lot of risk.

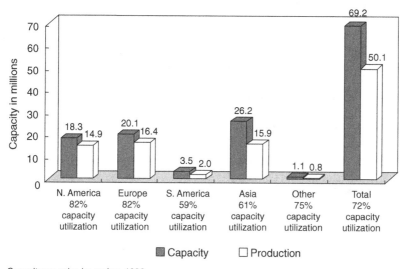

Capacity vs. sales by region–1998
Source: J.D. Power & Associates estimates
Reproduced in part by author

Figure 5.1 Industry structure – global overcapacity

Chrysler, a large-scale regional manufacturer centered in North America, was dominant in the under $25,000 per unit passenger vehicle segment for minivans and SUVs, while Daimler was known as a medium-scale, high-class, niche manufacturer,[3] with a worldwide reputation for its luxury vehicles. In terms of market and production bases, Daimler was a regional manufacturer centered in Europe. The natural conclusion was that neither of these manufacturers alone could have faced the challenges of global competition. Chrysler, even as a regional manufacturer in North America, would have had to strengthen production capacity to 1 million units and to begin to make huge new investments in engines and components.[4] Competing as a global auto maker through building presence in the weak European, Asian, and South American markets while at the same time shouldering the risk of huge investments would have been no easy matter. At the same time, Daimler could not have captured the growing Asian, Central American, and South American markets solely on the strength of the worldwide brand image of its luxury vehicles. This was even truer for the North American market – Daimler would have had to add both economical passenger cars and minivans/SUVs to its line-up.

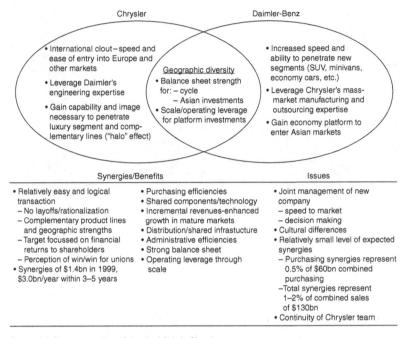

Chrysler · Daimler-Benz

- International clout – speed and ease of entry into Europe and other markets
- Leverage Daimler's engineering expertise
- Gain capability and image necessary to penetrate luxury segment and complementary lines ("halo" effect)

Geographic diversity
- Balance sheet strength for: – cycle – Asian investments
- Scale/operating leverage for platform investments

- Increased speed and ability to penetrate new segments (SUV, minivans, economy cars, etc.)
- Leverage Chrysler's mass-market manufacturing and outsourcing expertise
- Gain economy platform to enter Asian markets

Synergies/Benefits		Issues
• Relatively easy and logical transaction – No layoffs/rationalization – Complementary product lines and geographic strengths – Target focussed on financial returns to shareholders – Perception of win/win for unions • Synergies of $1.4bn in 1999, $3.0bn/year within 3–5 years	• Purchasing efficiencies • Shared components/technology • Incremental revenues-enhanced growth in mature markets • Distribution/shared infrastacture • Administrative efficiencies • Strong balance sheet • Operating leverage through scale	• Joint management of new company – speed to market – decision making • Cultural differences • Relatively small level of expected synergies – Purchasing synergies represent 0.5% of $60bn combined purchasing –Total synergies represent 1–2% of combined sales of $130bn • Continuity of Chrysler team

Source: J.A. Casesa and others: Schroders' DaimlerChrysler
Reproduced in part by author

Figure 5.2 Implications of the DaimlerChrysler merger

These two manufacturers with very different values, cultures, and characteristics therefore took the dramatic step of creating a large-scale cross-border alliance in order to survive in the face of stiff global competition. Figure 5.2 shows the mutually supportive effects of the Daimler and Chrysler alliance. Figure 5.3 shows the average price range and transitions in production volumes for passenger vehicles before and after the merger. Figures 5.4 and 5.5 show the ratio of light vehicles sold by region for each company individually before the merger, and Figure 5.6 shows the same ratios following the merger.

We should not overlook the impact of the globalizing financial system, which made such large-scale, cross-border alliances possible. Following the shake-up of the financial and stock markets, auto-mobile manufacturers and other companies no longer needed to rely on domestic banks, investments, bonds, and stocks to raise funds. Today, funds can be raised through global financial institutions and stock markets and the public estimation of the company can be

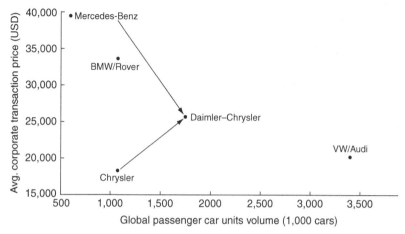

Source: Shreder's Report, p. 5

Figure 5.3 Passenger car volume vs. average price

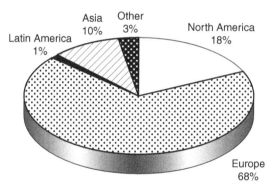

Source: Shreder's Report, p. 5
Reproduced in part by author

Figure 5.4 Mercedes-Benz 1997 light vehicle unit sales by region

systematically boosted through high cash-flow figures and economic value added (EVA).

As we can see in Figures 5.7 and 5.8, which show the production and cash-flow rankings for automobile manufacturers around the world, a wide gap has emerged in cash flow among the main manufacturers. Even manufacturers high on the production ranking have rather low cash flows.

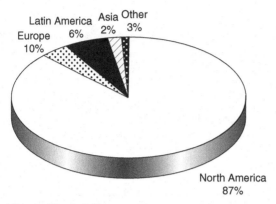

Source: Shreder's Report, p. 6
Reproduced in part by author

Figure 5.5 Chrysler 1997 light vehicle unit sales by region

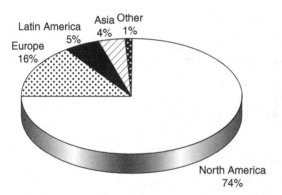

Source: Shreder's Report, p. 6
Reproduced in part by author

Figure 5.6 DaimlerChrysler 1997 pro forma light vehicle unit sales by region

Especially prominent are Japanese manufacturers such as Nissan and Mitsubishi. This is due mainly to the combined effect of the domestic recession in Japan and the economic crisis in Asia, with the collapse of the Japanese financial system and the stagnation of the main banking system. In contrast, cash flows for GM, Ford, and Chrysler are all high. However, this amount includes revenues from their respective finance companies, which manage huge amounts of capital and

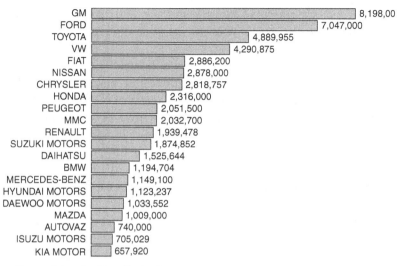

Source: Automotive News Yearbook
Reproduced in part by author

Figure 5.7 Global production ranking, 1997 (cars produced)

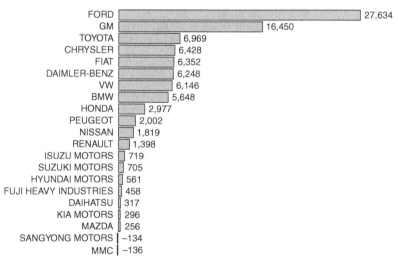

Note: Includes categories other than automobiles
Source: Prepared by ING Barings Securities
Reproduced in part by author

Figure 5.8 Consolidated cash-flow ranking, 1997 (US$ million)

reserve funds for employee health insurance. Differences in accounting systems are also responsible for the wide discrepancies between Japan and the US.

Regardless, one important factor here is the symbolism around GM, which prides itself on being the number one auto maker in the world, and the fact that it has been surpassed in terms of cash flow by Ford. Globalization has brought shifts in competitive power as rankings from the point of cash flow have become more important than those of car production, sales, and even market share. Cash flow is undoubtedly affected not only by domestic competitive power but also by global competitive power. It is easy to see from cash-flow levels that manufacturers such as Ford and VW have effective global strategies. The cash-flow perspective highlights the importance of global strategies, regardless of participation in alliances or mergers. Survival among auto makers in the twenty-first century will depend even more heavily on effective skills in designing global strategies, yet the economy of scale theory is often still used in discussions concerning cross-border alliances and collaborations.

Now to consider what drove the quick move toward large-scale international alliances and mergers. Foremost was the introduction of innovations based on digital design, which facilitated the sharing of global platforms as CAE and digital CAD CAM came into common use. The number of platforms, traditionally different for each model, could be reduced and the industry unified, thus lowering the barriers between manufacturers. This reduction in the number of platforms and increased common sharing was not new. Some manufacturers in the West had already begun this practice in the early 1980s, with some Japanese manufacturers starting in the early 1990s.

Today, reducing the number of platforms has become a common trend worldwide. For example, GM reduced its more than thirty-six platforms by half and was aiming at eight in the future, while Toyota and Nissan planned to reduce their more than twenty platforms to eight apiece. Honda, which foreshadowed common platforms, aimed to unify product development with a flexible world platform. Comparing current production numbers per platform in North America, small trucks and minivans manufactured by the Big Three occupy the top eight positions. Two basic types of small trucks account for the highest production number per platform at more than 1 million, and even the lowest production number is around 450,000.

As for Japanese cars in North America, the Honda Accord and Toyota Camry rank ninth and tenth respectively. Production is 440,000 and 430,000 per platform. A simple comparison reveals that small trucks, one of the US manufacturers' strong points, hold twice the scale merit compared with Japanese passenger vehicles. This is a source of high profits, at around $5,000 or $10,000 per unit (see Figure 5.9).

Unifying platforms brings a rise in production numbers per platform and a reduction in costs as the scale benefits go up. Taking this one step further logically, big mergers should bring increased scale benefits by establishing common platforms between the manufacturers involved. Moreover, there is a movement to unify basic components such as engines and transmissions as well as platforms. For example, Ford is developing a global engine series with an annual production of more than 2 million units. This trend also forms part of the thinking behind mergers and alliances.

One more point related to global mergers and cooperation is that global supplies make it possible to reduce component costs by narrowing down the number of component manufacturers. Advanced system unification also reduces costs by shaving the number of components and the manufacturing processes using module systems. A quick look tells us that mergers and cooperation bring about lower costs for component supply and promote module systems because of the resulting concentrated purchase of components and increased buying power.

Table 5.1 shows procurement strategies for the Big Three. Included are how the number of suppliers is being reduced, goals for reducing costs related to component supply and development, reduction of the number of platform types, and separation of intra-company component operations.

Further impetus to develop global strategies resulted from the increased importance of forming environmental strategies for handling such issues as CO_2 reduction and recycling, which will strongly influence competitive power in the automobile industry during the twenty-first century.

Full-scale global competition in the form of competitive strategies among auto makers was set off by the 1993 announcement of Ford's Project 2000, the company's flagship global strategy. More than anything, Project 2000 signaled the start of an era of global strategies in the worldwide automobile industry, and has since played a leading role in global strategies looking toward the twenty-first century.

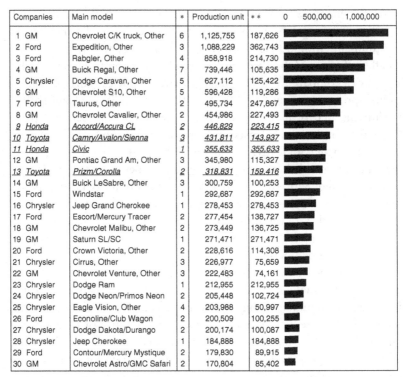

Companies	Main model	*	Production unit	**	0	500,000	1,000,000
1 GM	Chevrolet C/K truck, Other	6	1,125,755	187,626			
2 Ford	Expedition, Other	3	1,088,229	362,743			
3 Ford	Rabgler, Other	4	858,918	214,730			
4 GM	Buick Regal, Other	7	739,446	105,635			
5 Chrysler	Dodge Caravan, Other	5	627,112	125,422			
6 GM	Chevrolet S10, Other	5	596,428	119,286			
7 Ford	Taurus, Other	2	495,734	247,867			
8 GM	Chevrolet Cavalier, Other	2	454,986	227,493			
9 Honda	*Accord/Accura CL*	*2*	*446,829*	*223,415*			
10 Toyota	*Camry/Avalon/Sienna*	*3*	*431,811*	*143,937*			
11 Honda	*Civic*	*1*	*355,633*	*355,633*			
12 GM	Pontiac Grand Am, Other	3	345,980	115,327			
13 Toyota	*Prizm/Corolla*	*2*	*318,831*	*159,416*			
14 GM	Buick LeSabre, Other	3	300,759	100,253			
15 Ford	Windstar	1	292,687	292,687			
16 Chrysler	Jeep Grand Cherokee	1	278,453	278,453			
17 Ford	Escort/Mercury Tracer	2	277,454	138,727			
18 GM	Chevrolet Malibu, Other	2	273,449	136,725			
19 GM	Saturn SL/SC	1	271,471	271,471			
20 Ford	Crown Victoria, Other	2	228,616	114,308			
21 Chrysler	Cirrus, Other	3	226,977	75,659			
22 GM	Chevrolet Venture, Other	3	222,483	74,161			
23 Chrysler	Dodge Ram	1	212,955	212,955			
24 Chrysler	Dodge Neon/Primos Neon	2	205,448	102,724			
25 Chrysler	Eagle Vision, Other	4	203,988	50,997			
26 Ford	Econoline/Club Wagon	2	200,509	100,255			
27 Chrysler	Dodge Dakota/Durango	2	200,174	100,087			
28 Chrysler	Jeep Cherokee	1	184,888	184,888			
29 Ford	Contour/Mercury Mystique	2	179,830	89,915			
30 GM	Chevrolet Astro/GMC Safari	2	170,804	85,402			

Note: * number of models ** units produced per model
Extract from: Composed by ING Bearing Broker House, based on articles from *Automotive News*

In the Northern Market, the production scale of GM's C/K Pickup/Sierra/Suburban and Ford's F-series Pickup/Expedition, which represent the SUV segment that shares the same base as full-size pickup trucks, surpasses 1 million units per year. The merit of scale is twice of Honda's Accord/Acura (447,000 cars) or Toyota's Camry/Avalon/Sienna (432,000 cars). Because of this, it was said that the profit per car had reached about US$5,000 for pickup trucks and about US$10,000 for SUVs.
Following developments in the chassis, GM and Ford are expanding their merit of scale by integrating products' variation in the areas of engines and transmissions, which are basic components – for example, Ford's development of a global engine series which surpassed 2 million cars annually after the year 2000, and GM's plans to integrate power trains on a global base.

Source: Prepared by ING Barings Securities from *Automobile News*
Reproduced in part by author

Figure 5.9 Number of vehicles produced per platform (North America, 1997)

Under president Trotman, Ford set out a bold global strategy based on the recognition that the globalization of people, things, money, and information was proceeding rapidly, and that building of the appropriate corporate culture was necessary to keep up with the speed of change.[5] Therefore, Trotman promoted a strategic unification of the Ford

Table 5.1 *Component procurement strategies (Big Three)*

	General Motors	Ford	Chrysler
Key word	"Best Worldwide Supply"	"Ford 2000"	"Greatest Minimized Costs in the World"
Reduced number of suppliers	5,000–6,000 main component manufacturers in 1988 were greatly reduced to 2,500–3,000 in 1990, with further reductions planned for the year 2000 and beyond Demanding further development of module components	Aim to reduce the number of main component manufacturers from 2,010 companies to 1,000 in ten years The reduction of the number of component companies in North America from 1,500 to 1,000 by the year 2000. From these, 180 manufacturers are to receive two-thirds of future component orders Demanding further development of module components	Reduction from 1,500 main component manufacturers at present to approximately 150 by the year 2000
Goal of reduced component supply costs	Introduction of PICOS 30% cost reduction was achieved within three years of 1992. This program will continue	Requesting a 5% annual cost reduction and 20% overall cost reduction for the four years since 1995	Introduction of the SCORE program since 1989 Cooperation with suppliers to reduce costs A reduction of $2.67 billion by 1996 and overall target of $9.8 billion by 2001

Table 5.1 (*cont.*)

	General Motors	Ford	Chrysler
Key word	"Best Worldwide Supply"	"Ford 2000"	"Greatest Minimized Costs in the World"
Goal of reduced development costs	PICOS was introduced with the aim of reducing costs by 30% within three years of 1992. PICOS was later made into a regular program Requested improvements aimed at "zero defects" during the 1996 suppliers' meeting	Aiming at cutting back total costs for the year 2000 to the 1995 level through a product development-led system concentrated at five vehicle centers Shortening the development period from thirty-three months to twenty-four months	25% reduction in preparation time for manufacturing through the introduction of the CAM system, accompanied by reductions in related costs Aiming at zero annual defects per model
Reduced number of platforms	Reduction from twenty-five at present to a total of eight Reduced number of engine and transmission types	Reduction from twenty-four at present to a total of sixteen Increasing model variations from five types to eight types per platform Reduction from thirty basic engine structures at present to a total of fourteen by 2004	Integration of seven or eight platforms Expanding production per platform by integration of the platforms as well as increasing the production capacities

Table 5.1 (*cont.*)

	General Motors	Ford	Chrysler
	"Best Worldwide Supply"	"Ford 2000"	"Greatest Minimized Costs in the World"
Key word			
Movement away from intra-company component operations	Delphi Automobile Systems was established following the detachment of GM ACG (intra-company component operations) in 1994. Delco Electronics was then taken over at the end of 1997. An increase from 30% in 1996 to 50% by 2002 is planned for sales%ages excluding GM North America Operations (NAO). It is also said that a public stock offering is highly likely in 1999	Visteon Automobile Systems was established after intra-company component operations were detached in November 1996. Plan to increase reliance on sales outside of Ford from 10% in 1996 to approximately 20% between 2000 and 2002	Promote outsourcing except for main components such as platforms and power trains through the spin-off and sale of Acustar (intra-company component operations)

Source: Prepared by ING Barings Securities from *Automobile News*, etc.
Reproduced in part by author

family, including Ford Europe, Mazda, and Jaguar, and infusing a common global vision. Global unification of automobile chassis and platforms was promoted by carrying out worldwide unification of the development system. Then, related to this, a world-car concept was established with the Mondeo and Mystique light-vehicle series. This was the springboard for the debut of a basic world car, the KA series.

Overlap which had previously occurred in the development of similar concepts in North America, Europe, and Asia was halted, five vehicle centers were organized, and development functions were concentrated as much as possible in Dearborn. A strategy was developed to organize the division of labor and cooperation among North America, Europe, and Asia under a global development system. This was carried out mainly in development centers in North America with the introduction of common platforms, common components, and the global engine series. Under Ford 2000, a global strategy for component supply was established. Ford promoted the reduction and systematization of suppliers, establishment of module systems, the independence of Visteon, the intra-company component operations, and growth of global suppliers. In the process, thorough benchmarking was implemented by setting up a database of supplier capacity (cost competitiveness, price competitiveness, time for delivery, and technological/developmental ability). In this way, the groundwork for global sourcing was boldly laid, referred to as the best locations and supply worldwide.

The global strategy of Ford 2000 was formed with far-sighted vision and was very dynamic in nature. As is clear from the key words, "Think globally, act locally with agility," that Ford used in planning its world car, the company carefully considered the compatibility of products with local markets while taking into account complications surrounding local market needs and market changes.

At the time, Ford 2000 was considered too radical and bold a concept, and specialists in the US criticized the project as being too futuristic and carrying too great a risk. Some people saw the plan as lacking in reality and being a morale-boosting tactic to support Trotman's corporate culture reforms.

Conflicts and confusion occurred within the company after the strategy was implemented. The world-car concept was reconsidered and the direction of development-sharing with Europe was altered slightly. However, it later became clear that this bold global strategy would succeed when looking at increases in Ford's share of the world market, improved cash flow, and reduction of costs related to development and component supplies.

In an interview at Ford headquarters, I discovered that Project 2000 was not aimed solely at strategic global preparations. In order to even out the bureaucratic organization and make Ford even more active, promoting reform of the corporate culture at Ford was aimed not only at reforming the mentality within the company but also at making the best use of information technology. These reforms ranged from full implementation of databases to simplifying management procedures and organization. The main point of the project was to speed up business procedures and decision making.[6] This type of advanced global strategy, together with reforming the corporate culture, strengthened Ford's presence in the worldwide automobile industry and led to the establishment of global strategies by many other manufacturers, including VW and GM. In a way, this movement became the primer for worldwide reform as represented by the Daimler–Chrysler alliance and the Nissan–Renault merger.

3. The role of scale economy in global reorganization and systems that produced various models in different quantities

We have seen that the global strategy that received all the attention was Ford's Project 2000, which triggered the switch to global strategies. We will now look at global reorganization based on economies of scale – the 4 million unit theory. If annual production of 4 million cars is the magic number, below which companies will not survive, then merger fever is a natural phenomenon among automobile manufacturers and management. The question remains as to whether the economy of scale theory can explain the globalization of the worldwide automobile industry. Can it really be explained so simply?

If the international automobile market continues to undergo complicated and diversified changes, and movements in demand continue to roller coaster depending on the region and time, with no synchronization among regions, then there are alternatives to economies of scale as a competitive policy – for instance, lowering the break-even point for a limited production scale without sticking to the ideal of scale supremacy, developing creative products aimed at a specific niche market, being able to develop dynamic new products one after another with short lead times, and flexible production systems that can be adapted for different types and quantities.

Globalization of the automobile industry is proceeding in two directions. One is toward adopting a strategy based on economies of scale and the other is adopting a strategy of maintaining a flexible production system that can respond to any changes.

Expansion of scale benefits through mergers and cooperation surely brings an increase in production numbers per platform and reduces costs for component supplies. The problem, however, is that these points are not always accompanied by increased development ability, which is needed to guarantee improvements in product quality. Nor is there any guarantee that individual identity, as shown in distinctive product architecture, will remain after reducing the number of platforms. It is also possible for individual manufacturers with annual production of around 1 million units to reduce the number of platforms and to adopt common platforms in their own way. Narrowing the number of component manufacturers and moving toward modularity can meet demand through cooperation among networks of mid-sized automobile manufacturers even without mergers. An excessive move toward modularity, i.e., large-scale subassembly, will weaken the attraction of products and make automobiles standard products like personal computers. The charm of the product will disappear.

Another consideration is the diversification of needs and drastic changes in the automobile market. Competition in product development will heat up and quicker development will be required, with the increased use of electronic information in automobile design architecture for environmental, safety, and ITS countermeasures. In actuality, shortening development times is already happening, and 12–18 months has become a reasonable timeframe. A simple scale benefit theory does not fully explain how this copes with diversification and speed of change in the market. Competing with superior-quality products cannot be guaranteed just by increasing output.[7] In order to correspond to market diversification and speed of change, new production systems which make flexible production and variable quantities possible will be key. Scale is not the only way.

At present, reduction of supply capacity is proceeding and shortening of production lines is being planned. Japanese automobile manufacturers are pursuing flexible production and trying to create flexible production lines to adjust the rate of operations at plants or on production lines. The newest production lines at Toyota's Shimoyama engine plant and Honda's Suzuka plant are good examples.

As a case study, let's look at the new line at the Shimoyama engine factory.[8] Toyota's Shimoyama engine plant was established as the main plant, equivalent to the Kamigo plant, in 1975. Since then the plant has manufactured 25 million engines and now supports engine plants in Britain, North America, and Thailand. The new challenge for the Shimoyama plant was to start a new line to manufacture 30,000 ZZ-type engines per month, incorporating flexibility and shortening the lead-time for producing these lightweight, fuel-efficient engines. The ZZ engine uses a 4-cylinder, 1800-cc front-intake rear exhaust and has an aluminum casting liner. Flexibility to date had been aimed at handling variation changes within the same type of machine. The main characteristic of the new production system was to develop flexibility in handling design modifications as well as production fluctuations, in other words, flexibility to handle quantity.

It was difficult to establish stable production amounts at Shimoyama due to the stagnant domestic demand and because engine manufacturing was being transferred overseas. The aim was to organize the process to absorb fluctuations as much as possible, even if they could not "just fit" production fluctuations. They promoted a "no more transfer machine" process and eliminated computer integrated manufacturing processes that, although they could handle mass production, required a minimum production level.

To handle crank and camshaft processing, they lined up general-use machines and adopted a single shaft NC, and to handle block and cylinder head processing, they used multiple lines. Conventional CIM and production processes with transfer machines rely on high production levels. Because the additional cost almost doubled the initial investment, attempts to absorb the effects included reducing the production amounts at the lines. Multiple lines enable the plant to handle fluctuations in production, and mean that, in extreme cases, operations on one or more lines can be stopped, so that, for instance, when the plant reduces processing by 30 percent, they can switch the operators to the remaining lines. This can shorten the assembly and process lead-time and improve operability. Establishing new lines was accomplished with input from both production engineering management and the plant side.

In order to maintain high productivity while still accommodating production fluctuations and guaranteeing quality across multiple lines, it is crucial to train and develop operators by process rotation. This means they can be allocated to different processes and thus accommodate quantitative fluctuations. However, it is very difficult to rotate operators through all the processes, so processes are divided into three zones and operators learn of the relevant processes for one zone. These three zones contain related processes, such as blocks and heads, shaft-related processing such as cranks and rods, and assembly processing.

These methods are designed to handle operability fluctuations at 70–100 percent by creating flexible lines that can handle design modifications and production quantity fluctuations. Depending on the capacity, equipment such as presses may be shut down. The company is also considering establishing a module structure for equipment, so shutdown equipment can be used for another purpose on another line. This type of line structure has also been adopted in other companies in Japan.

Efforts to introduce production of various models in different quantities and process flexibility are linked to shorter product development times, faster preparation for mass production, and front loading (solving problems in advance during the trial process).[9] There are also some common aspects with limited small-scale production. Equipment investment will be less than that for existing production lines and yearly production limits will be established. This then pushes manufacturers to work with plants and production systems that can make a profit even with annual production at 50,000, or even 10,000 when needed. Honda is now carrying out an experimental trial in Turkey.

Large-scale international alliances or joining the 4 million club are thus not the only strategies for survival in the automobile industry in this global era. Even with these large-scale alliances, results depend on whether or not there is a true synergistic effect making the best use of the partners' different brand values and manufacturing characteristics. Examples of unsuccessful endeavors include the merger between BMW and Rover, and that between Renault and AMC. The conclusion is that the way to survive includes adopting flexible production systems while forming flexible and diversified cooperation networks, even if the scale is small.[10]

The founder of modern global strategies, Ford, did not pursue only scale benefits to standardize the platform or to supply components globally. Instead, its global strategies included careful considerations of global contents and the value side, focussing on the compatibility of the products in each community and the agility of business operations.

4. The direction of global structural change in the auto component industry

While assembler-level manufacturers in the automobile industry were pushing forward with restructuring efforts and global strategies, the same wave of globalization and structural change was also rolling through the automobile components industry. Structural changes were caused in part by the automobile manufacturers expanding their global outsourcing strategies. Another driving factor was the globalization of the automobile components suppliers themselves, which began to integrate, merge, and build network tie-ups of their own accord. The two trends were inter-related and fueled one another's evolution.

Western auto makers led the trend in reducing supplier numbers. Table 5.2 gives the sales rankings of the world's top component suppliers, and demonstrates the big changes in rankings that occurred between 1995 and 1997. Table 5.3 lists the brisk activity in mergers and acquisitions amongst automobile component manufacturers during this period, which impacted sales rankings. One of the reasons the outsourcing squeeze appeared first in the West was due to moves from the Big Three, but the targets of all automobile manufacturers and the processes they used to achieve those targets promoted mergers and acquisitions amongst components manufacturers and led to the emergence of global suppliers.

But what exactly are automobile manufacturers targeting by reducing the number of suppliers, and what kind of process are they using? Historically, there were distinct differences between the components procurement systems in the West and in Japan. In the US, most of the components were made in-house in what is referred to as an internal vertical system. Europe, meanwhile, used few in-house components, choosing instead a horizontal relationship with suppliers.[11] Though US and European automobile makers differed on internal manufacturing ratios, they were similar in the fact that they both

Table 5.2 *Worldwide sales ranking of automobile component manufacturers, 1995–1997*

Sales ranking			Company name	Worldwide sales		Regional business ratio 1997			
1997	1996	1995		1996 ($m)	1997 ($m)	North America (%)	Europe (%)	Asia (%)	Other (%)
1	1	1	Delphi Automotive Systems	26,000	26,600	75	15	5	5
2	2	4	Visteon Automotive Systems	16,400	17,000	85	15		
3	3	2	Robert Bosch Corp.	16,300	16,500	20	71		
4	4	3	Denso Corp.	13,000	13,104	18	5	76	2
5	5	19	Aisin Seiki Co.	7,790	7,790	9	7	82	2
6	9	16	Lear Corp.	6,249	7,343	68	26		6
7	8	17	Johnson Controls Inc.	5,942	7,280	68	29	1	2
8	7	5	TRW Inc.	6,493	7,032	50	42	3	5
9	14	14	Dana Corp.	5,450	6,217	80	12	2	6
10	20		Magna International	4,200	5,500	68	20		
11	12	6	Delco Electronics Corp.	5,350	5,350	81			
12	15	7	ITT Automotive	5,500	5,200	50	50		
13			Bridgestone Corp.	4,756	5,146	30	14	48	8
14	10	13	Valeo SA	4,600	5,000	22	74	3	1
15	6	20	Lucas Varity Plc.	5,100	4,471	40	50	5	5
16	17	15	Mannesmann AG	4,153	4,332		82		
17			Magnetti Marelli SpA	3,863	4,290	4	80		16
18			Bertrand Faure ECIA	–	4,000		95		
19	13	11	Groupe Michelin	3,620	3,980	32	54	8	6

Table 5.2 (*cont.*)

Sales ranking			Company name	Worldwide sales		Regional business ratio 1997			
1997	1996	1995		1996 ($m)	1997 ($m)	North America (%)	Europe (%)	Asia (%)	Other (%)
20	21	12	ZF Friedrichshafen AG	3,937	3,800		78		
21	25	24	Eaton Corp.	3,025	3,552	82			
22	23		GKN Plc.	3,423	3,381		66		
23			Goodyear Tire & Rubber Co.	3,370	3,360	50	24	12	14
24	19	18	Thyssen Budd Automotive GmbH	3,300	3,300	66	30		
25			Meritor Automotive Inc.	3,100	3,300	40	45		4

US Big Three have changed their purchasing strategies significantly since 1990. This movement is to select the primary component manufacturers to establish the supply chain without capitalistic relationships. This allows them to establish the system to expedite outsourcing, promote units' process, develop, and deliver on global bases. M&A among North US automobile component manufacturers continues. For example, a body- and engine-related component manufacturer, Dana, was planning a merger with Ericson in 2000 following the 1997 merger with Echlin. The result would be a giant company exceeding $13 billion. By merging with Ericson, which has the strong brand presence for the repair components, it could disperse the risk in the reciprocal market and stabilize the incoming cash flow.

Source: Automotive News, prepared by Bearing Holding Company; reproduced in part by author

Table 5.3 M&A of the automobile component industry, 1995–1997 (Automobile component manufacturers are already in action)

Date	Country	Initiating company	Description	Country	Non-initiating company
94.5	USA	Foamex International	Acquisition	USA	JPS Automotive
95.4	Norway	Walbro Automotive	Acquisition	USA	Dyno Ind. fuel system div.
96.6	UK	Lucas Industries	Merger	USA	Varity Corp.
95.11	USA	Tenneco Automotive	Acquisition	USA	Psefection Automotive Products
95.11	USA	Johnson Controls	Acquisition	France	Roth Freres S. A.
95.11	USA	Dana Corp.	Acquisition	UK	GKN
95.11	USA	Dana Corp.	Acquisition	Brazil	Rockwell do Brazil
95.8	USA	Lear Seating Corp.	Acquisition	USA	Automotive Industries Holding
95	USA	TRW	Acquisition	South America	Safety Transport Inter
96	USA	Borg-Warner Automotive	Acquisition	France	Societe de L'Usine de la Marque
96.2	USA	Dana Corp.	Acquisition	Argentina	Chassis, Piston ring
95.3	USA	T&N	Acquisition	France	Sintertech S. A.
95.3	Germany	Budd	Acquisition	USA	Resin Business of Complex Components
96.2	USA	Dana Corp.	Acquisition	USA	Business Department of SPX Corp.
96.2	USA	Dana Corp.	Acquisition	USA	Clark–Hurth Components
97.3	USA	Lear Corp.	Acquisition	Czechoslovakia	Acquired Empetek Autodily from ERPE
97.6	USA	Lear Corp.	Acquisition	UK	Acquired Dunlop Cox from BTR
97.6	USA	Lear Corp.	Acquisition	Germany	Automobile Seat Business of Keiper
97.7	USA	Dana Corp.	Acquisition	USA	Axle and Break Business of Eaton Corp.
97.8	USA	Lear Corp.	Acquisition	USA	Seat Components of ITT Automobile
97.9	USA	Eatin Corp.	Acquisition	USA	Clutch Business of Dana Corp.
97.9	Canada	Magna International	Acquisition	Germany	Plastic Interior and Exterior Decoration Department of YMOS

Table 5.3 (cont.)

Date	Country	Initiating company	Description	Country	Non-initiating company
97.7	USA	GM Delphi	Acquisition	Poland	Febryka Amortyzatorow S. A.
97.8	USA	Lear Corp.	Acquisition	USA	ITT Industries
97.8	Germany	Siemens AG	Share increase	USA	Ford
97.8	USA	Lear Corp.	Acquisition	Germany	Keiper Car Seating GmbH & Co.
97.9	USA	GM Delphi	Disposal by Sale	To be determined	Spin off of the unprofitable department
97.9	USA	Magna	Partial Acquisition	USA	GM Delphi
97.9	USA	Micronas	Partial Acquisition	USA	ITT Industries
97.9	USA	Textron	Acquisition	UK	General Rubber Goods Department (Pirelli)
97.9	Canada	Magna International	Acquisition	Germany	Ymos AG's plastic products division
97.9	USA	Eaton	Business Transfer	USA	Dana
97.10	USA	Federal-Mogul	Acquisition	USA	T&N
97.10	USA	Tenneco	Acquisition	Argentina	Fric–Rot
97.11	USA	Delphi Automotive Systems	Acquisition	USA	Delco Electronics
97.12	France	Ecia (PSA Peugeot Citroën)	Acquisition	France	Bertrand Faure
98.2	USA	Walton Johnson Group	Partial Acquisition	USA	Delphi Automotive Systems
98.5	USA	Dana Corp.	Merger	USA	Echlin Inc.

Note: The indicated dates are when the related articles were published but not the accurate merger or acquisition date.
Source: *Ward's Automobile Report* and extracts from companies' press releases; reproduced in part by author

used numerous component suppliers and numerous miscellaneous components. Even US companies, which used a high percentage of internally manufactured components, far outdistanced Japanese automobile manufacturers in the number of suppliers they retained. Take, for example, GM, with 6,000 suppliers, or Ford, with 2,000, and compare that with the roughly 200 primary suppliers for a Japanese company. European manufacturers also used many suppliers.

The components business of Western automobile manufacturers emphasized more than anything else cost evaluation on a short-term tender base. Because of the competitive bidding, component suppliers were changing constantly. Also, with the exception of the fuel pumps made by Bosch and transmissions made by Borg-Warner, functional components and system components were completely designed, developed, tested, and assembled by the automobile manufacturer, with no information being released outside of the company. These practices have had the greatest influence on the ongoing structural changes in the component supplies industry – the current outsourcing squeeze is the result of changes in traditional components business practices used in the West. In other words, Western automobile manufacturers are changing their component procurement practices and are now asking suppliers to deliver components as systems and units. Moreover, manufacturers are evaluating suppliers for their design strength, development strength, and engineering solutions needed to supply these systems and units, and additionally shifting their focus from inspected delivery to quality assurances from the supplier end. It looks like the West is copying Japan in the hope of gaining the stability inherent in Japan's vertical pyramid structure and business through affiliations. However, it has cost conventional automobile manufacturers time and money to reorganize their purchasing departments and form cooperative groups. The process has been helped, nevertheless, by the information revolution that has followed on the tail of these structural changes. Manufacturers are building a database of suppliers and a system for benchmarking quality, cost, delivery, and engineering, so they can see at a glance the capabilities and hidden potential of suppliers, a task that previously had left them groping around in the dark. Supplier integration and reduction have emerged as a clear policy, and the database of suppliers and benchmarking systems is being built not just for a single country but on a global basis.[12]

These structural changes have naturally invited dynamic mergers between component suppliers around the world. However, it is important to note that these mergers do not merely target expansion but a restructuring that can boost the suppliers' design and development strength and system-building capabilities. In essence, the restructuring we are seeing amongst components suppliers is not led by the automobile manufacturers but is the suppliers' own attempt at global integration. When the term "global outsourcing" was coined, manufacturers were trying to address the false assumption that volume components of a car, such as electronic components, had to be procured and supplied on a country base.[13] Now, a core element of global outsourcing is that suppliers also have to be capable of exchanging CAD/CAM and CAE data on a global scale. They have to incorporate their potential as the best location and best supplier into their global strategy. What this means, as Ryoichi Hara has pointed out, is that suppliers not only require the design ability that allows them to participate in development under the approved country system but also need the ability to propose basic development concepts. Things have turned out this way because automobile manufacturers need to focus development resources on advanced and basic technology in areas such as the environment and ITS.[14]

As restructuring continues along these lines in the global component industry, modularization is becoming a keyword. Modularization was originally introduced in Europe, by German automobile manufacturers, as a means of overcoming the high cost of labor and procurement that their horizontal supply business had created with the high number of components they had to deal with. These manufacturers built model plants in developing countries in Eastern Europe and Latin America, where modularization was first adopted. Watching this, global suppliers like Bosch, Delphi, and Visteon, which were targeting global business expansion, jumped on the design and development bandwagon and came up with a proposal to strategically use modular components.

This change constituted a completely different perspective on the prevailing notion of assembler leadership. One after another, Western manufacturers constructively adopted the modular approach, marking the start of a link between global outsourcing and component modularization. Japanese automobile manufacturers were generally circumspect about this trend, because their procurement system with domestic component suppliers was viewed as the most efficient in the world. They decided that there was no urgent need to promote modularization because primary suppliers were taking part in simultaneous engineering, modularization was progressing with procured competence, and sideline delivery was becoming customary with system components. They additionally pointed out that modular components would place restrictions on individual designs, and they found it hard to put modularization before the vehicle.

Nevertheless, over the past few years Japanese manufacturers have given modularization a second look and some are trying to introduce it. One reason for this is that the growth of modular components came at an opportune time, when increasing environmental concerns meant that manufacturers had to deal with recycling and low fuel-consuming vehicles, and also develop a next-generation vehicle based on ITS. Good results from Western manufacturers which have introduced modularization are another reason why Japanese manufacturers are changing their stance. Restrictions on the design work for modularization are being lifted somewhat thanks to improvements in digital design techniques and advances in architectural design.

Modularization is making it possible not only to reduce the number of component suppliers but also to greatly reduce costs, using inventions that divide and link suppliers and assemblers by their specialities. Japanese manufacturers are today promoting modularization by helping suppliers design doors, internal panels, and other components, while providing them with technical guidance along the production line. At the same time, they are promoting modularization in the design stage. What they need to do more than anything else is to improve their design capabilities and strength of architecture.[15] On this point, Masataka Ikeda feels that Japanese automobile manufacturers see modularization on the development level "as a wider range of development outsourcing." He cites the following reasons: (1) large cost reductions and the creation of added-value from business that is done on a modular base; (2) reduced development burden for the assembler; (3) the possibility of coming up with something innovative despite the fact that Japan is behind the West in modularization; and (4) the necessity to prepare for the eventuality that Japanese components manufacturers will be unable to participate as suppliers as Western automobile manufacturers shift from ordering components to ordering modules. Ikeda adds that, at the present time, European component suppliers outperform their Japanese cohorts in their ability to propose modular products. This should come as a warning to Japanese component manufacturers. It will determine both whether they need to form strategic alliances and whether they can.[16]

Japanese suppliers who have enjoyed the advantages of traditional subsidiary business are, not surprisingly, affected by this structural change in the global automobile industry. Global sourcing development has created similar strategies among automobile manufacturers. Two trends can be seen: one is to strengthen relationships with subsidiary suppliers, the other is to evaluate suppliers based on systems integration, their ability to establish a modular structure that goes beyond subsidiary relationships, and their ability to aggressively propose technologies. These two trends are not necessarily mutually exclusive, but rather the suppliers are expected to be global suppliers with superior technological abilities. The overall trend is that global subsidiary businesses are becoming networked and the business structure is changing to be more dynamic and unrestricted by nationality. Among these changes, Japanese suppliers are deciding whether to be primary global suppliers or secondary global suppliers utilizing their own technologies. This suggests that future changes are likely to be in the subsidiary businesses, such as global module trends, assembler-initiating reorganization, or global supplier-initiated reorganization.

5. Conclusion

Automobile and component industries worldwide have gone global. The Daimler–Chrysler and Nissan–Renault alliances alluded to the view that automobile manufacturers had to join the 4 million unit club to survive, but global strategies are the key, and pursuing individual purposes through joint ventures and alliances aimed at scale advantages are not the sole drivers for a global strategy. Joint ventures to merely match numbers carry the risk of being large scale without achieving scale benefits. Thus the Daimler–Chrysler alliance considered the survival risk in a global era and stressed mutual support by product and region. They cannot develop a standardized platform, which would be expected if they were aiming for economic advantage by global sourcing. What is important is therefore not only scale in numbers but also the ability to develop products that play a core competitive role. Competition among auto makers is centered on the production systems and components supply strategies that handle the developed products, and also the creation of brand identity through marketing. The pursuit of valuable competitive advantage can come from an ability to plan daring and dynamic product architectures, to optimize production systems and components supply systems so that different models can be produced in different quantities to accommodate rapid market changes, and to market the product promptly and flexibly.

Ford made the first move in planning and implementing a global strategy. It did not start by merely matching numbers but stressed flexible and prompt handling of local market changes and differences while advocating a world car plan. Ford implemented platform standardization and a world engine series in module production for Ford North America, Ford Europe, Mazda, and Jaguar. At the same time, each company within the group is pursuing economic advantage based on an operational focus. Mazda is working on its ability to produce various models in different quantities, while its hardest job will be to secure its product identity. It is necessary to focus on the fact that it is not merely about matching numbers; platform integration and global components supply would be meaningless if product values were lost.

Japanese auto and component makers have provided us with lessons for the production of a range of models in different quantities. Since there are many Japanese auto makers, why not start joint ventures to match numbers? Even manufacturers with annual production levels of about 1 million units have their own products and identities for their production technology, so joint ventures for the purpose of number matching without a certain level of identity in design and production ability, which creates the niche markets, would be meaningless. This qualitative gap suggests that network-type alliances with core abilities for development and product identity might be better. For example, retaining each product identity but still using global collaborative ordering for parts and components is not impossible, but would depend on collaborative development and mutual use of modularized platforms and components from overseas manufacturers.

The global components industry is also changing structurally. Expansion of global sourcing by auto makers and the integration of the global suppliers to accommodate this expansion seems to be economically advantageous. When we think about dynamic changes, such as environmental compliance for automobile components, the switch from electronic to information system integration, fuel cells, and ITS handling, the important point is how the basic and unique core technologies of suppliers can best be used. Once again, it is not just about numbers – suppliers must show an ability for developing and utilizing new technologies and the potential for dynamic system integration. They must have the creativity to develop architecture of component designs and the independence to supplement areas where they are lacking. Hence the need for strategic and network alliances among suppliers that produce a dynamic change in value.

Notes

1. K. Shimokawa, *Automobile Industry: Out of the Maturity Age* (in Japanese), Yuhikaku, 1985, pp. 131–132.
2. There was optimism over the prospects of the Asian market, due to the size of the population to be introduced by the participation of China and India in the global market. There are stronger views about the possible environmental issues raised along with the increase in car owners.
3. However, we must remember also that Daimler (Mercedes Benz) is the world's biggest large-size truck manufacturer, manufacturing 1,837,462 truck units (*Japanese Automotive News Automobile Industry Handbook*, in Japanese, 1999, p. 191).
4. According to the announcement made by Chrysler, it had a five-year plan, in which it aimed to invest $4 billion to keep the plants up to date and $4 billion into drive- and engine-related component plants (*Japanese Automotive News Automobile Industry Handbook*, in Japanese, 1999, p. 182).
5. "Ford 2000", Ford Motor Company, press release, October 1994; K. Shimokawa, "About the Ford 2000 Project" (in Japanese), *Japanese Automotive News*, 1999.
6. Interview at the Ford headquarters, September 1997.
7. T. Fujimoto, "Automobile Industry, 'Quality' First" (in Japanese), Nippon Keizai Shinbun, Keizai Kyoshitsu (Economics Class), April 19, 1999.
8. K. Shimokawa, "Impressions of the new line at the Toyota Shimoyama engine plant in Japan," *Japanese Automotive News*, March 19, 1999.
9. T. Fujimoto, "Shorter product development period with front-loading method problem solving" (in Japanese), Economics Research Section of Tokyo University Graduate School, International Japanese Economic Collaborative Research Center, Discussion Paper CIRJE-J-1, April 1998.

10. K. Shimokawa, "Global amalgamation and flexible production systems in Japan," *Japanese Automotive News*, May 15, 1999.
11. J. Womack, D. Ross, and D. Jones, *The Machine That Changed the World*, Macmillan, 1990, pp. 193–206.
12. K. Harada, "Strategies for the rapid progress of the US automobile industry" (in Japanese), Industrial Research Association, 1995, pp. 106–109.
13. During the author's annual US research, in May 1995, purchasing personnel at Chrysler and Ford expressed the importance of global supply. However, Japanese purchasing personnel at local factories and development centers saw global sourcing as a mid- to long-term issue, and one which could not be implemented immediately. Thus the views of purchasing personnel in the two countries were very different.
14. R. Minami, "Globalization and issues of the automobile components industry" (in Japanese), Japan Automobile Manufacturers Association, *Automobile Industry*, August 1999, p. 11.
15. K. Shimokawa, "New Trend for Component Modules" (in Japanese), *Japanese Automotive News*, April 1, 1999.
16. M. Ikeda, "Japanese automobiles and automobile component industry" (in Japanese), Japan Automobile Industry Association, *Automobile Industry*, August 1999, pp. 7–8.

6 | The restructuring of the world's auto-parts industry and the transfiguration of the keiretsu parts transaction

1. Introduction

In the 1980s, Japan's *keiretsu* parts system was singled out as a major reason for the international competitiveness of Japan's auto industry. Manufacturers in Europe and the US realized that high productivity and guaranteed production quality were not only the reasons behind the Japanese success, and that *keiretsu* transactions with suppliers were a very important contributor.

Japanese automobile manufacturers ordered more parts from external suppliers than those in Europe and the US. By adjusting trading relations with the *keiretsu* suppliers dynamically, purchasing was managed through a limited number of primary suppliers, and this purchasing system helped to develop and maintain long-term, stable trading relations. In contrast, manufacturers in Europe and the US used different trading structures. While there were differences between individual manufacturers and also between Europe and the US, compared with Japan both regions' industries had a higher ratio of production in-house, at more than 60–80 percent. This was a historical legacy, dating back to Ford's vertical integration of its parts policy starting in 1920, and GM and Chrysler integrating parts supply by buying up subcontract suppliers. The in-house production ratio for mass producers in Europe was only about 50 percent, although the ratio for the luxury-car maker Daimler-Benz was at a similar level to US manufacturers.

The European and US purchase systems functioned relatively effectively in a situation where the auto makers held sway over their own regional markets. Both European and US manufacturers developed and tested unit and system components by themselves, contracted out the parts, and traded on a short-term bidding base. This custom was historically established, and explained why both European and US companies had a large number of trading suppliers.[1] A mass production structure with large-scale, car-centered, model-change cycles was preserved for a long time among US auto makers, with scale benefits affecting not only the level of production of finished cars but also the production of parts and components. In this situation, the high ratio of production in-house was self-perpetuating because it promoted vertical integration. While the in-house production ratio was lower among mass-production manufacturers in Europe, they still made components such as transmissions, brake systems, and others for the hearts of the cars in-house. The model-change cycle for European cars was as long as 7–8 years, but the makers placed great importance on product identity, including the designs they developed. So, although small parts were made by their subcontractors, systematized unit and system components were produced in-house.

If both the *keiretsu* system and the European and US models relied on a large number of suppliers, why were the European and US supplier systems said to be so much less efficient than the *keiretsu* system? The main reason is that the European and US supplier systems began to fail under the pressure of international competition, especially after the 1980s, and they began to lose control over their regional markets.

The parts industry, which had been a regional-based one, began a worldwide reorganization after the 1990s aimed at structural reform and global operations. Japanese manufacturers began local production in North America and Europe, and thus Japanese parts makers appeared in foreign markets. European and US manufacturers changed their parts-buying strategies drastically after the mid 1980s, and by connecting this to reviewing and restructuring their development and production systems, they used it as a pillar for remodeling their business infrastructure. A global parts supply system emerged while the auto industry itself was restructuring.

Japan's *keiretsu* system was internationally valued and greatly influenced changes in the worldwide supplier system. Japanese makers moved to international procurement because of their emphasis on overseas production and local supply, and seven out of the eleven major Japanese companies made alliances with foreign capital. But *keiretsu* was not the perfect answer. Significantly, Carlos Ghosn, CEO of the Renault–Nissan alliance, declared that he was working toward global procurement by means of an alliance of parts suppliers – post-*keiretsu*.[2] Ghosn said that it was not that the *keiretsu* system itself had become out of date, but that not all *keiretsu* systems were efficient. There were cases where the *keiretsu* system functioned well and cases where it did not.

The latter was Nissan's experience, and therefore he chose to move post-*keiretsu*.[3]

It is perhaps helpful to review *keiretsu* transactions thoroughly from a global point of view. What kind of roles did the *keiretsu* transaction play historically? What characteristics of the *keiretsu* transaction were transferred to the European and US auto makers? How is Japan's *keiretsu* transaction system changing in the climate of global change in the auto-parts procurement and manufacturing industry? This chapter addresses those questions and is based on a long-term field survey.

2. Features of the *keiretsu* supplier system and its impact on the parts-purchasing systems of European and US auto makers

European and US auto makers began to examine the *keiretsu* parts transaction system in the 1980s, when they realized that the *keiretsu* supplier system was playing an important role in Japan's international competitiveness. At around the same time, the joint international auto research of the MIT (Massachusetts Institute of Technology) proposed a lean-industry revolution as a best-practice paradigm, including for the auto industry. The report emphasized Japan's advantage in its supplier system.[4] According to the research, the number of suppliers supplying one auto project was less than 300 in Japan, while the mass-production manufacturers in Europe and the US used between 1,000 and 2,500 companies. MIT pointed out that decentralizing orders to many suppliers can cause problems.

In a system of decentralized ordering, the bid range is given to the suppliers after auto makers have made detailed designs of each part, and eventually a short-term contract with a supplier is agreed. Suppliers cannot share information with auto makers, so they can deal with auto makers only by bargaining over the bid price. This short-term "trading by bidding" includes decisions not only about cost but also about quality and the date of delivery, plus penalties if the contract stipulations are not met.

The short-term bidding system puts pressure on suppliers to cut costs, and the decentralized ordering system prevents any chance of a collaborative relationship or information-sharing between auto makers and suppliers. The big-lot delivery-driven system means suppliers are not responsible for quality after delivery, thus there is little chance for improving the parts once a bid has been agreed.

In contrast, the Japanese *keiretsu* supplier system is a related parts-co-supply system, which means a close tie between the efficient procurement of auto parts and parts suppliers. Establishing a long-term supply relationship and an intimate collaboration between auto makers and parts suppliers makes it possible to cooperate on and increase the level of cooperation in the four fields of Q (Quality), C (Cost), D (Delivery), and E (Engineering). *Keiretsu* creates a total system of market mechanisms for Q, C, D, and E among parts makers, without relying on bidding. Advantages include quality guarantees by suppliers, efforts to bring down costs within a certain period of time according to a target, strict observance of the delivery date, and the possibility of the supplier participating in the design and development of parts for new models in the early stages, when the auto makers are developing new cars.[5] Importantly, the *keiretsu* system strives for targeted cost reduction based on a trust relationship, and allows for adjustments to reflect the results of technological improvement and streamlining, even though they might affect the delivery price.

Keiretsu has a pyramid-like trading structure, in which primary, secondary, and tertiary suppliers provide parts systematically. This enables a mechanism of mutual cooperation through cooperative associations of parts makers, setting up a total cooperative system with the auto makers at its top.[6]

The late Professor Banri Asanuma provided a clear theoretical framework for the *keiretsu* parts-trading system in Japan and undertook a field survey to support this framework. Asanuma studied *keiretsu* parts transactions based on the intermediate organization theory of Williamson and others. He pointed out that the system is synonymous with subcontract transactions under the dual structure of the economy. He criticized the theory that suppliers have a buffer-like function during risk of recession. He also pointed out that core companies have systems to share business risks with suppliers, and to share a certain risk over any changes of orders to suppliers.

Asanuma also pointed out that *keiretsu* transactions contributed to the auto industry in several ways.[7] He identified that the Japanese auto industry has a system which encourages suppliers to develop related skills. Suppliers range from those that are loaned drawings and make parts after seeing the drawings and the prototype, to those who design and manufacture parts based on their own ability, once they are shown the layout line. Suppliers can develop their capacity dynamically in the four areas of Q, C, D, and E. This notion of related skills is similar to the capacity-building ideas of Professor Takahiro Fujimoto, though they rely on different technological levels within suppliers. For example, suppliers loaned drawings focus on quality, especially the streamlining of cost and delivery, i.e., QC circles, VA activities, and just-in-time delivery. Suppliers approved to make their own drawings, meanwhile, focus not only on quality, cost, and delivery but also on VE, which includes designing ability, trial manufacture, and testing ability. As the former type of suppliers develop their skills, they can increase their ability to design and eventually become approved to make their own drawings. Professor Asanuma compared the auto industry with the electrical equipment and electronic industries, to see how skill-building ability differed according to type of supplier and component. He found that the ability to build skills was especially advanced in the auto industry, which has variety in parts and in technology, and that this was because the trading structure and system encouraged skill development (see Tables 6.1 and 6.2, and Figure 6.1). He also pointed out that *keiretsu* is a dynamic system and relations among organizations promote both evaluation by central firms and competition among suppliers in the form of plural orders.[8]

Professor Asanuma highlighted the most significant features of the *keiretsu* transaction system: adding value, which is gained when suppliers streamline their activities and their design proposals provide VA and VE per unit cost; reducing unit cost and maximizing profit; and sharing the risk, both in business investment and when orders decrease. These features demonstrate why the *keiretsu* transaction is similar to a long-term transaction, and why the number of suppliers that must be dealt with directly decreases. It also suggests that the *keiretsu* transaction has a certain universality, in the sense that it is not purely Japanese, and hence has elements that have greatly influenced changes in the supplier transaction system in the US and Europe.

The influence of the *keiretsu* system on European and US auto makers first appeared in the parts procurement systems of the US's Big Three companies, which were under threat of direct competition from Japan, and then began to be seen in the European auto makers. The most noticeable changes were a radical reduction of the ratio of parts manufactured in-house, a reduction in the number of suppliers, the

Table 6.1 *Classification of parts and suppliers*

Category	Custom parts						Market type parts
	Loaned-drawing parts		Approval-drawing parts				
	I	II	III	IV	V	VI	
Classification standards	Buyers indicate in detail even about the process.	Suppliers decide the process based on the loaned drawing.	Buyers submit a rough drawing, and entrust suppliers with completion.	Buyers have a wide knowledge about the process.	Intermediate range of IV and VI	Buyers have only limited knowledge about the process.	Buyers purchase goods from the sellers' catalog.
Examples	Sub-assembly	Small press-parts	Plastic parts for trim	Seats	Brakes, bearings, tires	Radio, fuel injection controller, battery	

Source: M. Asanuma, "Nihon no Kigyososhiki-kakushintekitekiou no Mekanizumu" (The mechanism of the revolutionary adjustment of Japan's corporate organizations), *Toyokeizai Shinbosha*, 1997, p. 215

Table 6.2 *The contents of related special functions in the main category for parts*

		Main elements of related special function		
Main category for parts	X1	X2	X3	X4
	Abilities which become visible through interaction at the early stage of development	Abilities which become visible through interaction at the later stage of development	Abilities which become visible at the delivery stage in the production process	Abilities which become visible at the renegotiation of cost in the production process
Market-type parts	(low visibility in the eyes of center firms)	(low possibility in the eyes of center firms)	1. Ability to assure quality 2. Ability to assure timely delivery	(low visibility in the eyes of center firms)
Approval-drawing parts	1. Ability to develop products according to specifications given by center firms 2. Ability which provides the improvement of specifications	1. Ability to develop the process according to the approved drawings (visibility varies from high to low possibilities) 2. Ability to reduce estimated costs through VE	1. Ability to guarantee quality 2. Ability to guarantee timely delivery	1. Ability to reduce costs through process improvement (visibilities vary from high to low) 2. Ability to reduce costs through VA
Loaned-drawing parts	(no relation)	1. Ability to develop the process according to a drawing which is lent 2. Ability to reduce estimated costs through VE (through proposals for improvements in design)	1. Ability to guarantee quality 2. Ability to guarantee timely delivery	1. Ability to reduce costs through process improvement 2. Ability to reduce costs through VE (through proposals for improvements in design)

Note: Center firm means OEM assembler.
Source: Asanuma, 1997, p. 115

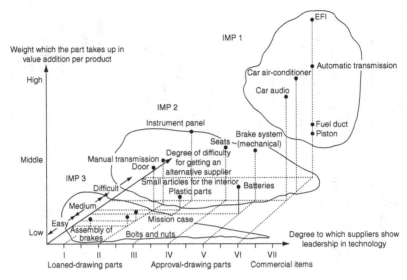

Note: IMP1 and IMP3 are dummy parameters to show the degree of importance
Source: Asanuma, 1997, p. 288

Figure 6.1 3D classification of parts and suppliers

introduction of a long-term relationship with related suppliers, and an emphasis on partnership. But it was not easy to change a supplier system which had become established over many years, and change was brought about through much trial and error.

3. Reorganization of the supplier system in the US and preparations for globalization

Until the 1980s, the proportion of parts manufactured in-house by US auto makers was over 80 percent for GM and more than 70 percent for Ford, and this took place in a vertically integrated system. The remaining 20–30 percent of parts were bought by the parts operation division, except for special unit parts, on a short-term basis and from multiple suppliers.

The US companies recognized the advantages of the *keiretsu* system in terms of quality, cost, delivery, and developing design skills (as seen in approval drawing and VE activities).[9] In particular, the following points were rated highly: having a thorough quality guarantee from suppliers; improving the quality and competitiveness of final products; auto makers and suppliers setting mid-term goals and sharing efforts to lower and streamline costs, "design-in and early participation in product development by VE-activities" improving technology in cooperation with auto makers, and shortening the lead-time for product development.[10]

US auto makers took the opportunity to review their supplier systems, in particular those companies that already had partnerships with Japanese auto makers. Some manufacturers had already begun copying *keiretsu* transactions in the first half of the 1980s. Chrysler, which was facing a bankruptcy crisis in 1980, immediately started selling and closing in-house production divisions, partly because the company had a low rate of in-house parts. Chrysler also tried to shift to a long-term transaction with Nippondenso (now Denso), and other Japanese suppliers, which they thought they could rely on completely. Ford and GM started copying the *keiretsu* system by establishing partnerships with suppliers, emphasizing long-term transactions and setting up a cooperative organization.

As mentioned, the US custom of supplier transaction meant that it was not unusual for suppliers to be decided by bids every year and for suppliers to change annually. Even now, US cars have a long model-change cycle, but they are given minor changes, or facelifts, every year. Long model-change cycles require a long-term contract with suppliers for the main components and those which need special technology, hence the high rate of component production in-house, although certain components were ordered from suppliers in large amounts. Suppliers were therefore under a lot of pressure from the order themselves as well as the pressure to supply products at the lowest price. Bidding also gave rise to extreme price changes, and it was common to change suppliers frequently. The Big Three attempted to copy the *keiretsu* transaction, because it would lead to stable and reliable long-term relationships that would promote trust-building between auto makers and suppliers, and make it easier to achieve continuous improvements in quality and technology. If it worked, suppliers could expect a guaranteed long-term transaction, making it easier for them to develop a business plan for their own R&D investment, and giving them better access to information and communication. GM and Ford established a vender association and launched the switch to long-term transactions with suppliers, equivalent to the primary suppliers in *keiretsu*. This was expected to be an important step in changing the supplier system in the US.[11]

However, merely copying the *keiretsu* system, although it started out with great fanfare, did not result in a true change to the US supplier system. Possible reasons include the fact that big companies, especially GM and Ford, had in-house parts divisions which were accustomed to mass orders and long-term, vertical inside transactions; it took time for suppliers to change their thinking because they were accustomed to the traditional, contract-driven methods; and, most importantly, GM and Ford did not have a system to analyze supplier transactions systematically and to evaluate the capacity-building capabilities of suppliers.

In the late 1980s, the US's auto makers realized that merely copying *keiretsu* would not improve their situation. They needed to develop new strategies and use information technology effectively, and decided that they had to change their supplier systems strategically.

What kind of strategic changes to the supplier system were necessary? The US's auto makers evaluated the efficiency, quality, and technology of their in-house parts production divisions and realized that levels were vastly different across business fields, with some divisions meeting international levels but others almost beyond recovery, which lowered their overall competitiveness. As a result, they decided to conduct a thorough reconstruction of their business units by cleaning up the parts divisions, improving units that were competitive and strong, and selling off those divisions that were not competitive. This clean-up led to some units being spun out. However, since the parts divisions were organized by members of UAW, and their salary levels were basically the same as the assemblers', it took some time before union opposition was resolved and the entire parts business could be spun out.

While reconstructing and spinning out their parts divisions, the US's auto makers were also employing their supplier policies strategically. The policy was to reduce the number of suppliers of outside transactions, and to conduct a systematic evaluation system of suppliers' competitiveness. In other words, they were rebuilding and applying a benchmarking system.

Although benchmarking systems vary among makers, all aim to evaluate suppliers' abilities across quality, cost, delivery, and engineering. The systems share information among different kinds of companies by setting common evaluation criteria and measurements, thereby establishing a kind of industrial standard. Each maker conducts evaluations according to its own criteria.

The business-field standards include the evaluation standard for general materials and for parts materials, which were set up by the AIAG at the beginning of the 1980s, the standardizing of parts racks and parts numbers, the introduction of a common bar code, and the setting up of a common computer protocol. Antitrust laws were excluded for conducting business by setting up industrial standards under the "law of national joint study," which was established by the Reagan administration in 1984 in order to strengthen industrial competitiveness.[12] This made it easier to use a common industrial standard as measurement for evaluating quality and other abilities of suppliers, and it also became easier to set up a database of quality and test-engineering evaluations for suppliers.[13]

The problems in basing measurement data on a common industrial standard are naturally connected to how individual companies develop their corresponding databases. Because of this, establishing a database about individual suppliers was promoted, and applied to the benchmarking of supplier evaluations. For parts makers and their parts, which are close to the market and easy to standardize, it is possible to build a database among individual companies and to exchange data.

The benchmarking system naturally reveals the individual character of each company.[14] Differences in purchasing strategies can be observed whether the evaluation of cost and quality is conducted over a short period or a long period, and delivery can be evaluated in relation to the order system.

Thus in the late 1980s, the Big Three companies chose to move to benchmarking strategies by building databases of suppliers, rather than by copying the *keiretsu* system exactly. There were, however, differences between companies. GM and Ford prioritized benchmarking for their own in-house parts divisions, whereas Chrysler, which already had a low ratio of parts produced in-house, had already restructured and sold off units in the early 1980s, so the company was especially enthusiastic about benchmarking and building a database of subcontracting suppliers.

Comparing Chrysler's supplier evaluation system, SCORE (Supplier Cost Reduction Effort), and GM's evaluation system, PICOS (see Table 6.3), clearly shows that Chrysler was taking the lead in this field.[15]

The information technology revolution played a major role in database and benchmarking activities, in particular connecting the databases together. This digital computerization was promoted not only for

Table 6.3 *GM, Ford, Daimler–Chrysler's strategies for suppliers*

	GM	Ford	Daimler–Chrysler (mainly former Chrysler)
Ratio of procurement from outsourcing (report base)	Approx. 30%	60–70%	70% (Chrysler)
Performance and aim of production cost	1997 performance $3.5 billion 1998 performance $4 billion 1999 performance $4 billion	1997 performance $3 billion 1998 Jan–Sep performance $1.9 billion 1999 plan $1 billion (1997–1999 total sum $6 billion)	Performance of SCORE program 1998 performance $2.1 billion total sum before 1998 $6 billion As Daimler–Chrysler 1999 plan $1.4 billion
Supplier evaluation criteria	• Evaluation criteria for the good supplier award started in 1991 were quality, service, cost, and engineering (engineering was added in 1998). • Began the best and the same cost procurement in the world • In 1999, it started a purchasing strategy to set evaluation criteria according to the quality and engineering levels by dividing parts into four groups.	• In addition to the traditional recognition of Q1 supplier, which is to evaluate the quality, a new system of awarding good suppliers started in 1999. The evaluation criteria were cost, delivery, and quality improvement. • In 1993 a program, Full Service Supplier, was started. Suppliers, which share in the development and design, were certified. About 200 companies were certified before 1998.	• Under the concept "Extended Enterprise," seeking participants for the development and improvement of production efficiency, the SCORE program started. • In the process of reducing the supplier base after the merger, it introduced a bubble chart to evaluate efficiency and efficacy.

| Program for cost reduction of parts | • In 1992, PICOS aiming to reduce cost by 30% in three months was introduced. After this, it routinely requested a cost reduction of 2–5% annually.
• In 1998, through a Current Saving program which guarantees future cost reduction caused by the improvement of production efficiency and the introduction of new engineering ahead of schedule, it is expected to relax the requesting item.
• Conducting world optimum procurement including net auction and cost reduction of materials through central mass purchasing by monitoring the market situation | • According to Ford 2000, it has requested a 5% cost reduction annually since 1995.
• In April 1999, set up Total Cost Management center
  It supplies a training facility for cost reduction and efficient production.
• Planned to start Supplier Owned Tooling Strategy in January 2000. It aims to promote low-cost procurement by shifting tooling and other procurement responsibilities to suppliers. | • In 1989 Chrysler introduced a program called SCORE. The SCORE program was also continued by Daimler–Chrysler. It expanded into Europe as well.
• As the reduction of purchasing and procurement cost is one of the best effects of the merging of D-Benz and Chrysler, the integration of the supplier base began. Central purchasing of raw materials and streamlining of processing of raw materials are being brought into view. |

Note: Apart from the detail mentioned above, each company is carrying out supplier–chain management, which is to provide total control of ordering, procurement of materials, inventory control, and delivery by computers.

Source: Fourin, Hokubeijidoshashagyo, 1999, p. 36

supplier databases but also for design development and factory local area networks (LAN). CADCAM (the system coupling of computer-supported design and computer-supported production) expanded in a very short period.

Benchmarking suppliers using databases would not have been possible without the digital information revolution. For example, the Big Three had a lot of buyers in purchasing divisions, and documents and data related to purchases were required for each part, so a huge amount of documents and data accumulated. According to a survey, GM had 20,000 employees in purchasing divisions at the beginning of the 1980s. In contrast, Toyota had about 500 employees in purchasing divisions, only one fortieth of the total at GM.[16] The reason why GM had so many workers in purchasing was because in-house production divisions depended on parts, and each division conducted its own procurement negotiations. At the same time, GM had many suppliers for its outsourced components and materials.[17] This extreme division of labor in both internal and external procurement meant that GM had vast amounts of data and documents on parts purchasing and transactions. However, such information was useless for evaluating suppliers and even more so for benchmarking. The data included information about bidding costs, negotiation processes, and inspection quality, but there were no data on the suppliers' efforts at streamlining or their ability to guarantee quality. Nor were there any data on suppliers' technology, especially their design development ability and technological know-how, since the suppliers kept this information as company secrets. This kind of information system could not measure the potential of a supplier to develop related skills, which Asanuma had identified as critical in evaluating suppliers.

Information technology made it possible to build databases about suppliers, and to benchmark and evaluate them, for example, across different factories or different kinds of parts. By benchmarking their internal divisions and comparing them with external suppliers, the Big Three were able to plan strategically which in-house production divisions to sell off or spin out, and to reduce the number of suppliers. This enabled them to improve the quality of suppliers and reduce their procurement costs. Many reports in the first half of 1996 described how much the quality and cost competitiveness of US cars had improved.[18]

Reconstructing the supplier system by the US's Big Three became a stepping stone for the globalization of the auto industry, which began in the early 1990s. The reconstruction of the supplier system led to the Big Three re-examining their parts-procurement strategies, and the reduction in suppliers strengthened the trend toward central purchasing, which led to ordering in bigger lots. Many parts and components, especially chassis seats (particularly for business cars), interiors, instrument panels, and electronic products, were suitable for big-lot orders from central purchasing. In addition, the relative increase in open-architecture auto types produced by the Big Three in the first half of the 1990s and the light truck segments (such as minivans, pickups, SUVs) were suitable for standardization, which also encouraged large orders. Ordering in big lots promoted the introduction of parts modules, which started in Europe and accelerated mergers and alliances among suppliers. As a result, this led to the emergence of mega-suppliers and the globalization and reconstruction of the parts industry. Global and mega-suppliers, including spin-outs like Delphi and Visteon, and the supplier system itself began changing from regional to global.[19]

4. Reform of the supplier system in Europe and the *keiretsu* transaction

The major European automobile manufacturers produced roughly 50 percent fewer of their parts in-house than the big US companies, and the main parts system relied on horizontal transactions via many suppliers and markets. Because European auto makers did not face direct competition from Japanese cars, their supplier system was reformed more slowly, even though the need for reform was recognized around the mid 1980s. Manufacturers in France and Italy had highly protected domestic markets, based on import restrictions, and labor relations were crucial for state-run companies like Renault and public enterprises like VW, which delayed reform. However, with the movement to European integration and a global economy, the European auto industry realized that solving the procurement cost issue was essential to improving competitiveness in all aspects of its cost structure.

The company that started the reform of the supplier system in Europe was Opel, an affiliated company of GM in Europe. Opel began adopting the Nummi production system, a joint project between GM and Toyota, in the latter half of the 1980s, and applying the results of research to the *keiretsu* system.[20] The Nummi production system was introduced in the Eisennache factory, which was built in 1990 in the former East

Germany. For suppliers, a new supplier control system was introduced, the core of which was a strategy based on what GM was doing in North America at the time. However, Opel's reforms did not end at copying the GM supplier-control system from North America. Opel began to integrate and reduce suppliers in a way that was radical at the time, realizing a drastic cost reduction (said to be more than 30 percent).[21] GM Opel reformed its supplier system under the leadership of Ignacio Lopez, who originally came from the Basque area in Spain. Lopez then became the executive vice-president of GM's headquarters in North America; he was in charge of purchasing and aimed to drastically reduce procurement costs. But according to the news reports of the time and my own research, his attempts to reduce procurement costs, which had been successful in Europe, did not have much effect because of the lack of cooperation from North American suppliers, which included Japanese-affiliated suppliers.[22] This was because there was still enough room to reduce procurement costs in Europe, but in North America costs had already been reduced significantly through restructuring, reducing delivery costs, and transferring responsibility for quality assurance in return for a long-term contract with suppliers. Lopez accepted an invitation from the chairman of VW, Ferdinand Piëch, to transfer to VW, and was preparing to reform the parts system at the German company, but problems over leaks of corporate data developed into a court case between GM and VW. In the end, VW apologized in a reconciliation with GM, and Lopez left VW.

However, inviting Lopez to VW stirred up the reconstruction of the supplier system in Europe. Although VW must have learned the methods of Lopez, the company did not copy them mechanically. In particular, VW's hang-up on quality, which included maintenance and extension of quality levels to primary and secondary suppliers, continued.[23]

Supplier reforms happened one after another among other manufacturers in Europe. However, the strategies varied, according to the brand identity which each maker sought for their cars, and whether they chose total performance or core competence as instrumental in strengthening their competitiveness (see Table 6.4).[24] Renault set a goal of 50 percent reduction in purchase costs when it set its strategic goal for TQM for the year 2000, in order to improve quality levels along with full-scale privatization, and at the same time began to reform its supplier system.[25] The number of direct transactions with suppliers fell for all the auto makers in Europe and system suppliers became important.

Table 6.4 *Two strategic alternatives*

Core competence approach	Total competence approach
Specialization in a number of core competencies	Retention of basic competencies in all strategic areas
Delegation of responsibilities to first-tier suppliers also in areas of quality control and design	Maintain the responsibilities for quality control and design
Decentralized management of the value chain	Central control of the value chain
Electronics/IT parts/knowledge transferred from external suppliers	Internal development of critical electronics/IT competence
Cautious and step-by-step approach to technological innovation	Leadership through innovation: hybrid vehicles and in-board navigation systems

Source: J. J. Chanaron, "Implementing technological and organizational innovations and management of core competencies: lessons from the automotive industry," *International Journal of Automotive Technology and Management*, 2001

Reform of the supplier system among European auto makers accelerated because they were inspired by the globalization of the auto industry in the 1990s. Fiat was the last company among European auto makers to instigate reform. While it was last, this meant that Fiat could review what Volkswagen, Renault, and other European makers had achieved, and apply those lessons to its own reform. Eventually, Fiat's reform was very similar to that conducted by other European makers, but Fiat's strategies were based on proper data, not on trial and error, as had been the case for the other companies. Parts were clearly categorized as "strategic" and "non-strategic." For non-strategic parts, Fiat left everything to the suppliers, using strict quality-assurance provisions. Strategic parts, such as engines and other parts with important commercial value, were developed in partnership with suppliers, but with Fiat taking the leadership role in development and production.[26]

In contrast, Renault selected and categorized its suppliers according to the categories shown in Figure 6.2.[27] An Optimal partnership defined the relationship as strongly inter-related and cooperative, confidential, and with openness and stability of transaction. Suppliers that fitted this definition were then categorized according to various criteria. At the time of writing, the number of Optimal suppliers was thirty-nine, but

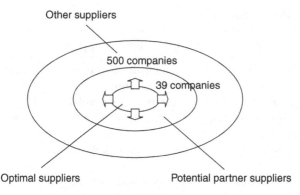

Other suppliers

Optimal suppliers   Potential partner suppliers

Source: Document submitted by the company at an interview at
Renault Technical Center in March 2002

Figure 6.2 Basic concept of Renault's supplier map

this number was scheduled to increase to more than fifty companies. As
we can see in Figure 6.2, the Optimal supplier is the core, and at its edge
are the Potential partner suppliers, which are approaching Optimal
supplier status. A further 500 suppliers exist outside these. Renault
uses twenty-two different evaluation criteria for selecting and categor-
izing suppliers. The criteria are mainly based on the suppliers' strategies
and results, competitiveness, international supply system and ability,
relations with Renault in transactions in recent years, costs and technology, and quality. In relation to this, Renault categorizes supplies
into (1) parts for system suppliers, (2) parts for modular suppliers, and
(3) parts for parts suppliers. Renault has different control systems for
each category.[28] By conducting this kind of evaluation and selection,
Renault reduced the total number of suppliers, but dynamic competition meant that Renault was moving toward increasing the number of
suppliers with which it did business directly.

There are similarities and differences between the reformed supplier
systems in Europe and the Japanese *keiretsu* system. While each auto
maker has a different approach to reform, on the whole they are
narrowing down the number of what are referred to in Japan as primary
suppliers, those which have direct transactions with the core company
and might supply systems, modules, or some other combination. The
horizontal transaction mechanism with many small-parts suppliers, top
suppliers, and auto makers led to numerous direct transactions.

By emphasizing a long-term transaction relationship with top suppliers and requiring a capability for design and development, the transaction mechanism has changed drastically. However, the horizontal transaction has not changed entirely to a vertical, pyramid-shaped *keiretsu* transaction, but rather has developed into a dynamic, network-style organization, with its main concern being changes in technology rather than the tight organization of what are referred to in Japan as secondary and tertiary suppliers.

In-house production in Europe was thought to rank somewhere in the middle between the US and Japan, where more than 70 percent of parts were outsourced. Fiat spun out the divisions responsible for seats and interior-related products, which had to integrate with the company's other suppliers. As a result, Fiat's in-house production has become as low as that of Japan (see Table 6.5). [29]

The modular system, in which suppliers are highly integrated, started in the 1970s and 1980s at VW and other European manufacturers (see Table 6.6). As part of the strategic move to a modular system, supplier parks have been built near the plants of European auto makers in recent years, and this trend is spreading to the plants of auto makers in North America (see Table 6.7). In Japan, suppliers are congregated in certain areas near plants, making just-in-time supply possible. In Europe and the US, the supplier park system, which is closely linked to the supply of module parts, is expected to expand further, and Japanese makers may see similar expansion around their own plants.

5. Formation of a global parts-procurement system and restructuring the global parts industry

The restructuring of the supplier system that began in North America not only brought a change in purchasing and procurement strategies but also encouraged the emergence of mega-suppliers that became active internationally, thus serving as a foothold for the globalization of the parts business itself. Especially in Europe, suppliers which reacted to this trend emerged rapidly, with some companies developing into mega-suppliers by establishing themselves as system suppliers.

The 1990s saw auto makers in Europe and the US start aggressively pursuing "global platform strategies" and "global sourcing strategies." Ford's global strategy, "Ford 2000," was based on global platform strategies. The idea was to standardize the platforms worldwide if

Table 6.5 *Business climate of the main parts of production in-house/outsourcing of European auto makers*

	Renault	PSA	DC
Transmission-MT	○ in-house Cleon (France) Cacia (Portugal)	○ in-house UMB (France) UMV (France)	○ in-house Unterturkheim (Germany) outsourcing Getrag (Vvto)
-AT	□ joint STA (France) (Schedule to procure from Nissan)	□ joint STA (France)	○ in-house Unterturkheim (Germany) ● outsourcing ZF
-CVT	(Considering procuring from Jatoco)	—	—
Seats	● Faurecia, JCI, CESA	○ Faurecia, ● Treves	mainly in-house ● Faurecia, JCI, Lear
Steering	● Sell-off to Koyo Engineering (in 1999)	● Sell-off to Koyo Engineering (in 2000)	● M-Benz Lenkungen (internal independent-affiliate company, plan for separation)
Partner for joint development production for engine	PSA, Nissan	Ford, Toyota, Renault	—
Misc.	● In 1998, sell-off of wire-harness plant to Labinal (now affiliate company of Valeo), cast and wrought products plant invests in Teksid (33.3%) and at same time business integration with Teksid, relegates five plants. In 2000, sell-off of LeMans' Constant-velocity joint division to NTN ● Plant for parts production in-house is for axle assembly, still having structure member production plant, and aiming to separate and sell off, established internal affiliated company Auto Chassis Inter 7	● Sell-off of rubber parts factory to Italy's CE Gomma (in 1999) ● Own a parts production affiliate company, Faurecia (shareholding 71%). Produce seats, exhausts, front-end modules, and misc. Expanding business of production in-house in M&A. Became a publicly held company in 1999, possibly for separation and sell-off	● Sell-off of electronics TEMIC in April 2001. Unterturkheim plant also makes axles. ● Made DC Powertrain, which produces engines for business cars, an internal independent company

Table 6.5 (*cont.*)

	VW	BMW	Ford
Transmission-MT	○ in-house Kassel (Germany) Prat (Spain)	● outsourcing ZF, Getrag	Semi-outsourcing Getrag joint plant (= former Ford plant, after joining, charged by Getrag)
-AT	● outsourcing ZF, Jatoco	● outsourcing Jatoco	
-CVT	○ in-house Kassel (Germany)	–	Semi-outsourcing ZF joint
Seats	● Faurecia, JCI, Lear Recaro	○ mainly production in-house	● Faurecia, JCI, Lear
Steering	○ production in-house Braunschweig (Germany) (● Some like Audi are by outsourcing)	● outsourcing ZF Lenksystem	
Partner for joint development production for engine	–	–	-PSA (DE full-line joint development)
Misc.	● Plants for production in-house are plants for axle and casting parts in Germany, molding plants in Spain. ● At Siemems-VW and 1/2 invested in VW Boardnetze, have joint production of wiring system	– In the US, seats are from outsourcing.	● Joint development with Benteler in chassis parts, and showing positive gesture in moving toward making orders to outside manufacturers ● In 2000 Mondeo production, most of the seats for main cars are from outside manufacturers.

Table 6.5 (*contd.*)

	GM	Fiat
Transmission-MT	○ in-house Russelsheim (Germany) Aspern (Austria)	○ in-house Mirafiori no.3 factory (Italia)
-AT	● outsourcing Jatoco	● outsourcing AISIN, AW, ZF
-CVT	○ in-house (Hungary)	● outsourcing Fuji Heavy Industries, ZF Betavia
Seats	● Faurecia, JCI, Lear Recaro	● Faurecia, Lear
Steering	(Delphi independent)	● sell-off to TRW
Partner for joint development production for engine	(GM–Fiat business integration)	(GM–Fiat business integration)
Misc.	–In summer 2002, began negotiations to sell-off Opel Bochum plant's axle production division to ThyssenKrupp	In 1994, sell-off of Sepi of sets production in-house to Lear, constant velocity joint division to GKN. In 1995 sell-off of steering division to TRW, in 1999 resin division to Ergom, in 1999 sell-off of suspension plant to ThyssenKrupp

Note: STA is a half-investment joint company between Renault and PSA which develops and produces AT

Source: Fourin, 2001, Oushu Jidosha Buhinsangyo, p. 77

Table 6.6 *Parts-procurement policies among European auto makers*

	Daimler–Chrysler	VW
Cost reduction	Pursuing cost reduction of small cars by joint development production with Mitsubishi	In new mid-term business plan of post4 platform policy, introduced eleven-module policy
Supplier policy	Reduction of price by SCORE and TANDEM	Control the core technologies which influence competitiveness by VW itself. Promoting a worldwide procurement policy
Module procurement	Trial introduction of seven-module assembly production in Smart production. Investigating the possibility of introducing module procurement in Z-car production	Procured front-end, cockpit modules and others
Online procurement	Set up Covisint. Covisint Europe (in April 2001)	Established own site ESL, started operation in October 2000. Tried to have cost reduction by online procurement. Declares not joining in Covisint

	Renault(–Nissan)	PSA
Cost reduction	Plan to halve cost production of €3 billion by 2003, and plant to cut €15.3 billion from purchasing cost	Making more efficiency by the integration to three chassis within group, Fauresia, which is a division of parts production in-house, increased competitiveness in M&A and expanded its business
Supplier policy	Started joint purchasing with Nissan which does international procurement. The number of Optimal suppliers became 150 companies.	Plan to build cooperative relationship with the leading eighteen suppliers. Cooperative partnering with Valeo, Delphi, and others in development of advanced technology

Table 6.6 (*cont.*)

	Daimler–Chrysler	VW
Module procurement	Procured 6–10 modules in France and Brazil	Cooperative relationship with the leading suppliers in module parts. No supplier park
Online procurement	Capital participation in Covisint. Covisint Europe (in April 2001)	Capital participation in Covisint. Covisint Europe (in April 2001)

	Europe GM–Fiat Auto	Europe Ford
Cost reduction	GM had capability reduction by closing plants in Britain. Fiat set up an efficient business system by selling off divisions of parts production in-house. By integration of purchasing business (€550 million) and integration of power-train business (€550 million), expect to have synergy effect of €1.4 billion by 2005	Capability reduction by closing plants in Britain. Pursuing efficiency by centralizing plants. In the middle of restructuring European business management
Supplier policy	By having integration of organization for purchasing with Fiat Auto in European GM, started joint purchasing which includes business in North America	Assigning to suppliers in a full-service supplier system. Along with standardizing the Ford–Mazda chassis, international procurement started for European and US Ford products
Module procurement	Gravantai plant in Brazil, which pursued a module system, started its operation. Opel also introduced a new production system at Russelshein plant in Germany.	Taking the lead in quantity and contents. Introduced supplier-park system to the leading mass-production plants. JIT supplying. Development was assigned. Stationed assembly plants of supplier-engineers
Online procurement	Established Covisint. Covisint Europe (in April 2001)	Established Covisint. Covisint Europe (in April 2001)

Source: Fourin, 2001, Oushu Jidosha Buhinsangyo

Table 6.7 *Names of plants and countries of supplier parks in Eastern Europe*

| Supplier parks in Europe in 1999 | | |
Name of plant	Name of country	Name of maker
1	Göteborg	Sweden	Volvo
2	Ingolstadt	Germany	Audi
3	Neckarsulm	Germany	Audi
4	Wackersdorf	Germany	BMW
5	Rastatt	Germany	Daimler–Chrysler
6	Melfi	Italy	Fiat
7	Saarlouis	Germany	Ford
8	Valencia	Spain	Ford
9	Antwerpen	Belgium	Opel
10	Ellesmere Port	UK	GM/Vauxhall
11	Liverpool/Halewood	UK	Jaguar
12	Sandouville/Le Havre	France	Renault
13	Abrera/Barcelona	Spain	SEAT
14	Palmela	Portugal	VW
15	Brussels	Belgium	VW
16	Mosel	Germany	VW
17	Gent	Sweden	Volvo
18	Trolhättan	Sweden	Saab
19	Hambach	France	MCC

Source: Larsson (2001) on the basis of Automotive News Europe 2000. Tenth GERPISA International Colloquium "Characteristics of the European automotive system, is there a distinctive European approach?" Ulrich Jurgens

possible, with chassis and bodies designed regionally in order to meet the particular characteristics of each market. Producing cars with completely different characteristics and appearance became possible with the application of advanced digital design technology, and thus the number of platforms could be reduced from nearly thirty to fewer than ten. Global platforms inevitably led to global instead of single-country procurement of parts, and these two new aspects combined suggested a drastic cost reduction for auto makers.

Global platform and sourcing strategies were quickly adopted outside Europe and the US, and Japanese auto makers recognized that, as they advanced into foreign markets, global sourcing was essential if

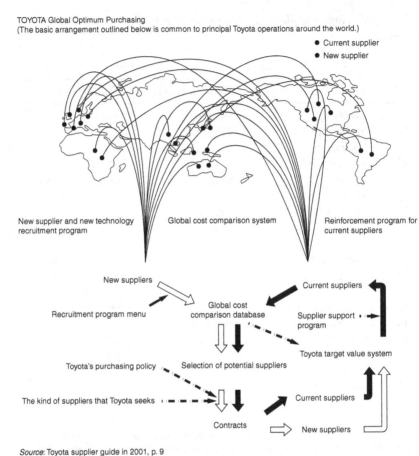

TOYOTA Global Optimum Purchasing
(The basic arrangement outlined below is common to principal Toyota operations around the world.)

● Current supplier
● New supplier

New supplier and new technology recruitment program

Global cost comparison system

Reinforcement program for current suppliers

New suppliers

Recruitment program menu

Global cost comparison database

Current suppliers

Supplier support program

Toyota target value system

Toyota's purchasing policy

Selection of potential suppliers

The kind of suppliers that Toyota seeks

Contracts

Current suppliers

New suppliers

Source: Toyota supplier guide in 2001, p. 9

Figure 6.3 Toyota global purchasing (1)

they were to make cars anywhere in the world. Even companies like Toyota, which have a high ratio of *keiretsu* transactions, could make cheaper parts if they broadened their view to Asia. "Comparative purchasing" became essential from the global point of view, and companies began to set up international procurement divisions (see Figures 6.3 and 6.4).

Globalization inspired Japanese suppliers to examine the need for structural reform, because they, too, were facing a situation where they could not rest on the *keiretsu* system but needed to act on global strategies.

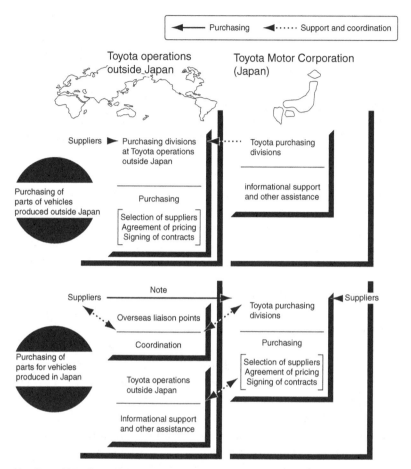

Note: Toyota Motor Corporation (Japan) sometimes purchases parts from overseas suppliers through Toyota operations outside Japan.
Source: Toyota supplier guide in 2001, p. 17

Figure 6.4 Toyota global purchasing (2)

In North America, as we have seen, Delphi separated from GM's in-house production division in the mid 1990s and became an independent parts supplier, and Visteon did the same in 2000. This had a significant impact on the parts industry in North America. The international ranking of parts suppliers changed drastically with the emergence of these independent parts suppliers, moving them ahead of Bosch and Denso.[30]

The restructuring began in response to efforts by GM and Ford to reduce the number of primary suppliers, but gradually suppliers started to realize the importance of developing their capability for proposing ideas, such as a module system that combined seats and meters like the cockpit in an airplane. The number of suppliers which could be involved in ideas and designing was restricted, which gave mega-suppliers the chance to grow into global suppliers.

Building modules and strategic M&A become an important key in the global strategies of suppliers, and M&A activity has since become borderless.[31] When suppliers that were traditionally making only certain types of parts decided to supply auto makers with parts in systems or modules, they had to obtain the ability to make the related parts. Because of this, the parts industry was restructured rapidly via M&A activities, some of which were driven by demands from GM and other auto makers, while others were for the purpose of building capabilities for their own strategies.

The global restructuring of the auto-parts industry and the re-examination of supplier transactions of auto makers in Europe interlocked. In Europe and the US, there was a strong trend toward auto makers taking the lead in or supporting the restructuring of suppliers.[32]

The problem which emerged from this situation was that strategic management started becoming very important in the parts industry. When different kinds of parts had been supplied horizontally in the past, even the basic design was designated by the auto makers, and it was enough for suppliers to make parts following the order. But as auto makers changed and started to demand that suppliers systematize or build modules of parts, the suppliers had to change their strategies. It became necessary for suppliers to establish strategic management by considering whom they should integrate with and how, or how they would sell their own technology in the network-like supply process. A passive business subcontract like the old style of supply was not acceptable any more. This trend was not limited to European suppliers but became an important issue for Japanese suppliers as well.[33]

6. Transformation of the Japanese-style *keiretsu* supplier system and its historical evaluation

The *keiretsu* supplier system fostered cooperative relationships that led to the constant improvement of quality, cost, and delivery, and helped make Japanese auto makers competitive, and the well-organized pyramid-shaped hierarchy helped suppliers to respond to the changing needs of auto makers. However, *keiretsu* was not a complete vertical integration, which involves transactions with only one partner. It was, rather, a semi-vertical integration, which has dynamic transactions with multiple partners. The resulting integration and competitive advantages coexisted.

But *keiretsu* also had disadvantages, most easily seen in recent years. For example, the delivery ratio of parts is concentrated and dependent on certain auto makers. In this case, it is inevitable that the management resources of suppliers place a disproportionate emphasis on certain auto makers, which causes them to focus only on those auto makers in dependent relationships and thus possibly lose their independent technological abilities. This is because the auto makers take the lead and the suppliers gain technological skills in only limited areas, restricting their possible future strategies. Furthermore, with guaranteed clients, the suppliers fail to develop marketing skills.

But then, what kind of environment did the *keiretsu* system function well in? The most important factor was that Japanese auto makers were highly competitive and so the amount of parts traded increased constantly. Along with this, cost competitiveness, quality competitiveness, and the shortening of delivery time improved, and the design abilities of drawing-approved suppliers were directly reflected in the competitiveness of auto makers and suppliers. In addition, *keiretsu* suppliers preferred traditional analog and specific technologies rather than the new digital technologies, and could display their strengths in an environment where their own analog and specific technologies, such as hyperfine processing, en bloc casting, and en bloc processing, could be fully used.[34]

However, the environment in which *keiretsu* flourished changed drastically because of the development of global competition, the strong yen, and the long slump in Japan's domestic market. This change triggered the transformation of *keiretsu*.[35]

The most influential element behind changes to the *keiretsu* system was the shift of auto makers to global procurement, which was made possible by information technologies that brought new parts procurement methods, such as net procurement, and enabled benchmarking of suppliers. The traditional Japanese *keiretsu* supplier system was partly supported by the confidential relationships which arose from personal connections. Information technology took auto makers and suppliers beyond these personal connections when attempting to answer questions such as which supplier to use, who and where should be integrated as a system supplier, and what kind of strategies are needed to develop this supplier into a module supplier. Essentially, the IT revolution made it possible to adopt a strategic and systematic approach toward the restructuring of the supplier system.

At the same time, there are arguments against such dynamic innovation. For example, issues such as the introduction and diffusion of fuel cells and demand for recycling and other environmental technologies are emerging. In response to this, positive steps are being taken to introduce intelligent technologies in the electronics field, develop and introduce new materials, and examine the possibilities of a new system integrated through the renovation of parts-processing technology.

In this new era, suppliers that can achieve a development policy that goes beyond the basic idea of "design-in" to "concept-in" become important. While suppliers already use their own technologies in designing parts that realize the policies and specifications of designs decided on by auto makers, the idea of "concept-in" involves suppliers proposing and negotiating the use of their own, completely new design concepts for parts. Suppliers lacking in the ability to propose their own ideas will disappear.[36] A supplier that becomes the sole provider of a specific technology can assure itself of a strong position even in an era of restructuring.

There has been a trend toward the formation of mega-suppliers through M&A and spin-outs from auto makers around the world. However, paths offering new challenges are still available for small-scale suppliers. For instance, analog technologies will continue to be important in the future because, although simulation has become possible with the development of digital technologies, collecting data for simulation and understanding those data still relies on analog skills. Many Japanese secondary suppliers have latent competitiveness in analog technology. Because of this, foreign auto makers and leading suppliers will have their eyes on these promising suppliers. It will become more important for such suppliers to be able to sell their own technological abilities without being entrenched in the framework of *keiretsu*.

An immediate issue today, however, is how to deal with the impact of the cost revolution in parts and components from other Asian countries. China's participation in the market in various ways has caused a cost revolution in small and standard parts. It is important for Japanese suppliers to have the appropriate global and engineering strategies to respond.

7. Conclusion

We have examined the restructuring era of the global auto and parts industries after the 1980s, and the reform and restructuring of the supplier system in the early twenty-first century in response to the impact of the *keiretsu* system. The beneficial aspects of the *keiretsu* system influenced reform and restructuring of the supplier systems in Europe and the US in various ways, in particular the notion of long-term, confidential relationships between auto makers and suppliers. This played an important role in narrowing down the number of trading suppliers and the selective integration of system suppliers and module suppliers, as auto makers had to choose the suppliers they wanted to have such long-term relationships with, focussing on those with capabilities in quality assurance, cost reduction, and delivery.

However, it is not easy to build such relationships quickly. For European and US auto makers, the solution to strategically reforming and rebuilding their supplier systems came from information technology, which made databases and benchmarking suppliers possible. While it is questionable that a database of suppliers can rival a long, historical relationship, the more detailed the database, the better the auto makers' ability to evaluate their suppliers.

Strategic integration and the necessary building of databases and benchmarking of suppliers to promote integration had immediate results: in-house production divisions were spun out, the numbers of suppliers fell rapidly, and long-term transaction relations were strengthened. As auto makers concentrated their trade on a much smaller number of suppliers, procurement costs fell dramatically. But US and German auto makers have different opinions on whether this drastic reduction and the guarantee of quality level by suppliers are balanced. GM Opel faces a problem of deteriorating quality, despite its dramatic success in reducing procurement costs. VW maintained its obsession with quality whilst learning from the supplier integration of GM Opel. Chrysler still faces a problem with deteriorating long-term quality levels (which influence the price of used cars), and Daimler is still focussed on quality even after its merger with Chrysler. This shows the contrast between the immediate benefits of supplier integration and the quality problems which still exist.

The introduction of global platforms and global sourcing began to transform Japan's *keiretsu* system. Japan's auto makers themselves had many local plants overseas and expanded their parts procurement to get the best procurement globally, through global supplier competition and international procurement as well as *keiretsu* transactions with their domestic suppliers, as shown by the international group purchasing set up by Nissan and Renault in recent years. Globalization in supplier systems began influencing the form of the traditional *keiretsu* transaction, with suppliers increasingly needing skills in strategy building and marketing, and the ability to move from being design-in suppliers to being concept-in suppliers. Those working with analog technologies had to move to become sole providers of their particular technology.

Although *keiretsu* has changed in the face of globalization, it is too early to conclude that it has become outdated or lost its efficacy. A full understanding of the *keiretsu* supplier system and why it functioned effectively shows us which parts of *keiretsu* should be maintained and which reformed.

As long as *keiretsu* functions effectively, it offers an effective model for a customer-oriented system. Even though rooted in a Japanese style based on, for example, hierarchical, confidential relationships and group unity with suppliers as partners, *keiretsu* had important lessons for restructuring the supplier system to raise QCDE levels and suppliers' abilities.

Keiretsu functioned most effectively during the boom in Japan's automotive industry, although, as Carlos Ghosn pointed out, it did not necessarily function well in every situation. In particular, auto makers had different experiences when looking for *keiretsu* suppliers with the potential to build their skill and improve their abilities effectively. Nissan and other auto makers had to shoulder extra costs in order to support and maintain *keiretsu* suppliers by making extra financial contributions, dispatching administrators, and assuming debt. However, these problems with *keiretsu* did not come to the surface when the competitiveness and strength of Japan's auto makers were growing in the boom years but rather as the gaps in competitiveness became apparent when the economic situation deteriorated.

If we focus on cases where *keiretsu* worked well, for example, at Toyota, Honda, Daihatsu, and Suzuki, we can see such characteristics as the emphasis on long-term transactions, quality assurance, cost-reduction by VA, emphasis on delivery time, and emphasis on design-in abilities with VE proposals. Even at Nissan, which declared its abandonment of *keiretsu*, these principles endure. To support the partnership with suppliers, the outcomes of efforts at VA cost-reduction, building systems for evaluating and promoting improvements in VE designing ability, and the risk burden taken by auto makers caused by changes in orders are shared in various ways by the different manufacturers.

The merits of the *keiretsu* system are still seen today, but relying on them is no longer sufficient. *Keiretsu* is being changed by global sourcing, collective global transactions, and open global competition. The new module strategies, in which European and US companies are taking the lead, may also cause further changes in *keiretsu* transactions in the future. There are two approaches to building module systems. One approach is to delegate the construction of modules completely to full-service suppliers, which is favored by US makers. The other is to keep module building in-house in order to lower the influence of having a "black box" in designing and developing parts. The differences among auto makers in module-building strategies cannot be discussed without mentioning the architecture and identity of products and brand identity. Each strategy offers many options for each auto maker, and global sourcing also offers many ways to operate. Under these circumstances, it will be interesting to see how the *keiretsu* supplier system changes in the future.

Notes

1. K. Shimokawa, "Nichibeiou jidoshasangyo ni okeru keiretsutorihiki shisutemu no hennkaku" (The change of the keiretsu trading system in the Japanese, American and European auto industry), *Management Trend*, vol. 6, no. 2, p. 89.
2. Nihon Keizai Shinbun, October 19, 1999. Speech by Mr. Ghosn entitled "Nissan Ribaibaru Puran nitsuite" (About Nissan's revival plan) on October 18, 1999, excerpted from Nissan Jidosha Koho-shiryo. In this speech, Mr. Ghosn said that although Nissan was purchasing parts and materials from 1,145 companies across the world, by centralizing and globalizing it would reduce this to 600 companies by 2002. He also said, regarding equipment and services, it would reduce the number of trading companies from 6,900 to 3,400, and would make no exception for purchases from Nissan-related companies. Nissan also declared that it would sell its shares of *keiretsu*

suppliers except for the main four companies, including Calsonic Kansei and Unisia Jecs, and it pursued this policy later.

3. See above.
4. D. Roos, J. P. Wormack, and D. Jones, *The Machine That Changed the World*, Rawson Associates, 1990, pp. 140–142.
5. K. B. Klark, and T. Fujimoto, *Product Development Performance*, Harvard Business School Press, 1991.
6. B. Asanuma, "Nihon no Kigyososhiki-kakushinntekitekiou no Mekanizumu" (The mechanism of the revolutionary adjustment of Japan's corporate organizations), *Toyokeizai Shinhosha*, 1997, pp. 174–184.
7. Ibid., pp. 203–206.
8. Ibid., pp. 207–219.
9. Chrysler was the first company to recognize this advantage of the *keiretsu* transaction. Chrysler, which faced near-bankruptcy in 1981, operated drastic reductions and sell-offs in its parts division. For example, it switched its transaction to Japanese electrical equipment, including electrical components, air conditioners, and radiators. (Heard from President Takeuchi, a former chairman of Denso in the US, in August 1985 and September 1987.)
10. D. Roos, et al., p. 186.
11. GM made a GM Japan Kyoryokukai in Japan as well as in North America, composed of eighty-two Japan-related suppliers. The author made speeches at the association as an advisor in 1987 and 1988.
12. K. Harada, "Beikoku Jidoshasangyo yakushinn no senryaku" (Strategy for promotion of the US's auto industry), *Kogyochosakai*, 1995, p. 29.
13. Ibid., pp. 50–53.
    K. Hirano, "Biggusurii no buhinntorihiki no naitekihennsei" (Internal organization of parts transactions of the Big Three), edited by T. Fujimoto, T. Nishiguchi, and H. Ito, "Sapuraiya Shisutemu" (Supplier system), *Yuhikaku*, 1998, p. 219.
14. K. Harada, p. 93.
15. Ibid., p. 103. According to a questionnaire for suppliers conducted by the SAE (Society of Automotive Engineers) in 1994, Chrysler was using the expertise most effectively.
16. Toyota's purchase division at headquarters controls all domestic and international purchases. But the number of workers was still about 500 (interview at the headquarters of Toyota in June 2002). The purchasing authority was transferred to factories and affiliated companies overseas, but still this is a lean organization.
17. P. F. Drucker, *The Practice of Management*, Butterworth-Heinemann, 1956. Translated into Japanese under the editorship of Noda, Kazuo, Jiyuminshato, pp. 43–44.

18. K. Harada, p. 120.
19. K. Shimokawa, "Gurobaru jidoshasanngyo no saihen to jidoshabuhin sanngyo no kouzoutennkann"(Reconstruction of the global auto industry and the structural change of the auto parts industry), *Keiei Shirin (Hosei Business Journal)*, vol. 36, no. 4, January, 2000, pp. 14–18.
20. K. Shimokawa, "Gurobaru soshingu no yukue"(The fate of global sourcing), *Daily Automotive News*, October 3, 1995.
21. Hearing at Nippondenso America Co. Ltd., September 1993.
22. Ibid.
23. K. Shimokawa and A. Takeishi, Research notes. "Nijyuisseiki wo mukaeta oushu jidousha sanngyo no shinndoukouchousa – VW, Runo, Konchinental, PSA wo chushinni" (Research into new trends in the European auto industry in the 21st century – especially at VW, Renault, Continental, PSA), *Keiei Shirin (Hosei Business Journal)*, vol. 38, no. 3, October 2000, pp. 59–60.
24. K. Shimokawa, "Runo wa dou kaikaku wo susumetaka" (How Renault conducted its reform), *Daily Automotive News*, April 17, 2000.
25. U. Jürgens, "Characteristics of the European automotive system: is there a distinctive European approach?" Tenth GERPISA International Colloquium Keynote Speaker article coordinating competencies and knowledge in the auto industry, p. 14.
26. Fiat began strategic co-designing in which suppliers participated in 1989. This began bearing fruit from 1993, with the small-size car, the Punto. Fiat started a system that placed importance on system suppliers in 1997. K. Shimokawa, and A. Takeishi, Research notes. "Sekaiteki gyokai saihenn no kachu niaru oushu jidousha sanngyou no kihonndoukou to sono jittaichousa" (The basic trends and actual conditions in a survey of the European auto industry, which is in the midst of worldwide industry reconstruction), *Keiei Shirin*, vol. 37, no. 4, January 2001, pp. 146–147.
27. Interview at Renault Technical Center in March 2002.
28. Ibid.
29. K. Shimokawa, see note 1 above, p. 91.
30. Ibid., p. 92.
31. Ibid., p. 93.
32. K. Shimokawa, "Guroobaru buhinnsanngyo no kouzoutenkan" (Structural changes in the global parts industry), *Daily Automotive News*, September 30, 1999.
    K. Shimokawa, "Guroobaru sapuraiyaa" (Global suppliers), *Daily Automotive News*, July 21, 2000.
33. K. Shimokawa, "Sekaisaitekichoutatu to buhinnsanngyo no kouzohennka" (The most suitable procurement in the world and structural changes in the parts industry), *Daily Automotive News*, December 14, 2000.

Japan and the Global Automotive Industry

34. K. Shimokawa, "Sapuraiyaa no dokujigijyutu" (Specific technologies of suppliers), *Daily Automotive News*, June 8, 2001.
35. K. Nobeoka, "Nihon jidoshasangyo niokeru buhinnchoutatukozou no henka" (The changes of the structure of parts procurement in Japan's auto-industry), *Kokumin Keizai Zasshi*, vol. 180, no. 3, December 1999, pp. 59–69.
36. R. Hara, "Jidoshabuhinsangyo no gorobarizeshon to kadai" (Globalization and problems of the auto-parts industry), *Jidoshakogyo*, vol. 33–8, August 1999.

According to Mr. Hara in *JAMA* (Japan Automobile Manufacturers Association) monthly magazine, "in the traditional model-development, design-in, in which design was made according to the specifications given by automakers, was common in the first step of development, including the product and cost planning. But the automakers were in demand for concentrating their resources for product development on environment-related technologies and other precedents and on component technological development. Because of this, parts makers are often asked to participate from the higher levels of planning and making concepts. In order to promote a concept-in-type development, an element of self-sustaining management – which includes abilities for products proposition, cost planning and quality planning – based on the value approved in markets, becomes necessary. But parts makers which have relied completely on automakers don't have enough elements of such management." This comment is highly suggestive about the fate of the parts industry and strategic issues in globalization. However, how the movement toward "concept-in" is happening and what kind of models of "concept-in" are demanded, because of the difference in the purchasing strategies of auto makers, are research issues for the future.

7 | Global M&A and the future of the global auto industry – the light and dark sides of merger and re-alignment

1. Introduction

GM and Ford's sudden fall into deficit caused a stir. The benefits yielded by the merger of Daimler and Chrysler in 1988 were not as significant as expected, and the Chrysler division remained in deficit for many years. The direct cause of the deficits for all these makers was the business slump in North America, but the so-called legacy costs – health insurance, pension funds, and others agreed under a longstanding labor contract with UAW in North America – were blamed, rather than errors in global strategies. This seems to be an unreasonable and strained excuse.

However, it is undeniable that the three companies showed a pioneering spirit in meeting the challenges of globalization at the beginning of the twenty-first century. Environmental issues of global magnitude, emerging markets – such as Eastern Europe, Russia, and Asia, especially China and India – and global deployment of the entire auto industry were all top of the agenda. Yet despite this pioneering spirit, fundamental errors were made. This chapter looks at those strategic errors and compares them to the successful Renault–Nissan alliance, in particular problems arising from strategic integration and respecting different corporate cultures.

Japanese auto makers are performing well in the age of global restructuring, despite being once seen as lagging behind in the deployment of global strategies and suffering directly as a result. This good performance is seen not only among Toyota, Honda, and other purely Japanese makers, but also among foreign-affiliated makers (except for Mitsubishi Motors). Good performance is no longer due to the export-oriented business style of the old days but rather is supported by overseas production and global businesses, and the evolution of unique global strategies and management based on a huge variety of experimental trial and error.

In comparing the contrasting global strategies of auto makers in Japan, the US, and Europe, this chapter will discuss the pioneering role of US and European makers and the reasons why they could not use their leadership effectively. It will also look at the learning process in Japanese auto makers, and the historical significance of global restructuring and the modern deployment of global business.

2. US and European auto makers, in particular Ford and GM, proved their leadership in exercising global strategies

Ford was the quickest to react to the end of the Cold War between East and West and the globalization of the world economy in the early 1990s, and proposed clear global strategies in response to global changes. It was followed by GM and Volkswagen, which focussed on the end of the Cold War, especially the integration of East and West Germany, and of Europe. Volkswagen showed its uniqueness and leadership in its strategies for global platforms and for implementing common modules. However, the company that mapped out global strategies with a clear view was Ford, and it was Ford that proved its leadership in this area.

Ford's bold global strategy, Ford 2000, was developed under the leadership of chairman and CEO Alex Trotman and launched in 1993. Ford 2000 laid out a global strategic vision that focussed on Ford in the twenty-first century, aiming to work for a global and one-dimensional integration of business activities around the world and faster strategic decision making. The slogan for Ford 2000 was: "Think Globally, Act Locally with Agility." Previously, Ford's overseas enterprises had functioned autonomously as an Asian entity in Asia, a North American entity in North America, and a European entity in Europe, with no cooperation or integration, especially in product development and sourcing. Ford 2000 meant that the company would improve its weak points and try to implement a global integration, while also being able to respond to regional complications, the diversity of brands in the market, and regional needs. "Agility" meant the ability to respond to rapid changes and complications in global competition, reduce the development period, create effective sourcing with the application of IT, and respond quickly to situational changes, such as production flexibility. These are still issues for the world's auto makers.

3. What kind of global strategies did Ford conduct under its global vision?

Ford at first tried to integrate its European and US development divisions to eliminate the duplication of product development and to integrate business activities. The company also decided to put out a series of medium-size, low-grade world cars to represent its global strategy, the Contour and the Mystique.

Ford's global strategies were rolled out with great fanfare, but did not yield the expected results. Concentrating the development divisions of North America and Europe, for example, was conducted by transferring thousands of engineers to Dearborn in Michigan from European Ford. But Ford could not contribute to the development of cars which met the needs of the European market, and this process was later reversed in relation to the business alignment of European Ford. The two world-car models proved to be disappointing in both North America and Europe, and did not emulate the earlier success of models like the Taurus. Thus Ford's global strategy seemed to end in anticlimax.

In the latter half of the 1990s, Ford made high profits in the light-truck segment, with models such as the SUV Explorer in the North American market, and took this as an opportunity to emphasize global M&A and brand control. In addition, the company placed an importance on strategies of global concentrated production and standardization of components.

Previously, Ford had bought Japan's Mazda and Britain's Jaguar. It then bought Aston Martin and Range Rover, as well as the Swedish luxury car maker Volvo in 1999. Certain companies within the group, such as Mazda or European Ford, were given the responsibility to develop platforms, engines, and other components of small- and medium-sized cars, and the company tried to standardize and establish components as global platforms and global engine series.

GM and Daimler responded to Ford's lead in developing global strategies. GM already had strong ties with Japanese makers, including a capital and business affiliation with Isuzu and Suzuki. In 1998, GM invested in Fuji Heavy Industry, and affiliated 100 percent with Korea's number three maker, Daewoo. In Europe, GM affiliated with the Swedish passenger car maker Saab 100 percent, and decided to tie up with the well-known Italian maker, Fiat. Through these tie-ups, GM deployed M&A-oriented strategies toward aggressive global re-alignment in, for example, co-development of engines and some models. The tie-up with Fiat was dissolved after seven years.

Daimler entered the global re-alignment business in 1998, when it merged with the US's number three maker, Chrysler. At that time, Chrysler's future was the subject of much public attention. The merger was touted as the merger of the century across the Atlantic and was cited as the real beginning of global re-alignment in the world's auto industry. The Daimler–Chrysler merger had an impact on the auto industries in Europe, Japan and Korea. In Japan, auto makers, except Toyota and Honda, began to develop relationships with foreign companies. In Korea, two out of the four big auto makers merged with GM and Renault and became foreign-affiliated companies, while the other two domestic makers, Hyundai Motors and Kia Motors, merged.

The Daimler and Chrysler merger was expected to have a synergetic effect though the mutual use of their specialized markets. The two companies could not only maintain basic lines to ensure high added value by producing a small number of high-class cars but also put their mass-produced models and models which had not previously been produced by Daimler, such as minivans and SUVs, into product lines. It was assumed that this synergy effect would also spread into joint development and mutual exploitation of platforms, collaborative development, and the joint purchase of components and parts. In addition, the huge cost required for development technology, especially technology for environmental protection, was expected to be relieved in the long term.

The global re-alignment of the auto industry which began with Ford has not yielded the expected results. Business operations in some companies have become deadlocked and others are making strategic errors, in spite of having shown leadership and a sure eye.

4. Why did global restructuring end in deadlock?

The business slump that GM and Ford faced in the US sent the companies into a vicious cycle of falling sales and disappointing globalization strategies.

The reconstruction of business in North America is obviously a priority in response to this vicious cycle, but it is impossible to escape only by rebuilding business in North America. The global strategies tried to date must be thoroughly examined to find out why they did not go as well as expected, and which basic concepts were mistaken. While the legacy costs mentioned earlier have been a major burden for business in North America, solving only this problem will not necessarily rebuild business there.

To break the vicious cycle, these companies have to restructure their product capabilities so that they are able to respond to rapid changes in market forces in North America. They will have to rethink their previous strategy of avoiding competition with Japanese passenger cars which, although it enabled them to make profits in the pickup truck, minivan, and SUV segments, did not push them to improve development capabilities.[1] The light truck models have a relatively long model-change cycle and the number of parts is relatively small, which suited the giant mass-production system which US makers historically specialized in, and provided both high added value and low costs. However, failing to improve development of passenger cars led to a delay in creating a brand that could respond to drastic changes in the US and global markets, and meant these manufacturers were slow to respond to the growing tendency toward fuel efficiency caused by the hike in the price of gasoline.

Failing to focus on the development of highly competitive passenger cars meant that these companies fell behind on engine technology and so did not make the necessary large investments in development and factories. The stagnation in engine technology is easily connected to stagnation of the brand value, not only for passenger cars but for all types of cars.

The bodies of the larger SUVs and light trucks were frame–chassis oriented, making them unsuitable as platforms for the bodies of passenger cars, delaying the emergence of cross-over models that could divert passenger car production to SUVs and use platforms for passenger cars for small-size SUVs. In contrast, Japanese auto makers, which started late in the light truck segment, commoditized platforms of passenger cars to small-size SUVs and other models, developed fuel-efficient engines, and introduced cross-over models one after another. (Figure 5.9 shows the production number of cars per platform by Japanese and US makers in North America.)

The US makers, especially Ford and GM, also preserved non-flexible, mass-production, high-volume factories and production systems, in which one model is produced for a long period of time in a make-to-stock production system. This helped them establish substantial discounts by increasing the production ratio of factories to a certain level so that the mass-production effect of models rose, and large incentives and rebates were paid, and substantial discounts given, to maintain supply capability at a certain level. Incentives and rebates are usually paid by auto makers temporarily to adjust demand and supply, but the payments made by US makers are extremely high and structurally established. It is difficult to raise the brand capability of new models in this situation, and thus leadership in increasing the development capability of products cannot be exercised globally.

In addition to problems related to business operations in North America, one of the biggest reasons why these companies' global strategies became deadlocked was in the content and basic concepts of the strategies themselves. The premise of the global strategies for business integration and business restructuring adopted by Ford, GM, and Daimler was based only on economies of scale. Jacques Nasser, the former chairman of Ford, stated that only five auto makers would survive in the restructured global auto industry, and this sentiment was amplified by the idea of the 4 million car club – that survival was possible only for companies producing more than 4 million cars a year. Obviously this idea focusses only on economies of scale rather than creating an auto business that can evolve to cope with the complications and diversification present in a globalizing world, and relates to the two principles that are essential for global strategies: (1) integration of global platforms, and (2) global sourcing strategies for parts.

If the integration of global platforms is tried mechanically through developing IT and digital design, speeding up design, and automating production processes, then the brand identity of the products will be lost. Integration of global platforms involves consolidating the designs of platforms which are different by region, but if integration is conducted by simply imposing the use of one platform on some areas, models which do not meet the market needs of each area are produced, and while this may bring economies of scale, brand value will fall. Moreover, platform integration can cause conflict between the conventional and unique design divisions and the corporate cultures of production divisions. Honda, which is conducting a simultaneous, global establishment of its Accord and Civic models, is standardizing platforms as much as possible, but is adopting a policy of developing some models locally while trying to meet local needs flexibly. Toyota, which develops platforms in Japan but then undertakes local development of models, does not aim at a mass-production effect with standardized platforms, but rather tries to meet different needs and changes locally through flexible operations.

As to global sourcing of parts and components, which is at the core of global strategies, Ford and GM in North America increased the ratio of outsourcing, especially of parts. However, they were choosing areas where sourcing was possible at lowest cost and where logistic problems were smallest, and procuring parts from these areas intensively and liberally. This procurement concentrated especially in Eastern Europe, China, Mexico, Central and Southern America, and India. Development of IT and the spread of database and net sourcing seemed to help global sourcing and quick decision making on purchasing by allowing the exchange of information in real time.

However, since the basic concept of the three companies in Europe and the US was low-cost purchasing in large amounts, they were still fixated on economies of scale. There was a strong tendency to ignore detailed and individual evaluation of quality and technology capacities, or to evaluate the integrity of quality and technology capability for parts as a group. Today's rapidly developing technology for cars and global competition in quality make the dynamic evaluation of parts, quality, and technology, as well as the potential of parts makers, indispensable. Expanding global sourcing with a cost focus may have led to immediate cost reductions, but it ignored the important long-term factors of quality and technological capability, especially in the development and design potential of parts makers. Such a strategy let total quality stagnate and increased warranty costs for quality guarantees, and caused parts makers to be slow to respond to new needs for environmental and fuel-efficiency technology.

Since the platform and sourcing strategies that were the foundation for Ford, GM, and Daimler's global strategies concentrated only on pursuing economies of scale, they risked slowing the companies' ability to respond flexibly in evolving their brands and design development capabilities, and neglecting the critical areas of quality and technology.[2] Deadlock was due to the fact that they ignored these risks underlying their global restructuring strategies.

5. Management crisis and GM, and lessons from global strategies

Despite the many changes occurring in auto markets due to oil price increases, business and sales movements in North American auto markets are not deteriorating significantly. This suggests that the problems for Ford and GM are not caused by a business recession or other temporary causes but are structural problems caused by strategic errors.

As we have seen earlier, some blame the problems on the high legacy cost, but this is only an excuse. The crisis is due to strategic errors. It should be noted that though the strategy in North America and global strategy appear to be completely separate because of their market characteristics and product strategies, these strategies are mutually and closely related in, for example, platform strategies and global sourcing of parts.

Mergers and acquisitions were the focus of the global strategies of Ford, GM, and Daimler as a means toward global integration. But their confidence in how this strategy would bring economies of scale of merit was misplaced. Ford, for example, placed enormous emphasis on the development of a global brand, and so Japanese Mazda and Swedish Volvo are the only companies within the group which maintain their brand value, purely due to their efforts to preserve their identity and brand value. By contrast, other brands within the group, for example, Jaguar, Range Rover, and Aston Martin, are failing to increase their brand values. Even Jaguar, acquired more than ten years ago, has standardized platforms with Lincoln, a luxury car brand in North America, and the establishment of European Ford's Halewood factory in England as a production site for Jaguar and an important wing of the world premium group has had no significant effect so far.

In the case of GM, its affiliation with Fiat and Opel in Europe was dissolved after five years because of dissent in operating the business. The passenger division of Swedish Saab, which was supposed to strengthen its cooperative ties with Opel, has not maintained its brand identity. As to GM's dealings with Japanese makers, GM invested in Isuzu, Suzuki, and Fuji Heavy Industry, and at one time these Japanese companies were listed in its consolidated financial statements. But GM's ties with the Japanese companies have weakened and GM started selling its holdings because of financial problems. GM relinquished its stocks of Fuji Heavy Industry to Toyota in 2005, and began selling most of its holdings in Isuzu and Suzuki (in the case of Isuzu, 45 percent of the holdings were sold.) The stocks were relinquished by the makers in which GM had invested or by related general trading companies, and its controlling share has largely decreased. Though the investment ratio has lowered, the actual cooperative ties based on the alliance have continued with Isuzu and Suzuki; the supply of Isuzu's small-size trucks as a GM brand, technical tie-ups, and the supply of diesel engines as well as the supply of Suzuki's small-size cars from overseas factories will continue.

In Asia, the affiliation between GM and Japanese makers was not completely equivalent to M&A, apart from the establishment of Korean GM after 100 percent acquisition of Korea's number three maker, Daewoo. In the future, GM is likely to rebuild its global strategy in Asia using Korean GM as one base, by making a partial investment in the FAW group in China, which is already producing good profits, and by placing emphasis on India and other growing markets.

GM's global M&A, which once drew much attention, ended in anticlimax, and GM is now learning lessons from the past and examining possible restructuring. GM's experience has demonstrated that it is meaningless to conduct mergers that are only about numbers, without having real business-integration strategies.

While Ford and GM were able to fund their M&A activities with the huge profits they made in the 1990s in North America, their profit performance shows volatile fluctuations even with a small change in the market or the economy. This is because the management culture of the two companies is still focussed on mass production and high volumes with a high break-even point, thus when sales increase, profit increases. The first attempts at global restructuring for Ford, GM, and Daimler left the high-cost structure in their home countries in place, failed to reform the production systems for factories and sourcing, neglected many problems, and placed too much confidence in economies of scale. Daimler sold out Chrysler stock in 2007.

Preserving their mass-production, high-volume style meant that Ford and GM continued with product development and production systems which were suited to this strategy, and continued make-to-stock mass production to increase factory utilization rates. As a result, they injected huge sums into promotion costs (such as incentives, rebates, and interest-free loans), and this caused a vicious cycle of high production costs to maintain effective factory utilization rates and high promotion costs. Figure 7.1 shows the changes in promotion cost per car over the years 2000–2003.

So the question is, how should Ford and GM break the vicious cycle? What is urgently needed is to raise the level of total quality, which will

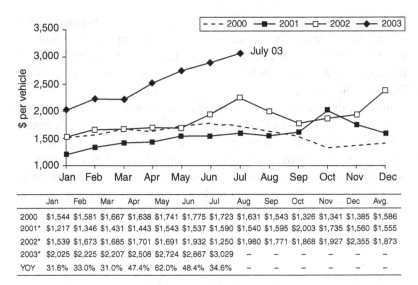

	Jan	Feb	Mar	Apr	May	Jun	Jul	Aug	Sep	Oct	Nov	Dec	Avg.
2000	$1,544	$1,581	$1,667	$1,638	$1,741	$1,775	$1,723	$1,631	$1,543	$1,326	$1,341	$1,385	$1,586
2001*	$1,217	$1,346	$1,431	$1,443	$1,543	$1,537	$1,590	$1,540	$1,595	$2,003	$1,735	$1,560	$1,555
2002*	$1,539	$1,673	$1,685	$1,701	$1,691	$1,932	$1,250	$1,980	$1,771	$1,868	$1,927	$2,355	$1,873
2003*	$2,025	$2,225	$2,207	$2,508	$2,724	$2,867	$3,029	–	–	–	–	–	–
YOY	31.6%	33.0%	31.0%	47.4%	62.0%	48.4%	34.6%	–	–	–	–	–	–

Source: Autodata
*Starting in August 2002, the methodology for tracking US retail promotion costs was revised. 2002 and 2001 figures have been restated; however, data prior to 2001 have not been revised, and comparability is skewed

Figure 7.1 Promotion cost per car by monthly trend in the last four years

reduce warranty costs, and to rebuild product and brand value through reforming product development. This means rebuilding global product development, taking into account not only the advanced markets but also emerging markets. These companies must close or combine mass-production factories and reconstruct flexible factories with a new concept. This would make it possible for them to respond quickly to changes in market needs and to eliminate pressure for excess supply and the vicious cycle of huge promotion costs.

In short, the first auto makers to undertake global restructuring forgot to focus on the reality of competition because they were too busy with nominal and surface competition. And while they used IT technology positively in exercising global strategies, they lost touch with real business because they were overconfident about the effects of the IT revolution. In order to use IT as an effective tool, proper and concrete strategies are required. IT itself will not provide strategies or decision making. These repeated strategic errors led to mistakes in the allocation of management resources and a lack of constancy and continuity in strategies.

6. Problems relating to marrying different enterprise cultures under international M&A

Global restructuring and mergers bring problems of combining different enterprise cultures and creating a synergy from the best characteristics of each company. The marriage of two different corporate cultures does not mean forcing the culture of one side on the other. It is essential to have a mutual respect for both cultures, to learn from each other, to find new directions from each other, and to learn about creativity and organization. But early attempts at integration saw the initiative taken by the acquiring company, and placed the emphasis on unifying the corporate culture, which was mistakenly believed to be relatively easy. This was most marked in the case of the merger between Daimler and Chrysler and the contrasting experience of Renault and Nissan.

In the case of Daimler and Chrysler, their strong points in producing models, and in targeting customers and markets, were different, and thus they could have been mutually complementary, as Figure 5.2 shows. Daimler, which set up the merger, was a global maker of luxury cars and medium and large trucks, and made high profits out of its brand capability and high added value even where production volume was small. When the world auto industry was still in the globalizing process, a clear segregation was possible between the makers of luxury cars and those of mass-production models. However, this kind of segregation became difficult due to global competition in the auto industry, and some mass-production makers began producing luxury cars. Moreover, the future of the global auto markets was dependent on the future of Asia, BRICs (Brazil, Russia, India, and China), and other emerging markets, as well as the development of environmental technology, and thus entry into businesses with a future could be hindered by limiting production to luxury cars. Therefore what Daimler targeted was basically acceptable. In addition, by affiliating with Chrysler, Daimler could ensure a strong position in the North American market, in which Daimler was relatively weak, and the minivan and SUV could be added to Daimler's production line. Chrysler also could improve on its weak points in long-term quality, development capability in engine technology, the slow adoption of environmental technology, and European and Asian markets.

Put this way, the aim of the restructuring and merger of Daimler and Chrysler was reasonable. But they took the challenge of mixing the two different corporate cultures and exploiting mutual synergy too lightly. Jurgen Schremph, the former chairman of Daimler, in particular failed to grasp the seriousness of this problem, focussing only on Daimler's culture and driving out former Chrysler executives who advocated respect for Chrysler's culture and realistic reforms. The marriage of the two different enterprise cultures was thus more difficult than expected. As a result, the Chrysler division, despite good business performance, suffered from deficits for many years after the merger, and was saddled with huge financial and personnel burdens by Daimler's headquarters.

Now we must consider the dissonance of corporate cultures between Daimler and Chrysler. Traditionally, Daimler and Chrysler had different concepts in design and products. They had different ideas for design, for example, platforms, engine power trains, and interiors. They were different in sourcing and designing parts. While Daimler placed importance on self-production and sticking to its own methods of design in outsourcing, Chrysler placed emphasis on outsourcing ratios and focussed on the selection of suppliers and the outsourcing of design. The two companies were also different in product-quality criteria, methods for quality control, and production systems. For example, the quality-gate system carried out by Daimler, which emphasized durability and quality, was suited to luxury cars. But this system fundamentally conflicted with Chrysler's quality-control system, which was oriented toward mass-production models and which placed emphasis on shop floor-oriented improvements in quality and QC activities. The two companies also had different labor practices in their factory production systems. Chrysler valued the JIT approach in terms of shop floor-oriented improvement or proposals, while at Daimler, engineers and skilled laborers exerted considerable influence.[3]

Integrating such different cultures cannot be achieved without mutual understanding of both sides' strong and weak points, and mutual respect. Daimler lacked this understanding, and attempted to force its own culture on Chrysler. Thus, no immediate effect could be expected in the integrity of platforms and joint procurement, which were the original impetus for the merger. Since their concepts for design, brand, and products were completely different, an adequate response was needed. However, as we have seen, it is not an easy thing to do and a speed-before-quality response causes failure. Latterly, some adjustments were made under the control of Dieter Zetsche, who succeeded in returning the Chrysler division to profitability after many difficult years.

Ford and GM stand on the same ground in the sense that both took the integration of two different enterprise cultures too lightly. Both companies had the same idea – that they could impose their own cultures on the companies they merged with. They have been making adjustments based on their experiences ever since. For example, Ford approves the independence of European Ford, is integrating global business with Mazda and Volvo, of which it became the biggest shareholder, and is trying to change into a company that respects different corporate cultures and their brand values. Ford leaves Mazda to take charge in development and to supply its small-size engine as a global engine, and has tried to support Volvo's enterprise culture and brand identity by respecting Volvo's assertions in safety criteria and even making some changes in design in order to meet those assertions. Though Ford sent three presidents to Mazda, it eventually promoted a Japanese executive, who succeeded in developing brand identity at Mazda, to the position of president. In this way, Ford is beginning to respect and utilize Mazda's corporate value while making sure of Mazda's role in the Ford group.

The alliance between Renault and Nissan suffered few of the problems that Ford and GM faced. This was because Renault, which led the alliance, believed that synergy was possible through mutual learning and understanding, focussing on the strong points of the cultures and management of the two different companies. For example, Renault and Nissan operate an alliance committee, and representatives of both companies can discuss business plans relating to cooperation or creating synergy. In this committee, one side cannot force proposals on the other side, nor can proposals be refused by one side.[4]

So what kind of cooperation and learning were achieved through this alliance? The most effective result of the cooperation was the joint purchasing of parts. It began with basic parts, which are easy to standardize. Compound components were purchased jointly after first going through a process to review the basics of each other's design, if required. Mutual independency over basic parts such as engine power trains, brakes, and absorbers, which relate to brand identity, was given more importance than mechanical integration, and design standards were reviewed if there was merit on both sides. Platform standardization is another example of what was achieved through their mutual cooperation. This can be seen clearly in the unification of Nissan's Micra (called March in Japan) and Renault's small car, the Clio. However, this does not mean that Renault left all the platform development to Nissan. A joint team of Renault and Nissan engineers was based at Renault technical center in the suburbs of Paris. The two companies had not yet reached agreement on their luxury-class models, and at the time of writing they were working on this.

Renault and Nissan have a cooperative relationship between complementary businesses, thus they both use the Nissan sales network, which is strong in the North American market, and the Renault sales network, which is strong in the Central and Southern American market, and they also both use surplus production capacities. For example, Renault's commercial and other cars are assembled in Nissan's factories in Spain and Mexico.[5]

Renault and Nissan use each other's strong points and support each other while collaborating in a process of mutual learning. They learn from each other in many areas, such as a mutual study concerning factory systems, or mutual study into co-developing a supplier-support system with suppliers, or how to set up a database for technology. Renault dispatched a president and important personnel from a strategic division to help Nissan develop its strategic leadership. But Renault did not force its methods on Nissan unilaterally, instead emphasizing commitment toward getting each worker from top to bottom to take responsibility for Nissan's new strategies and revival plans. Renault proposed reforms in management quality and introduced TQM as a part of restructuring, but did not use TQM in the same way that it eventually appeared in Nissan's revival plan. Renault taught Nissan about brand management as well as car design. In return, Renault learned many things from Nissan about factory production systems, including QC-circle activities and the concurrent production which Nissan operates. In product development, Renault learned about reducing lead times and development numbers from Nissan. They also exchanged designs and technology for engines, components, and other basic parts.

Renault and Nissan are clearly making efforts to promote a mutual synergy, to respect their different corporate cultures, and to maintain the spirit of mutual respect. So far, the alliance of these two companies is showing obvious effects in their moves toward global restructuring, indicating the importance of mutual respect as a methodology for integration of different company cultures in the process of restructuring.

7. Recent trends and global strategies in the Japanese auto industry

Japanese auto makers seemed to delay the start of their global strategies, but recently they have produced high profits from overseas business. The major reasons why Japanese makers waited to exercise global strategies were the dive in profitability due to the restructuring of the Japanese auto industry and the second hike in the yen in the early 1990s. Overseas production and factories in North America were still in development at the beginning of the 1980s, and the accumulation of investment and a stagnation of factory operation ratios contributed to the slump in profitability.

In what seemed a symbol, in 1993 Nissan (Japan's second largest maker), Fuji Heavy Industry, Mazda, and Isuzu had deficits, and Honda's operating profit was less than a quarter of its highest level in the past. Even Toyota, the top Japanese maker, declared monthly losses. Following this, the Japanese yen rose in value from 120 yen per dollar to over 80 yen per dollar in the second hike of the yen, and exporting completed cars from Japan resulted in huge losses. Consequently, Japanese auto makers faced severe pressure to restructure, but there were also intrinsic reasons to face the crisis.

Importantly, the domestic auto market had seen annual production rise from 2 million cars to 5 million cars between the latter half of the 1980s and the beginning of the 1990s because of the business boom, and luxury cars or high-class versions sold well because of the shift to higher-class models. Trying to get ahead of the competition, each auto maker invested in new and powerful automatic factories. This increasing capability resulted in excessive domestic plant and equipment and a high break-even point. And because luxury cars and high-specification models sold well, the number of models and model versions was increased, and consequently development and production costs increased. In 1992, the boom ended, and the structurally high-priced system was exposed.

Japanese auto makers faced troubles both at home and abroad, and began bold restructurings. Table 4.1 shows a summary of cost-reduction plans for restructuring conducted by each maker. All of them looked to reduce the number of models and types, reduce parts units, and emphasize standardization and commoditizing. According to a White Paper by the Japanese government, the basic models of Japanese cars doubled to 400 models in the ten years before 1991, and the number of named cars reached two or three times that of European and US leading makers in the ten years before 1990. In order to reduce and standardize the number of models and types, as well as parts, design development, which was a sanctuary for auto makers, needed to be reviewed. In addition, VA and VE needed to be established with suppliers. Reducing the number of workers was carried out in different ways. Some companies closed factories and others reduced their production lines. Every auto maker placed importance on reducing staff numbers, especially office staff. Key workers in factories, who had been trained in multiple areas, were retained, and this largely contributed to the comeback of Japanese auto makers later.

Restructuring among Japanese auto makers was carried out at different rates, depending on whether the top management shared the sense of crisis with their workers quickly. But on the whole, it yielded good results; the break-even point was lowered and the structurally high-priced system was corrected, largely through the various measures and policies described above.

Furthermore, in the latter half of the 1990s, Japanese auto makers also began to reap the profits from their global business. Previously, overseas factories had received investment, production, sourcing, and development support from headquarters, and this was hugely expensive. However, as overseas factories were localized, the factories became profitable, cleaned out their accumulated losses, and contrariwise to the past, began contributing profit to the headquarters. Locally produced cars began making profits in overseas markets at around the time when the profit earned from exports was injected into the local factories, and as a result, the system shifted to being one close to an exchange rate-free system, in which profitability is assured without influence from exchange rates. Profitability from production sites is not limited to North America; the European and Asian production sites are also profitable. Today, Honda, Nissan, and Mazda make more than 70 percent of their entire profit overseas, and even Toyota, which was domestically strong, is catching up with them.

Strategic restructuring happened quickly at Toyota and Honda, where a sense of crisis and tension became widespread among the workers from top to bottom. Both companies adopted a TQM approach, to foster responsibility in decision making and quality of management by executives. Alongside this, both companies conducted bold changes in design development within a short period by reducing the number of designers, simplifying tests by simulations using three-dimensional digital design, reducing the number of prototype cars, simplifying models and variations, and standardizing and commoditizing parts.

Suppliers play an important role in restructuring. Instead of forcing a severe cost reduction on suppliers, efforts were made to raise their technology and design capability, increase their participation in design development, simplify design by going back to basics, and raise suppliers' ability to propose their own design simplifications. Toyota succeeded in reducing costs by as much as 40 percent, as targeted in its CCC21 plan, and profit was shared with suppliers at a constant rate. As a result, Toyota's primary suppliers were increasing their profitability every year.

Toyota and Honda were quick to revise design development, utilize three-dimensional design, simplify excessive design, standardize and commoditize parts, encourage the participation of suppliers in the first steps of design development, and apply other measures and policies important for restructuring. Other Japanese auto makers followed with similar measures and policies.

The fact that the strategic effects of restructuring became apparent immediately, and also that lowering the break-even point for domestic production was successful, increased global competitiveness. At the same time, Japanese auto makers established strategic activities which allocated resources to the development of economical engines, environmental technology and key parts, and to setting up flexible production systems.

Japanese auto makers improved their domestic competitiveness by a thorough restructuring, not by simply focussing on reducing the number of workers, but by returning to their origins in design development, reducing costs by involving suppliers in development, and establishing flexibility in factories. In contrast, Ford, GM, and Daimler ended up postponing structural reforms in their home countries, and laid off employees when business slumped. As we have seen, global M&A, while postponing reforms in their home countries, did not yield the desired results.

8. Global competitiveness and the development of global business by Japanese auto makers

The Japanese auto industry was divided into two groups following global restructuring. One group comprised national and independent makers with no foreign investment, such as the Toyota group and Honda. The other was a foreign-affiliated group that included Nissan, Mazda, Mitsubishi, Fuji Heavy Industry, Suzuki, and Isuzu. Though they are foreign-affiliated companies, only Nissan and Mazda have foreign holdings of more than 37.5 percent, which confers influence over the selection of the president and important decision making, while the holding ratio is fluid in the other groups. Mitsubishi Motors Corporation spun off Mitsubishi Fuso Truck. GM sold its Fuji Heavy Industry stocks to Toyota, Isuzu stocks held by GM have been proportionally transferred to Toyota, and Suzuki's GM holdings have largely reduced. But some of these manufacturers are continuing business relationships, supplying cars, engines, and components.

Global restructuring forced Japanese auto makers to realize the severe reality of global competition. Up until then, Japanese auto makers had not had a clear global strategy, but they began reviewing their conventional business structures with a global vision. Until then, business inside and outside Japan was controlled separately, and cooperation was set up if it was needed. Overseas factories were established in response to trade conflict and auto makers focussed on their production systems where labor practices were different, encouraging Japanese suppliers to increase local sourcing of parts, and establishing a cooperative relationship with local suppliers. Product development was left completely to headquarters in Japan at the beginning.

Overseas factories began to change from simply being complementary existences to profitable businesses. Before long, localization of production systems and sourcing were being pursued, and then the Japanese auto makers began to localize development. One after another they succeeded in localizing product design by setting up independent development centers, and this led to localization of interiors, press parts, and body design. Engine power trains and platforms were localized depending on models. For example, Honda's Accord in the US was developed in a development center in Ohio, and is completely distinguishable from that developed for the Japanese market.

Localization makes it possible to develop new models quickly in response to local needs, and, coupled with cooperation, makes global development and the inter-supply of parts possible. For example, Honda's Accord was developed in the US and produced in factories in China, and standard models such as the Civic were produced in leading areas globally and simultaneously. Toyota developed models like the IMV (Innovative Multipurpose Vehicle), aimed at the Thai and other South-east Asian markets, through cooperation between headquarters and local factories, and then produced them in major producing countries. Nissan unified the standards for parts – which had become different depending on area as a result of an increase in sourcing of parts and progress in localization – as much as possible. Digital design has been instrumental in making global platforms and global components possible.

Thus, unlike Ford, GM, and Daimler, which conducted bold M&A activities aimed at market share as part of a magnificent vision, Japanese auto makers carried out their globalization strategies through cooperation among their business units around the world, continuing the necessary domestic restructuring and promoting localization and profitability overseas. The continued restructuring was not simply about reducing employee numbers, and effort to establish good profitability overseas helped Japanese auto makers to become globally competitive. Before long, synergy effects resulted in a significant improvement in production efficiency in overseas factories and cost reductions in sourcing became apparent, especially in North America, South-east Asia, and other Asian countries. Japanese auto makers' strength – the ability to respond quickly to changes in demand – became prominent. Table 7.1 lists sales volumes and consolidated profits of the top ten auto companies in the world; the sudden business recovery of three Japanese companies is obvious.

In the twenty-first century, differences and changes by area are becoming more prominent than unifying demand in the global auto industry. In the North American market, demand is shifting to medium and small SUVs and passenger cars with good fuel economy. The Asian markets vary, and include low-cost and light cars in the Indian market, small pickups in the Thai and Indonesian markets, and medium-sized passenger cars in the Chinese market, although the ratio of small cars is increasing. In European markets, diesel engines are popular and luxury cars maintain a certain share, but the ratio of medium and small cars is

Table 7.1 *Ranking of ability of ten leading auto makers (2001)*

	Sales volume in 2001 (1000) (year-on-year)	Consolidated profit/loss (US$ hundred million) (year-on-year)
GM	8,560 (–0.4)	14 (–70)
Ford	6,991 (–5.8)	–54 (–)
Toyota	5,928 (2.0)	48 (30)
VW	5,084 (0.5)	26 (12)
D-C	4,479 (–5.7)	–6 (–)
PSA	3,133 (11.3)	15 (29)
Honda	2,634 (4.5)	28 (56)
Nissan	2,580 (–1.7)	29 (12)
Renault	2,409 (2.4)	9 (–2)
Fiat	2,216 (–11.9)	7 (–)

Source: *Nihon Keizai Shinbun*, May 26, 2002

also high and a shift from passenger cars to SUVs is occurring. In the Japanese market, though the market has reached its peak, the ratio of light cars is increasing and the shift toward SUVs is rapid. Moreover, eight auto-makers are competing intensively over new models and thus the addition of new models occurs frequently.

The characteristics of these markets can change in a moment. When global markets are unified, economies of scale can be expected by mechanically integrating and unifying platforms, as attempted by Ford and GM. But if the global auto market is characterized by differences and frequent change, then an effective response cannot be made using unified and rigid methods. The ability of Japanese makers to respond to such differences and changes is significant and their lead times are short. A short, effective development period means that models can be put out as needed according to the movement of markets. To realize this, close cooperation between development and manufacturing, especially the rapid set-up of new models, swing production among factories, and flexibility of manufacturing, is indispensable. This production flexibility, which is a speciality of Japanese makers, is conducted across all Japanese factories, whether in Japan or elsewhere in the world. Furthermore, although production flexibility in Japanese overseas factories is much higher than it is for European and US makers, it is not yet at the same level as the factories in Japan. Figure 7.2 shows the degree of quality, productivity, lean production ratio, and the degree of

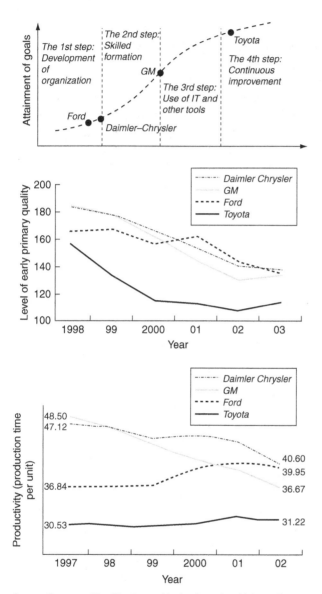

Source: Composed by Chuokoronshinsha, based on Haboun Report

Figure 7.2 Comparison between the US Big Three and Toyota in competition over quality and cost (1997–2003)

achievement of Toyota and the Big Three in recent years. Lean production ratio includes the degree of flexible production.

The sudden expansion of global business has also caused problems
for Japanese auto makers. The rapid increase in overseas business sites
has caused a shortage of trained personnel, especially production technology veterans, multi-skilled employees, engineers with concrete ideas
and instinct, and those with global management capability, overseas
experience, and development ability, which are particularly important
to second-tier and other suppliers. In response, Toyota, Honda, and
Nissan are promoting localization and aiming at independent, self-
sustainable management.

9. Conclusion – the sequel and future of global restructuring

Despite the fanfare with which it was announced, global restructuring for
Ford, GM, and Daimler in the late 1990s did not yield the results
expected. Strategic errors included focussing on economies of scale; failing to restructure thoroughly across the business, for instance, factory
reform, development systems and sourcing, much needed by businesses in
North America and Germany; overconfidence in the impact of IT in
producing synergies; and failing to address the problems that arose
from mixing different brands and business cultures. In contrast, Renault
and Nissan, which chose the path of their alliance carefully, achieved
synergy effects through respect for corporate cultures and inter-learning.

Even if eliminating duplication of global platforms is excellent as an
idea, the necessary volume will not be assured without having a product
concept that improves brand value and identity. And while global
sourcing can be achieved effectively using IT databases and networks
in the parts trade, this only suits trade in countries with low labor costs,
including China, India, South-east Asia, Central and Southern America,
and Eastern Europe, where parts are merchandized with a standard of
measure. Global sourcing does not suit trade in high-tech parts and
components, because quality and the integrity of parts cannot be effectively evaluated or guaranteed.

Japanese auto makers came late to the global restructuring game and
started with revising the basics of development and sourcing systems
and reforming production systems. They confronted global restructuring with a sense of crisis, and returned to the starting point of lean
production, which had been forgotten during the economic boom.

Japanese companies started to emphasize the structuring capability of strategies that could respond to global competition. They used the fruits of the IT revolution in their own creative ways, by digitizing design, improving efficiency by introducing digital simulation tests, and conducting development by sharing design information, integrating production, and exchanging design information with suppliers. Consequently, a more evolved supplier system was constructed, and the seeds of a global supply chain were sown.

But what about the future of global restructuring? First of all, though restructuring did not achieve the expected results, it is not necessary to return to where things were before, but rather to revise restructuring strategies. Further international M&A will not take place except in emerging countries, because such M&A activity brings big risks. Business structures are being revised in the light of M&A experience, in particular those where brand value was lost. Brands with a high contribution, such as Mazda, Volvo, and GM Daewoo, will be emphasized in future, along with brands with strength in emerging markets such as India, Asia, China, and Latin America.

Though possibilities for the further spread of global M&A will fall off, the possibility for alliances without mergers still exists. Alliances involving environmental technology and new technology development, the inter-use of suppliers, and alliances with clear themes will expand in various ways. In these cases, strong and weak points in management and technology should complement each other, and synergy effects should be expected.

Emerging countries, represented by the BRICs and others in Southeast Asia and Latin America, will be important in the future. Areas where business opportunities expand as markets expand will decide the future of global competition. There is also the possibility that successful local makers in these areas might enter into global restructuring. China's FAW Corporation and India's financial clique, TATA, could be candidates, and a case like that of the Mittal Steel Company in India in the iron and steel industry could occur in the auto industry. However, the global iron and steel industry represents economies of scale, which we have seen is of limited benefit in the global auto industry. Considering environmental problems and oil and other energy issues of the future, an auto industry which can respond to economic resource issues and environmental technology is suitable for emerging areas, and the lean and flexible production systems adopted by Japan form the direction which makers in emerging areas should pursue.

Amplifying these, technologies for the environment and safety are the key to the future of global competition. These technologies will require closer cooperation with the electronics industry, the telecommunications industry, and related industries such as materials and fine processing technology, and tighter cooperation with suppliers and a supply-chain network will be essential.

Global restructuring among suppliers is more likely to draw attention than global restructuring at the level of auto makers. We can see this in the fact that supplier mergers and integration, which were stimulated by global restructuring at the assembler level, are ongoing, and the world ranking of suppliers is changing every year. Table 7.2 shows the sales ranking of suppliers in the world in 2004. Delphi, which separated from GM, was number one for a long time, but has now fallen in the ranking. Delphi became eligible for Chapter 11 due to the recent business slump at GM, and is now in a state of bankruptcy. The same situation is seen with Visteon, which separated from Ford. The urgent restructuring of these leading parts makers will include the disposal of underperforming businesses, which will inevitably influence restructuring in the parts industry. In contrast, Bosch and Denso, with potential in technological development, will restructure with a focus on high and prior technology development, without depending on simple M&A. Canada's Magna, along with Johnson Controls and Lear, are parts makers which have already established a

Table 7.2 *Sales of the best ten auto-parts makers in the world*

Ranking	Companies	Sales (hundred million) (y/y)
1	BOSCH (Germany)	344 (15.5)
2	DELPHI (USA)	287 (2.0)
3	DENSO (Japan)	251 (6.4)
4	MAGNA International (Canada)	207 (34.6)
5	JOHNSON Controls (USA)	205 (20.0)
6	VISTEON (USA)	187 (5.6)
7	LEAR (USA)	170 (7.7)
8	AISIN (Japan)	163 (10.7)
9	FORLESIA (France)	146 (14.2)
10	VALEO (France)	129 (10.2)

Source: *Foreign Automotive Monthly*, April 2003

global base, and will deploy global strategies with a focus on quality, using M&A as necessary. Parts makers have used M&A to achieve economies of scale across regions, and this will be repeated in the future, but strategies will be modified to take account of the many lessons learned from the global restructuring of assemblers. Engineering quality and skills will be key factors for restructuring that targets mergers across countries and the integrity of new technologies, especially environmental and safety-related technology in the electronics and communications fields and the new materials industry, and fine processing technology and other multi-fusion technologies that are essential for processing. These are being conducted at the second and third levels, and some specialized financial institutes exist to support this. Small- and medium-sized suppliers that have original technology or which are finding ways to combine processing and integrated technologies will aim to create business models with added value in order to survive in the face of global competition.

Global competition is not temporary, and will expand in the future. Global restructuring will show its true value only if the foundations for real business competition are established both inside and outside the home country, based on a global vision that has alliances and strategic construction as its core.

Notes

1. K. Shimokawa, "Nichibei jidoshasangyo koubou no yukue" (Direction of rise and fall of Japan and the US auto industry), *Jijitsushinsha*, 1997, pp. 126–127.
2. K. Shimokawa, "GM kokusai koubaitanto fukushachou Baugh Anderson kaikenki" (Interview with GM Vice President Baugh Anderson), *Nikkan Jidosha Shinbun*, September 12, 18, and 25, 2004.
3. K. Shimokawa, T. Fujimoto, Y. Konno, S. Orihashi, and K. Seunghwan, "Global senryaku to kannkyou senryaku no kyouka wo hakaru oushu jidoushasangyou no senryakudoukou to nikkeijidousha meika – buhinnmeeka no oushusenryaku to koujyou nojittaichousa" (Strategy and trend plant field survey of EU auto industry and Japanese car makers, Japanese suppliers which strengthen global strategy and environment strategy), *Houseidaigaku keieishirin*, vol. 39, no. 4, vol. 40, no. 1, April 2003, p. 118.
4. K. Shimokawa, Y. Konno, D. Heller, and H. Katou, "Nissan jidousha ribaibaru purann to Nissan jidousha Hanawa kaicho, Carlos Gohn shacho intavyukiroku" (Interview with Yoshikazu Hanawa and Carlos Gohn on

228   *Japan and the Global Automotive Industry*

Nissan revival plan), *Houseidaigaku keieishirin*, vol. 40, no. 3, 2004, p. 59.
5. K. Shimokawa, S. Orihashi, D. Heller, and H. Higashi, "EU kakudai no nakadeno global senryaku no saikouchiku wo hakaru oushuujidousha meika oyobi Nikkei meika no shinndoukou to koujyouchousa" (New trend and the plant field survey of European and Japanese auto companies which pursue reconstruction of global strategy in extension of the EU), *Houseidaigaku keieishirin*, vol. 41, no. 4, vol. 42, no. 1, 2004.

Bibliography

T. Abo, et al. "Amerika ni ikiru nihonnteki seisan shisutemu" (Japanese production system in America), *Toyokeizai Shinposha*, 1991.
T. Fujimoto and K. B. Clark, *Product Development Performance*, Harvard Business School Press, 1991.
K. Shimokawa, "Ajia niokeru nihonjidoshasangyo no kokusaibyungyou no saihyouka" (Reconsideration of international division of labor by Japanese auto industry in Asia), *Kokusai bijinesu kennkyugakkai nennpo*, 1999.
K. Shimokawa, "Ford motor shacho Nick Sierria shi kaikenki" (Interview with Ford President Nick Sierra), *Nikkan Jidosha Shinbun*, December 4, 5, 2002.
K. Shimokawa, "Ushinawareta jyunen' ha norikoeraretaka" (Does Japanese business change overcome "Lost Decade"?), Chuoshinsho, Chuoukouryon shinsha, 2006.
K. Shimokawa and T. Fujimoto, "Shinkyokumenn ni haitta hokubeijidousha shijyo to jidousha meikadoukou no jittaichosa" (North American market in new dimension and field survey of auto maker trend), August 2002.
K. Shimokawa, T. Fujimoto, T. Matsuo, S. Orihashi, H. Katou, and N. Kato, "Global brando senryaku no kyouka to seisan shisutemu kaikaku ni noridashita oushu jidoushameika no doukou to chutouou no kyouka wo hakaru jidoushameika to buhinmeeka no doukou ni tuiteno jittai-chousa" (Trend of European car makers which strengthen global brand strategy and reform of production system, and Japanese car makers which strengthens mid and Eastern Europe), *Houseidaigaku keieishirin*, vol. 40, no. 4, March 2003, vol. 41, no. 1, 2004.
A. Takeishi and T. Fujimoto, "Jidoshasangyo nijyuisseiki eno shinario" (The scenario of the automobile industry in the 21st century), *Seisanseishuppan*, 1994.
A. Takeishi and T. Fujimoto, "Nouryoku kouchiku kyousou" (Competition of capability building), *Chuokoronshinsha*, 2003.

A. Takeishi and T. Fujimoto, "Seisanshisutemu no shinkaron" (Evaluation theory of the production system), *Yuhikaku*, 1997.

"Toyota oyobi Toyota gurupu kigyou no ASEAN jigyotai ni kansuru chou-sahoukokusho" (The Report of Toyota and Toyota Group Company's ASEAN Business), *Meijyodaigaku chiikisangyo shuuseki kennkyusho*, 2006.

8 | The Asian and ASEAN automotive industries in the global era

1. Introduction

As the automobile industry has become increasingly global, the rapidly growing industry in Asia has attracted attention. Asia is now recognized as a prospective growth region for the automobile industry in the twenty-first century, with its potential to be the world's largest automobile market given the huge population (1.4 billion in China, 0.8 billion in India, and 0.5 billion in Association of South-east Asian Nations (ASEAN) countries). The automobile markets in developed countries have reached maturity and have almost no growth potential.

However, although Asia has seen remarkable industrialization and economic growth from the 1980s onwards, steady progress is not always guaranteed – as seen during the currency crisis – and this holds equally true in the automobile industry. The South Korean automobile industry has an overproduction capacity of nearly 1 million cars annually, and automobile production in Thailand once reached 0.6 million per year, but declined by more than half due to the Baht crisis in July 1997.

During the economic crisis, most of the automobile manufacturers reduced production. Now there are signs that the financial order of the Asian region is starting to stabilize and recover. Japanese, European, and US automobile manufacturers have started to increase production in the region again. Sooner or later, it is expected that the automobile industry in Asia will be revived. However, after two years of economic crisis and falling production levels, it is also expected that an innovative system of international divisions of labor will be established after the existing limited system has been re-examined. It was established with a focus on technology transfer, and the production and supply systems were aimed at the domestic markets of each Asian country.[1] It is believed that the currency crisis led to improvements in domestic production of auto parts (because of the high cost of imported parts and improved intra- and inter-regional divisions of labor), while at the same

230

time promoting exports outside the region due to the depreciation of the regional currencies.

This chapter examines the development of the automobile industry in Asia following the currency crisis, which marked a turning point, looking at the presence of Japanese automobile manufacturers in Asia, particularly in terms of direct investment, trends in international labor, the impact on technology transfer, and the auto parts industry.[2, 3]

Before the Asian currency crisis occurred, the strategy of Japanese automobile manufacturers in the Asian markets was to expand international production, especially in ASEAN countries, while establishing a foothold in China. The international divisions of labor linking ASEAN countries, Taiwan, and South Korea was only regionally oriented. Its aim was to develop regional production while contributing to domestic production in each country, in expectation of the development of markets within the region. The underlying idea was to gradually develop international competitiveness through an expansion of international production by AICO (ASEAN Industrial Cooperation), in anticipation of the establishment of AFTA (ASEAN Free Trade Area), which was scheduled in 2003. Companies were not prepared for the rapid price increase of imported parts when currencies declined, or for the export drive for completed cars.

Japanese automobile manufacturers faced two options in the wake of the Asian economic crisis. One was to hold off on expansion until the economic crisis was over. The other was to take aggressive measures to enhance competitiveness in exports by increasing domestic production rates, though this was a little risky. It is quite contrary to trends in the electric and electronics industries, which have made progress in complementary international divisions of labor and are now reinforcing this as part of a global strategy and increasing exports outside the region.

While there will not be any drastic movements for the time being, in the future the way automobile production is organized in Asia will be re-examined, looking at it as a production base with the potential for global development.

2. The presence of Japanese automobile manufacturers in Asia and the history of local production

The presence of Japanese automobile manufacturers in Asia has become more and more significant in various ways. The influence of Japanese automobile manufacturers is most noticeable in Taiwan and ASEAN

Table 8.1 *Automobile market in thirteen Asian countries (units: thousand)*

	94	95	96E	2000E
South-east Asia total	3,526	3,561	3,790	5,800
Korea	1,556	1,556	1,600	2,200
China	1,337	1,403	1,550	2,700
Hong Kong	57	60	60	60
Taiwan	576	542	580	740
ASEAN total	1,202	1,459	1,561	2,165
Thailand	486	572	610	900
Malaysia	200	286	310	400
Indonesia	326	384	400	600
Philippines	103	28	145	240
ASEAN 4 countries	1,116	1,370	1,465	2,040
Singapore	38	42	45	45
Vietnam	28	22	25	50
Myanmar	19	25	26	30
South Asia total	539	739	920	1,500
India	470	629	800	1,300
Pakistan	69	110	120	200
13 Asian countries total	5,266	5,759	6,271	9,365

Note: 95 actual is an estimated total for China, Hong Kong, Vietnam, Myanmar, India, and Pakistan
Source: TED seminar, Mr. Mashu Kato, "Trends and prospects of ASEAN automobile market and automobile/parts industries," September 1995

countries, followed by South Korea. The continental nations of China and India have started technological tie-ups and other projects on a trial basis (see Table 8.1 and Figure 8.1). China has adhered to a policy of accepting only a limited number of newcomers in projects favorable to the three big, three small, and two tiny state enterprises. As to large-scale projects, Japanese automobile manufacturers allowed Volkswagen to get ahead of them with the Shanghai Project. Japanese companies have made progress in production and related technological tie-ups, but do not have major production bases there. However, Daihatsu has established a production base for mini-cars in Tianjin as a joint venture with Tianjin Automotive Industrial Group Company. This production base has given Daihatsu a foothold for opening a factory for small cars and an engine factory. Honda started assembling operations for the Accord at

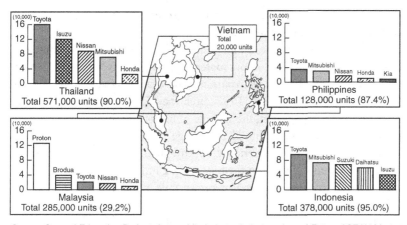

Source: General Education Project, Automobile Industry in Indonesia and Future ASEAN Market, seminar material by Mr. Osamu Masuko, p. 53 (July 1996)

Figure 8.1 Automobile market in five ASEAN countries

the Guangzhou Automotive Industrial Group Company after the French automobile manufacturer Peugeot withdrew. In addition, Honda and Suzuki motorcycle projects are starting to make progress in various locations in China. However, all of these projects are in the so-called seed stages, with another 10–20 years to go.

India has the second largest population following China. Suzuki established a major base in India with an annual production of more than 0.2 million Multi-model type cars, modelled after the Alto mini-car, as a joint venture with Multi Udyog Ltd., and is making profits as a preceding manufacturer. European and US manufacturers have also entered the Indian market, and Toyota and Honda have begun to establish themselves there.

In South Korea, three major automobile manufacturers, Hyundai, Kia, and Daewoo, dominated the market. Production under license, capital and technological tie-ups had long been established between Hyundai and Mitsubishi, Kia and Mazda, and Daewoo and General Motors. However, around 1988, when the Seoul Olympic Games were held, these South Korean manufacturers began to establish systems for their own development and relations with the Japanese manufacturers started to gradually weaken. Since Toyota and Honda had not histori-cally been involved, tie-ups between assemblers had been limited, but parts manufacturers had made quite a few technology tie-ups and joint ventures, especially in sophisticated electronics, press parts, cast parts, engine parts, and underside parts.

The South Korean automobile industry had been trying to enter the world market, and also import materials and parts from Japan, which was a not insignificant cost, particularly when the yen strengthened sharply between 1985 and 1987 after the G5 summit. Despite high costs due to the strong yen, the volume of imports from Japan continued to increase, which contributed to a huge trade deficit between South Korea and Japan. In addition, the South Korean government approved Samsung Group's entry into the automobile industry, putting an end to the domination of the three major automobile manufacturers. This move fueled competition and the total production capacity reached 3.5 million cars per year, an excess of more than 1 million. Then the financial crisis broke out in 1997. In the process of financial and economic reconstruction under strict International Monetary Fund (IMF) supervision, the big financial groups and business exchanges were restructured. Then Kia went bankrupt and fell under legal control in 1997 and Samsung Motors Inc. also went bankrupt. These incidents led to the domination of Hyundai Motor Co. and Daewoo Motor Co. in the South Korean automobile industry. However, Daewoo Motor Co. is now facing turbulence over the issues of dissolution of the group and financial support. Nissan and Mazda used to have ties with the two failed manufacturers but have almost totally backed off, only Mitsubishi maintaining a limited tie-up with Hyundai Motor Co. at the assembly level. South Korea virtually abolished import tariffs on automobiles and opened the way to total liberalization, but Japanese automobile manufacturers' export efforts do not seem to have made very much progress so far.

Therefore, it is not too much to say that ASEAN countries and Taiwan are the only countries in Asia where Japanese automobile manufacturers maintain a strong influence or a presence in the region. Around 90 percent (or over 80 percent) of the cars domestically produced in Taiwan and ASEAN countries are developed by Japanese automobile manufacturers and produced by joint ventures with them.

In Taiwan, 0.44 million cars are produced annually by as many as twelve manufacturers and most of them have been developed by Japanese manufacturers, including Mazda cars produced by Taiwan Ford, the second largest automobile producer in Taiwan. Toyota, Nissan, Mitsubishi, Honda, and Taiwan Ford produced 80 percent of the automobiles.[4] In Taiwan, there are few huge industrial groups, like in South Korea, and many companies have formed joint ventures with Japanese manufacturers. However, there are many owner-operated companies, which prevented joint consolidation against the government's intentions and, unlike South Korea, no manufacturers with large-scale production (over several hundreds of thousands of cars) have been developed in Taiwan.[5] The total investment to Taiwan Ford was NT $555 million, 70 percent of which came from Canada Ford.

Compared with this, the ratio of direct investment by Japanese automobile manufacturers is low. In 1986, Toyota Motor Corp. finally invested, after a request by the Taiwanese government. A total of NT$2 billion was invested into Kuozui Motors and 49 percent came from Japanese companies, 22 percent from Toyota Motor Corp., 25.2 percent from Hino Motors Ltd., and 1.8 percent from Mitsui and Co. Ltd. Among the remaining companies, Nissan Motor Co. invested 25 percent of the total capital of NT$1.6 billion in Yuron Motors, Mitsubishi Motors Corp. and Mitsubishi Corp. invested 15.95 percent and 5.47 percent respectively of NT$667 million in China Motor, and US Honda invested 13.5 percent of NT$4.868 billion in Sanyang Industries.[6]

Seeking entry to the World Trade Organization (WTO), Taiwan reduced the tariffs on European and US cars to 30 percent and imported cars, mainly passenger cars, which account for over 30 percent of the market. The 90 first-tier suppliers and some of the roughly 200 small and medium parts manufacturers in Taiwan have excellent technology and quality. Both public and private sectors in Taiwan have been making efforts to incorporate these suppliers and parts manufacturers into a network of global parts suppliers.[7]

The parts manufacturers of Toyota and Nissan groups entered the market via joint ventures and have been actively carrying out technology transfer. It is possible that Taiwan will become an auto parts supply center for the world in some fields, just as Acer is for personal computers. With its location and given positive developments with the Chinese mainland, Taiwan could develop various automobile-related projects. However, it is uncertain how relations between China and Taiwan will develop after the return of Hong Kong to China. Rather, divisions of labor in ASEAN countries, where Japanese automobile manufacturers have a strong influence, are more likely to be practical.

The ASEAN region, where Thailand, Malaysia, Indonesia, and the Philippines produce 1.4 million cars annually, has been attracting the most attention in Asia, as this region has tremendous potential for demand. As mentioned at the beginning, the Asian currency crisis occurred in the ASEAN region, and caused a decline in the demand for automobiles in 1997. Although this decline in demand was expected to continue for the next two to three years, demand will recover eventually, after these countries implement operational adjustments and restructuring.

Japanese automobile manufacturers have tremendous presence in the ASEAN region, and 90 percent of all cars domestically produced in this region are produced through cooperation with Japanese manufacturers in domestic production and technology transfers.

Toyota and Mitsubishi began operations with SKD (semi-knockdown) as early as the late 1960s and early 1970s in response to requests by local governments for cooperation in domestic production. Today, Toyota and Mitsubishi have the most influence in the ASEAN region followed by Honda, which started with motorcycle production, and Nissan, which is trying to catch up. As far as the automobile industry was concerned, direct investments from Japan were relatively low in ASEAN countries. This is because while ASEAN countries, especially Malaysia and Thailand, implemented positive measures to increase foreign imports in home electrical appliances and electronic equipment such as color televisions, video tape recorders, and air conditioners, they favored domestic production and domestic capital for the automobile industry, so promoted indirect foreign investments for domestic capital rather than accepting direct foreign investments, especially from Japan.

Figure 8.2 shows the expansion of the automobile industry in the ASEAN region. Assembly production, in the form of SKD production, KD (knocked-down) production and CKD (complete-knocked-down) production, has been carried out from the early stages of importing completed cars and repair. The domestic market was protected at the same time. However, although protecting the domestic market has promoted technology transfer and domestic production to a certain extent, production volume was limited and cost penalties were inevitable due to high tariffs on imported parts for domestic production. As a result, there was a high cost dilemma, twice as high as Japanese-made, and lower quality, compared with the international standard. In order to ease this dilemma, ASEAN Complementation (an agreement for reciprocal complementation in automobile production) was concluded among the five founding members of ASEAN in 1969. However, it ended up only as a desk plan since it was difficult to decide which country would produce

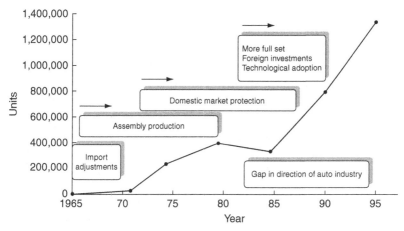

Source: "Small to mid-size finance corporation investigation dept., automobile industry trends in ASEAN and effects on our domestic small to mid-size parts manufacturers," Report by Japan Finance Corporation for Small Businesses, no. 98-1, April 1998

Figure 8.2 Shifts of the automobile manufacturing units of ASEAN and industrial development

which auto parts, due to conflict of interests in auto-parts trading between the countries. In the background lurked the differences in automobile industry policies in each ASEAN country, which emerged in the 1980s.[8] However, the major problem lay in different policy decisions regarding foreign investment in order to promote the introduction of more sophisticated technology for full production of automobiles, and whether they should actively prepare for free trade areas in Asia, especially AFTA (ASEAN Free Trade Area), or protect domestic industries. Through trial and error, ASEAN countries gradually developed local production and technology transfer, and the expansion of domestic markets seemed under way. Then the financial crisis hit Asia.

3. Dividing labor in Asia and technology transfer

The development of complementary divisions of labor in components and parts production among the four major ASEAN countries should not be overlooked when it comes to the automobile industry in the ASEAN region. If production is divided among countries rather than all parts being produced in each country – for example, engines produced in country A, transmissions in country B, and pressed parts in country C – costs will be reduced considerably because of economies of scale. The ASEAN Complementation program to promote divisions of labor for auto-parts production and reciprocal complementation, initiated in the late 1960s, was intended to achieve this.

The complementation plan failed because each country had its own domestic production plan and there was a conflict of interests over allocation of parts to be produced. It was difficult to solve because some countries would have surplus and others would have deficits in the auto-parts trade. Underlying causes of the failure were the low standards, and the different degrees, of industrialization in ASEAN countries.

In the late 1980s, the industrialization of the four major ASEAN countries and domestic automobile production plans started to get on track. The BBC (Brand of Brand Complementation) was started. In this scheme, a specific automobile manufacturer offered reciprocal complementation for parts of a specific brand car, and import tariffs on the parts was considerably reduced. Some manufacturers, such as Toyota, Mitsubishi, and Nissan, started to use this system. This concept of complementary division of labor was expanded to parts and materials among ASEAN countries. AICO (ASEAN Industrial Cooperation) was established as a comprehensive and full-scale reciprocal complementation agreement to respond to the sharp reductions of import tariffs to be implemented under AFTA, scheduled for 2003[9] (see Figure 8.3 and Table 8.2). The ASEAN Secretariat approved BBC projects, while AICO applications required approval of the Ministry of Industry of each country, which delayed implementation of AICO.

The notable point about AICO was that it would help promote divisions of labor and cooperation among parts manufacturers and also help form a network, not only within the region but beyond the region.

AICO came into effect in November 1996, and nineteen companies, mainly Japanese, applied. But none has actually operated under AICO. Thailand approved the AICO application of nine companies, including Japanese automobile manufacturers like Toyota and Honda, auto-parts manufacturers (e.g., Denso Corp.), and home electrical appliance manufacturers (e.g., Matsushita Electric Industrial Co.), as well as Volvo and Goodyear. However, Malaysia and Indonesia did not approve any companies, due to concern about the impact on domestic industries. Later, in 1998, Matsushita and Volvo were given AICO approval.

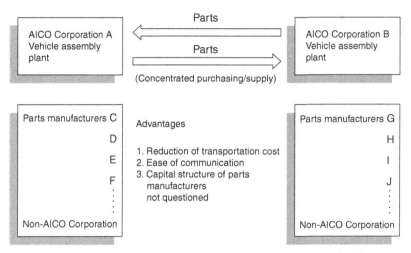

Source: Previous TED seminar, Mr. Fumio Yoshimi, Current Situation of ASEAN Automobile Industry and Strategies of Automobile Manufacturer

Figure 8.3 Complement of AICO arrangements

According to Japanese automobile manufacturers which applied for AICO, each country demanded a foreign currency balance (import–export balance between two countries) from each manufacturer when making the AICO application.

There is no doubt that the basic concept of AICO will greatly contribute to the development of regional labor in the ASEAN region if it functions full scale. However, there are differences in expectations and degrees of domestic automobile production among the ASEAN countries, and the problem of balancing auto-parts trading remains to be solved.[10] The currency crisis in 1997 discouraged many countries from liberalizing trade in important industries; however, if ASEAN countries hold off on trade liberalization for a long time, the ASEAN market will become less attractive due to non-tariff barriers, and direct investments to ASEAN will stagnate. ASEAN will then be unable to compete with China and India in attracting more direct investment. Therefore, though AICO is not functioning at the moment, if the ASEAN economy recovers by the time AFTA and CEPT agreements are established, a production and supply network for auto parts will be established linking Japan, Taiwan, and other countries.

The outlines of the BBC regional reciprocal complementation plans of Toyota and Mitsubishi are shown in Figures 8.4 and 8.5. The

Table 8.2 *Comparison of BBC and AICO plans*

	BBC	AICO
Contents	(1) Expansion of mass production effects (2) Resolve obstacles for the private business plans by reducing high tariffs set to protect the domestic parts industry and reducing the vehicle production cost. This enables support for the distribution of the specific parts of the specific model of the specific brand in the local participating countries.	Promote the establishment of the infrastructure toward the trade deregulation of WTO through the trade/investment expansion in order to enhance the mutual profits and competitiveness in each country for the promotion of economic development in the ASEAN region CEPT adoption was advanced to 2003, thus temporarily adopted the AICO plan in 1996 in order to make adjustments for each ASEAN country for 2003. Also, ASEAN automobile industry is expected to improve in the long term in the aspects of income and technical standards. But the recognition of the necessity of each country to reduce cost by promoting the localization and mutual complements among countries was one of the factors for the advanced adoption
Background	Originated by the AIC approved by the 14th ASEAN Foreign Ministers' Conference in 1981. In 1982, Mitsubishi Automobile Industries proposed to	

Table 8.2 (*cont.*)

	BBC	AICO
	"(1) reduce the import parts tariff to half, (2) consider the import parts as the domestic parts and include in the calculation of the domestic production ratio, when each country mutually accommodates the parts with higher priority in cost." In 1987, at the 3rd Summit, agreement was reached to promote as BBC plan by the Manila Declaration, and in 1988 it was approved and signed at the ASEAN Cabinet Economic Ministers Council.	
Items included	Automobile parts	Finished products/mid-process products/raw material
Applicable term	From October 1988 until the issue of AICO	Until the issue of CEPT (2003)
Applicants	Domestic automobile manufacturers (brand owners)	Manufacturers in each country
Authorizing party	ASEAN office	Industrial ministry in each country

Terms and conditions	• Limited to the automobile parts
	 • BBC products fulfill the regulation of the place of origin by PTA (ASEAN Patent Tariff Agreement).
	   a. Single ASEAN content exceeds 50%
	   b. Cumulative ASEAN content exceeds 60%
	 • Manufactured based on the International Quality Assurance Standards
	 • Competitively priced for the general market place
		• Established in "each ASEAN member country" and operate business
		 • Minimum 30% of country's share
		 • Sharing the material, or corporations cooperate with each other
		 • Corporations conducting business established by multiple participating countries, which cooperate to manufacture AICO products.
		 • Designated parts domestic manufacturing ratio exceeds 40%.
		 • Approved as AICO products when the raw material import CIF amount is less than 60% of the export FOB amount

Table 8.2 (*cont.*)

	BBC	AICO
Benefits	• Domestic manufacturing approval • 50% exemption of the CDK tariff	• To be included in the domestic manufacturing ratio • 0–5% performance tariff is applied (available only for the participating companies which handle AICO approved parts)
Issues	• Advantages and disadvantages become evident for the governments in each country due to their domestic automobile, domestic manufacturing programs. • Each country advocate to produce more value added parts (engines and transmissions), which leads to conflicts. • BBC has the special program for the large automobile manufacturers, thus the early shift to the CEPT is necessary. Also, more opinions are indicated for a program to promote small to mid-size local industries. • After submitting the application to the ASEAN office, opinions of each country's MITI must be asked. Complicated process due to the approval necessary by all ASEAN participating countries	• Each country's pace is not the same. • Approval by the government (of importing and exporting countries) is done simultaneously and the importing and exporting countries need to negotiate. Both government benefits and losses will be evident and conflicts may affect the surrounding industries – for instance, automobile-related industries may experience delay in receiving permits. • In order to balance the trades, it is possible that the CKD package export, which gathers the parts by the parts manufacturers under the control of each country's automobile companies, may not be approved.

Source: Small to mid-size finance corporation investigation dept., previous document, p. 26, as recreated from ASEAN office documents

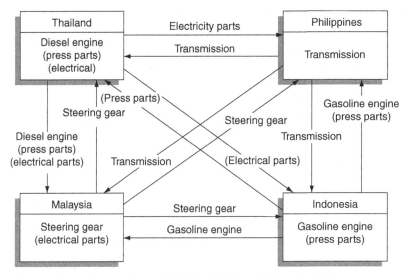

Source: Toyota Motors, Automobile Market in Asia and Oceania, 1990

Figure 8.4 Outline of Toyota's components complementation plan 1990

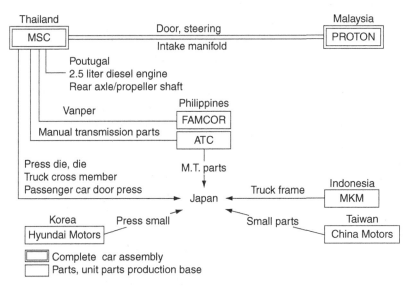

Source: Mitsubishi Research Institute, Automobile Industry Report 1, 1994

Figure 8.5 Outline of Mitsubishi component complementation in ASEAN

currency crisis occurred when operations were starting to shift from BBC to AICO. It is believed that Japanese manufacturers will improve domestic production rates, strengthen the international divisions of labor, and start exporting outside the region sooner or later due to the high cost of imported auto parts from Japan.

Major Japanese automobile manufacturers are also trying to establish full-scale production systems for Asian cars through division of labor, especially in Thailand. Cars produced in this region originally were largely commercial vehicles due to road and traffic conditions in ASEAN countries. For example, Toyota developed an original commercial vehicle model, Kijang, which was mainly produced in Indonesia.[11] However, the prospect of market expansion for passenger cars began to attract attention and production of Asian passenger car models, such as Soluna by Toyota and City by Honda, started, mainly in Thailand.[12]

The BBC requires 50 percent of ASEAN content, and it is imperative to improve local content and regional division of labor as currency rates make it costly to import parts from Japan.[13] Table 8.3 shows the general trend in the amount of imports of major products in Thailand, Malaysia, the Philippines, and Indonesia between 1990 and 1996. According to the figure, during the period up to 1996, the year before the economic crisis, Thailand and Malaysia saw an increase in domestic production rates for each major auto part, while imports from Japan declined considerably. It is inferred that local production of parts and components increased during this period. On the contrary, the Philippines and Indonesia saw an increase in imports, except for certain parts.[14] In Thailand, local production of power trains and engine supplements made progress, reflecting the effect of local production regulations. Meanwhile, import of bodies and accessories increased, probably because demand shifted to various passenger cars with the development of the domestic market.

However, other than bodies and accessories, the progress of domestic production was outstanding in general. Malaysia, thanks to the domestic production policy for national cars, became less dependent on imports in all areas. The Philippines became less dependent on imports of underside, transmission, and steering parts, while imports of power trains, engine supplements, bodies, and accessories were on the rise. This trend implies that demand for high value added passenger cars expanded along with the political stability in the country, while

Table 8.3 *Summary of parts production capability of each country (1990–1996)*

	1990–1996	Individual items
Thailand	Generally localization progressed	• Items other than car body/accessories showed localization. • Improved the production of power train/engine supplement equipment
Malaysia	Localization developed for all items	• Low dependency for import on each item • Even more development in electronic accessories in recent years
Philippines	Localization developed for some items	• Mainly electronic accessories, foot area, transmissions and steering parts • Structure of the car body and accessories is easy to increase imports
Indonesia	Little change	• Space to localize in the power train/ engine supplement equipment • Higher local production capability for the foot area parts

Source: Mid to small-size finance corporation investigation dept., previous report, p. 42

domestic parts production was not making progress. Indonesia did not see much change on the whole, but it is worth noting that local production of engine supplements and power trains lagged behind while domestic production of underside parts made progress.

In conclusion, there are considerable differences in the degree and content of domestic production among countries because each country has a different domestic production policy and is at a different stage in developing its automobile market. In order to develop complementary regional division of labor in the ASEAN region, political adjustments are needed for such issues as tariffs for domestic production and the trade balance. But more importantly, as shown in Table 8.4, intensive production covering the whole region should be carried out by all levels of manufacturers, from finished car manufacturers to parts manufacturers. The economic crisis may have helped promote such intensive production.

Table 8.4 *Summary of intensive production prospects*

Finished vehicles	
Finished vehicle	Possible intensive production at plants other than Proton, larger-scale plants in Thailand and Indonesia
Internally manufactured parts	Cause for the intensive production is high because of the expected mass-production effects with power train and press parts
Parts manufacturers	
Power train / engine supplements	Not many items are duplicated in production except for the belts for engines (current status continues).
Transmissions/steering	Possible intensive production for clutch-related parts and steering wheels
Foot area parts	Wheel and tire production is duplicated in each country. Possible to adjust production centers
Car body/accessories	Automobile glass, seats, windshield wipers, weather strips, anti-vibration rubber, seatbelts, headrests, various trims and instalment panels may have mass-production effects, thus possible for intensive production
Electronic accessories	Possibility for the intensive production for wiring harness lighting equipment for vehicles, electric wires, cable, switch, relay meters, alternators, batteries
Other products	Production of car air conditioners, car audio is duplicated in each country, but mass-production effects are already seen for car audio from outside region exports. Thus, limited possibility for intensive production

Source: as Figure 8.6, p. 44

4. The Asian economic crisis and countermeasures taken by Japanese automobile manufacturers

The Asian economic crisis was triggered by the Thai baht crisis in July 1997 and involved mainly ASEAN countries. Japanese automobile manufacturers were forced to re-examine their strategy of regional complementary divisions of labor and take emergency measures to change direction

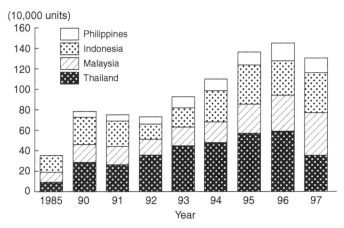

Source: Fourin, Automobile parts industry in South-east Asia, Taiwan, Oceania, various media reports, etc., Ms. Minako Morimoto, "Japanese Automobile Manufacturers Aiming to Establish the New Production Network in ASEAN," Japan Automobile Industry Association, *Jamagazine*, vol. 32–7, p. 6

Figure 8.6 Shifts in automobile sales units in four ASEAN countries

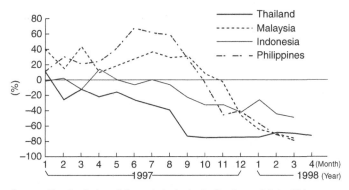

Source: Fourin, Automobile parts industry in South-east Asia, Taiwan, Oceania, various media reports, etc.

Figure 8.7 Comparison of monthly vehicle sales units with the previous year after January 1997

temporarily. Figure 8.6 shows changes in sales volume of automobiles in the four major ASEAN countries up to 1997, and Figure 8.7 shows changes in monthly sales volume in those countries from 1997 to April 1998. According to these figures, the total annual sales volume of automobiles in the four major ASEAN countries was close to 1.5 million

Table 8.5 Trends of Japanese automobile manufacturers after the currency crisis

Production reduction	• Place of origin/temporarily terminated operation • Terminated outsourcing production • Froze the investment plans • Postponed the introduction of the new model
Reduction of employment	• Temporary workers/full-time workers reduction
Measures for sales	• Increase in sales price due to the rise in imported raw materials • Implementation of the sales promotions • Special implementation of auto loans
Local parts manufacturers' support	• Advance payments • Increase in the parts purchasing price • Council to discuss the support measures by cooperative efforts among Japanese finished-automobile manufacturers

(Temporary measures)

Changes of purchasing/ clients	• Promotion of local/regional supply purchasing • Expansion of exports (finished cars/parts)
Financial support for the local corporations	• Increased investment and investment ratio by Japanese companies
Concentration of plants	• Concentrate on the domestic manufacturing center by closing the old plants
Technology/quality system plants	• Implement employee training in Japan • Obtain ISO, etc.

Source: Previous documents, paper by Ms. Minako Morimoto

in 1996 and declined to 1.3 million in 1997. After August 1997, the sales volume declined drastically compared with the period up to July. Compared with the same month in the previous year, the volume declined from –60 percent to –80 percent, a drastic fall. This implies the factory operation rate declined to the level of about 30 percent or 40 percent and the sales volume is believed to have declined by more than half after 1998.

Faced with this crisis, Japanese automobile manufacturers took both short-term and long-term measures (see Table 8.5). Short-term measures included reducing production, temporarily suspending operations, freezing investment plans, postponing the introduction of new models,

		Post-currency crisis			
Background factors	Market size	No growth in ASEAN market (Sufficient production capacity not available domestically) (Room for economical scale)		Growth in ASEAN market (Able to secure a certain level of production capacity domestically)	
	Deregulation	Trade deregulation	Trade deregulation terminated	Trade deregulation	Trade deregulation terminated
Pattern of mutual complements and divisions of work		Promote more active mutual complements of parts in order to obtain mass production effects = intensive production of parts	Concentrate and organize the production centers in each country	Product discrimination work for the finished cars. Divide work to suit the area of expertise of each country rather than the mutual parts complements by the mass-production effects	Do not nurture competitiveness in the long term, which will prevent market growth Do not nurture outside regional export competitiveness
Key points for mutual complements and divisions of work		Which parts can we expect the mass-production effects from? Is there room for the mass-production effects of the finished cars to take place?	–	What are the "areas of expertise" for each country?	–

Source: "Make creation," report by Japan Finance Corporation for Small Businesses, p. 30

Figure 8.8 Prospects of regional mutual complements/divisions of work toward AFTA 2003

reducing the workforce, and increasing prices. Most notably, they also carried out advance payment and purchase price increases and had meetings to discuss joint support measures in order to prevent local parts manufacturers from going bankrupt. This shows that the Japanese manufacturers realized the importance of supporting local parts manufacturers, which they had helped develop, for their post-crisis strategies. While reducing the workforce, they tried to keep skilled workers who played a central role at the workplace, and trained them in Japan. Long-term measures included promoting intra-regional procurement and expanding exports of both finished cars and auto parts outside the region. In addition to these fundamental strategic measures, Japanese companies continued to invest in local corporate bodies and prepare intensive production bases.[15]

The Japanese manufacturers adopted these measures on the assumption that the ASEAN market would eventually grow in the mid to long term and that regional trade liberalization would continue to progress. Figure 8.8 illustrates the prospects for regional reciprocal complementation and the structure of the divisions of labor leading up to the establishment of AFTA in 2003. The section "Post-currency crisis" shows the situation after the crisis and suggests that approaches should be considered from two aspects in the face of stagnant market growth: when trade liberalization makes progress and when trade liberalization gets strangled. It also suggests that these post-crisis approaches are to be considered in anticipation of the growth of the ASEAN market in the post-AFTA era and trade liberalization. A competitive edge in exports should be achieved not only through the progress of reciprocal complementation in auto-parts production with mass-production effects but also through specialized division of labor according to the forte of each country.

5. The outlook for division of labor in Asia after the economic crisis

There are interesting differences in how the electric appliance and electronics industry and the automobile industry engaged in international division of labor during the Asian economic crisis. These differences are attributed to their structural differences in pursuing strategies in Asia.

The great difference in unit price and the difference in degrees of improvement in infrastructure caused a gap in the scale of these markets leading up to the crisis. The market for electric appliances and electronics was growing while the market for automobiles was just about to grow. Therefore, the degree of damage inflicted by the economic crisis was quite different between these two industries. Since the electric appliance and electronics industry had a certain degree of market scale and some products were strongly export-oriented, the industry incurred relatively little damage. The automobile industry, meanwhile, was investing in factories with a view to expanding production when it was hit head on by the economic crisis.

The electric appliance and electronics industry had switched from import substitution in the early stages to export-oriented production relatively quickly. This and the expansion of the market for electric appliances and electronics products in Asia helped considerably. The advancement of set makers, or assemblers, into Asian countries, including parts manufacturers, was carried out in a relatively coordinated way. Since automobiles are sophisticated and complicated, transfer of electronics-related or precision manufacturing-related parts and sophisticated parts and materials, such as metal molds and rough casting materials, tended to lag behind. So local assembly and domestic production of parts did not advance smoothly or in a balanced way. Furthermore, since production in the electric appliance and electronics industry had been transferred relatively smoothly, the industry was able to shift to high-tech fields, such as high-definition televisions and information appliances, in order to alleviate the hollowing out of the industry. This helped promote production separation transmitted through a kind of horizontal division of labor. This might be achieved in the automobile industry in the future, but it would have been difficult to switch to horizontal division of labor under current conditions to the same extent as the electric appliance and electronics industry.

It is undeniable that the economic crisis hampered the development of regional division of labor for Japanese automobile manufacturers in the ASEAN region. The crisis happened just when the industry was about to see growing demand for automobiles in the region and the emergence of a fully fledged market for public consumption, like the one for the electric appliance and electronics manufacturers, toward the year 2000. In addition, international division of labor on a global scale, involving China, was not yet developed in the automobile industry. In the midst of the economic crisis, many of the Japanese factories in Thailand, Indonesia, and Malaysia were forced to introduce temporary closures and reduce production. These countries were due to become the core of division of labor in the ASEAN region, but such division of labor now had to be postponed.

However, there are signs of recovery in automobile production in Asia, especially in the ASEAN region, along with overall recovery from the economic crisis. During the two years of recession, though still insufficient, gradual progress can be seen in reforms of the financial system, transparency of the business of industrial groups, elimination of special enterprises, and liberalization of entry of foreign capital. This region still has great potential demand for automobiles just as it had for electric appliances. Besides, the economic crisis also made Japanese automobile manufacturers realize that it was risky to rely on the automobile market of only one country, so strategies focussed on international division of labor will continue.

The conflict of interests over trade in auto parts, deciding which parts were to be allocated to which country, was the biggest impediment to dividing component production labor regionally. However, since the schedules for AFTA and CEPT toward 2003 are agreed, the problem should be solved eventually. At the moment, Thailand is playing a central role and the issue is now centered on adjusting interests between Malaysia, which prioritizes its national interests and national manufacturers, and the most powerful ASEAN country, Indonesia. However, in the twenty-first century, they will be forced to give up their minor differences in order to accomplish a common goal.

Another impediment to dividing labor across the region was that auto-parts technology transfer did not reach the local, lower-end suppliers. During the recession, support was provided for local suppliers, but smaller suppliers with no competitive margins were forced out of business through restructuring. This put the focus on production recovery while improving competitiveness in cost and quality. The currency crisis brought the prospect of an advantage to local producers due to a substantial competitive edge in exports and the rise in costs of imported parts and materials, and this made it imperative to shore up parts suppliers at the lower end. The economic crisis also brought a kind of strategic turning point, switching local production from domestic-oriented to export-oriented.

Of course, the currency conditions favorable to exports do not directly lead to cost, quality, and technology meeting international standards. In order to enhance competitiveness in exports, it is essential to improve workers' skills. Honda and Suzuki sent several hundred local workers from their factories in Thailand to their Japanese factories for six months' training while they cut back on factory operations in Thailand. This policy had mid- and long-term aims, to enhance competitiveness in exports and to prepare for international division of labor. Recovering from the Asian economic crisis, preparations for reinforcing regional international division of labor are under way, with the ASEAN region as the core but with long-term plans for division of labor on a global scale.

6. The automobile industry in Thailand, an emerging global production base

The automobile market in Thailand experienced an extreme drop in production, from a maximum of 580,000 cars in 1996 to 130,000 in 1998, but it recovered to 400,000 in 2002 and is expected to recover to the maximum level of the past (see Figure 8.9). Currently, more than

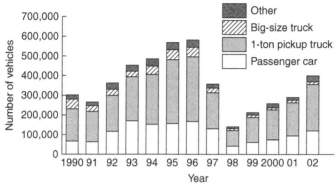

Source: MMC City Pole material

Figure 8.9 Transition of the automobile market in Thailand

200,000 cars are exported from Thailand annually, and this is likely to increase.

In response to such a situation, the Japanese automobile makers that had entered Thailand changed their basic strategies dramatically, going from a strategy of cooperating with Thailand to produce cars domestically and placing Thailand as a labor base within ASEAN, to a strategy that aimed to build Thailand into an important base for global business.

During the 1997 economic crisis, Thailand experienced a large fall in production and many plants were closed. The leading automobile makers guaranteed the employment of full-time workers while firing many term workers. Training for full-time workers was conducted in Japan, or by off-JT through collaboration between the Japanese and Thai governments. As a result, the retention rate of mid-level executives, skilled workers, and other important workers improved and their absentee rate decreased, while wage and salary costs were lowered because of the recession. Some makers and suppliers also restructured their plants. In addition to output cuts, exports were expanded in order to prop up the availability ratio of plants. This was helped by the exports of finished cars, KD parts, and components, which were favored by the cheap baht. Though there were many complaints about the quality of their products, this taught the workers a lesson about the difficulty of working in an international market, and improving quality was emphasized along with the need to expand exports.[16]

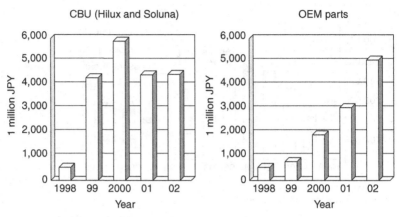

Source: Materials supplied by Thai Toyota

Figure 8.10 Export performance of Thai Toyota

In Thailand in the 1990s, the local content ratio of parts expanded and many Japanese suppliers expanded their business. The number of local suppliers increased and their technical levels and supply systems for materials and intermediate goods improved. Taking this situation as an opportunity, European and US automobile makers and parts makers expanded their businesses in Thailand. As a result, the ASEAN automobile industry became concentrated in Thailand and the infrastructure of the parts industry improved. This continued even after the crisis in 1997, and the local content ratio of parts increased after the abolition of nationalization control in 2000, surpassing 80 percent.

The international division of labor mandated by the AICO, which had stalled because of the 1997 crisis, began to be re-established, and Japanese automobile makers accelerated their use of the scheme. Table 8.5 and Figure 8.10 demonstrate how Thailand was seen as a global production site in the division of labor. A representative example is the IMV project conducted by Thai Toyota, with the aim of completion in August 2004. This was a quite ambitious project which aimed to use Thailand as a global production base for Hilux-level small-size MPVs, and to export finished cars to eighty countries and CKDs to nine countries. A total of 450,000 of the exported cars were to be assembled all over the world, and 180,000 of them were to be manufactured in Thailand (see Tables 8.6, 8.7, and 8.8). Without waiting for the completion of the IMV project, each automobile maker devoted its

Table 8.6 *A list of export destinations of Thai Toyota*

OEM parts (for Toyota headquarters, CKD plants)	Japan, Malaysia, Indonesia, the Philippines, Kenya, South Africa, etc.
Spare parts	Australia, Singapore, Hong Kong, New Zealand, the Philippines, Brunei, etc.
Engines (from STM)	Japan, Malaysia, Indonesia, the Philippines, New Zealand
Hilux	Australia, Laos, Cambodia, the Philippines
Soluna	Singapore, Brunei, Sri Lanka, Indonesia, the Philippines (from April 2003)
Tooling (die, jig)	Australia, Malaysia, Indonesia, the Philippines, Turkey, Taiwan, France

Source: Materials supplied by Thai Toyota

Table 8.7 *Thai Toyota – outline of IMV project*

Entire shift of control of Hilux manufacturing in HINO automobiles, Hamura plant, to Thailand

Establishment in Thailand in August 2004, then establishment of CKD base
Export finished cars to 80 countries, CKD to 9 countries (including Argentina, South Africa, Indonesia – currently only to Australia. The number of specifications largely increased from 57 to 282).
*450,000 cars all over the world (180,000 in Thailand). Twofold increase in the number of the cars, ten-fold for export, and eight-fold for OEM parts
Setup of IMV model
IMV1: B cab, IMV2: C cab, IMV3: D cab, IMV4: SUV, IMV5: Kijang, subsequent (manufactured in Indonesia)

Source: Materials supplied by Thai Toyota

newest models to Thailand. For example, Honda started producing the Accord and Civic simultaneously around the world, Toyota began producing cars loaded with the newest common-rail technology in diesel engines, Isuzu introduced a new model cab consisting of three partition-style frame chassis pickup trucks, and GM began using Thailand as its production site for Opel's newly developed MPV Zafira. The Thai automobile industry, outgrowing its crisis, is thus developing into a global production site.

Table 8.8 *Thai Toyota – contents of IMV project*

A huge investment → received approval from BOI at the zone 3 level. Reduced the initial cost by 30%
Six important points: Local procurement, moulding ability, development, IMV-Q, regulation-certified schedule, IS (IT) Established Thai Virtual Company (Thai-VC), and allocated 16 selected Thai staff to "IMV control room" as specialists Countdown board: to see the progress of each theme at one glance Conducted supply-chain activities for the first time overseas Purposes are to compose a database for crisis control and to flush out the problems of rectifying supply chains Implemented also with Thai Denso, Thai Hino, Saiam Thai

Source: Materials supplied by Thai Toyota

Table 8.9 *Thai Toyota – self-support project (a part of IMV project)*

Improving merits of plants as a way to respond to the increase of complications and changes of production, which co-exist with diversification of points of destination
Giving a five-step evaluation in comparison to the level of Toyota headquarters in the eight areas of management, manufacturing, quality, cost, safety, manufacturing control, distribution, and maintenance Mechanism to improve effectively toward the IMV project in 2004 Lead by Motomachi plant. Conducted in Indonesia and Thailand Try not to be swayed only by figures

Source: Materials supplied by Thai Toyota

7. Conclusion

The development of the automobile industry in Taiwan, ASEAN, Korea, and other Asian countries cannot be explained without mentioning its relationship to the Japanese automobile industry and parts makers. European and US makers also paid attention to Asia and some automobile makers in Korea, Taiwan, the Philippines, and Thailand tried affiliations with European and US makers. But

European and US makers placed more importance on competition in North American and European markets, because they decided that it was meaningless to focus on Asian markets where a quick profit could not be expected. Only Japanese automobile makers tried hard in ASEAN countries. When almost all of these efforts had started to prove fruitful, Asia was hit by the economic crisis of 1997, and this changed Japanese automobile makers' strategies in Asia enormously. In a sense, the economic crisis prompted a movement toward large economic change and a structural adjustment in shifting to the globalization of Asian economies. With this, the automobile industry had to shift to a strategy of building a more global strategic base, with Thailand providing a typical example.

Japanese automobile makers have had a long relationship with Asian markets. From the early 1990s, industrialization, especially in ASEAN, has been significant and Asian countries are becoming a dominant profit source, next to advanced countries, for some makers. During this period of progress the Asian economic crisis took place, and Mitsubishi Motors Corporation, for example, suffered from a big deficit of consolidated accounting. Thus, Japanese automobile makers have been forced to take a bold decision for developing ASEAN production toward a global strategic base. Furthermore, a major problem occurred during this strategic changeover: the appearance of China as a great country for automobile production.

Since its entry into the WTO, China's presence in Asia's economy is growing with every passing year. China is also taking aggressive steps in home electronics, electronic devices, and two-wheel vehicles using its low wage levels. It has improved its industrial and transport infrastructure and is not only increasing exports but also bringing in foreign investment from Japan, Korea, and other advanced countries. China is thus having a big impact on the allocation of production bases and the international division of labor in Asia. Competition and a prosperous co-existence with China is a pressing necessity for ASEAN countries.

Measures to attract industries to China, with its cheap wages and abundant labor force, have had a big impact on Japanese home electronics, electronic-device makers, and other related parts makers, and this has influenced the division of labor in ASEAN. For example, the allocation of production bases among makers has changed in Malaysia and Thailand, and a shift to China is occurring in labor-intensive fields. In ASEAN, vertical specialization was the main international division of labor for home electronics, electronic devices, and their parts. But the re-allocation of production bases and horizontal specialization have started because of the rise of China.

Will car manufacturing in ASEAN face the same situation as home electronics and electronic devices because of the growth of China? To answer this question, it is important to consider how the Chinese automobile industry will obtain its competitiveness in exports and how the automobile industry differs from home electronics and electronic devices. As to China's competitiveness in exports, it will need some time to reach international competitiveness since it needs to learn the technologies that are related to cars – technologies that are progressing rapidly, including the area of environment-related technology. China also needs to improve the infrastructure of its parts industry. Furthermore, unlike home electronics and electronic devices, the automobile industry requires large investments and is not labor-intensive, so it is difficult to shift to China only because of low wages. Technology and the industrial infrastructure which have been accumulating over many years in Thailand and other ASEAN countries are not easily shifted.

The economic crisis in 1997, globalization, and global restructuring caused a turning point for the automobile industry in Asia and ASEAN. The appearance of China as a significant country for autos produced a major shock for, and applied pressure to, other Asian countries. Movements in Asia for the future will be decided by how Japanese and Korean automobile makers build Asian strategies, while some makers may affiliate with European and US makers. The biggest issue is how to make an approach to China, which is capable of becoming the world's largest market, while still putting a lot of work into the globalization of the ASEAN automobile industry.

Notes

1. C.K.K. Koko (Small to mid-size Finance Corporation) Research Dept., "Automobile industry trends in ASEAN and effects to our domestic small to mid-size parts manufacturers," Chusho Koko Report, no. 98–1, April 1998.
2. C.K.K. Koko, "Japanese small to mid-size companies go through the economic crisis in Asia," report by Japan Finance Corporation for Small Businesses, no. 99–2, July 1999.
3. K. Kitamura, *Advancement of Industrial Structure in East Asia and Japanese Industry*, Asia Economic Research, 1997.

4. M. Kawakami, "Capital and technological introduction from Japanese corporations in the Taiwan automobile industry," *Asia Economy*, vol. 36, no. 11, 1995.
5. T. Hayashi, "Development and international divisions of labor for the automobile industry in East Asia," *Economic Management Theories*, vol. 8, no. 1, 2, March 1989, Yachiyo Gakuin University.
6. K. Ishiro, "Current situation and parts supply of NIES equipment industry," *Asia Economic Research*, 1991.
7. K. Shimokawa, "Taiwan automobile industry in the transition phase," *The Economist*, July 24, 1990.
8. K. Shimokawa, "Accelerating Asia and ASEAN strategy," *Nikkan Automobile Newspaper*, May 23, 1995.
9. K. Shimokawa, "Development of direct investment and international divisions of labor of Japanese automobile industry in the Asia region," *Keiei Shirin*, vol. 35, no. 3, October 1999.
10. K. Shimokawa, "Starting the ASEAN Automobile Association," *Nikkan Automobile Newspaper*, July 27, 1997.
11. K. Shimokawa, "Summary of visit to the Toyota Astro," *Nikkan Automobile Newspaper*, August 6, 1996.
12. K. Shimokawa, "Background of the Asian car," *Nikkan Automobile Newspaper*, March 20, 1995.
13. K. Shimokawa, "Dark and bright side of the ASEAN automobile market," *Nikkan Automobile Newspaper*, May 23, 1995.
14. Ibid.
15. K. Shimokawa, "Asian economic crisis and the Japanese automobile industry," *Nikkan Automobile Newspaper*, February 9, 1998.
16. K. Shimokawa, "Afterward Asian International Division of Labour," *Nikkan Automobile Newspaper*, November 22, 2000.

9 | China's automotive industry in the global era, Japanese auto makers, and their China strategies

1. Introduction

China, which joined the WTO around the millennium, has rapidly modernized and industrialized in recent years. In fact, China's development has been so great that it has been called "the factory of the world," and its automotive industry is about to undergo change, too. The Chinese automobile market is expanding quickly and total production has reached 5 million. Sooner or later, domestic demand will increase beyond 10 million. Therefore, China will become the main field of global competition.

One of the key factors for the global restructuring of the world's automotive industry at the end of the twentieth century was the business strategies in Asia, especially in China, which has the potential to be the world's biggest market. However, there are still many obstacles and problems to be overcome before China becomes the world's biggest automotive market and automobile-producing country. These are macro and micro problems, including problems of how to tolerate the social allocation of resources and personal mobility, including traffic, environmental and energy issues, as a social system.

China has become one of the leading producer nations for appliances, electronic devices, personal computers, and two-wheelers surprisingly quickly, and, depending on the product, has even become the world number one. However, in order to succeed in the automotive industry, you need the ability to construct complicated parts, advanced technologies for electronic devices, and information and communications, and also extremely advanced technologies for design, development, and production. There is still a question of whether China will become a leading automobile manufacturing country, notwithstanding its success in appliances and two-wheelers. There is also the question of whether having the world's biggest population of 1.3 billion means that China will be the world's largest automotive market.

What we must acknowledge, in order to answer these questions, is that China has been run under a socialist planned economy, which is different from other developing countries in Asia. This tradition still exists, despite the path to reform and opening up initiated by Deng Xiaoping, and the contradiction in being a country with a socialist market economy, between the public position and reality, goes unchallenged.

In spite of this, China has made rapid changes and development since it joined the WTO, and the acceptance of foreign investment and the reform of the state-owned enterprises are resulting in dramatic progress. Other completely new movements, such as the entry of local private enterprises into the automotive industry, are beginning to emerge. In this chapter, we will examine China's existing automotive industry and its related policies. We will study how participation in the WTO has changed things, and what kinds of strategies Japanese automotive makers are adopting in order to approach the Chinese market. Finally, we will examine what China's automotive industry might look like in the future.

2. The automotive industry and auto industrial policies in China

China's automotive industry was formed during the honeymoon period of the former Soviet Union and the People's Republic of China. Though an automotive industry existed in the industrial city of Shenyang, in former Manchuria, and in other industrial cities in the north-east part of China,[1] the main facilities were removed during occupation by the former Soviet Union, just after Japan's defeat in the Second World War. The former Soviet Union started mass production of big and medium-size trucks with technical assistance and facilities provided by Ford and other US companies before the Second World War. Then, the former Soviet Union shifted its mass-production technology for mainly trucks to state-owned automotive factories in Changchun, Beijing, and other places. To understand the subsequent development of China's automotive industry, we should acknowledge that China adopted not only the style of the former Soviet Union, in which mass-production factories were concentrated at large-scale bases, but also another style of automotive production, which was to place repair yards in many local areas.[2]

In the 1960s, the ideological conflict between China and the former Soviet Union developed into political conflict. As a result, technical assistance from the Soviet Union stopped, the technicians returned home, and the relationship between the two countries was broken off. Before long, China entered the era of the Cultural Revolution and the People's Commune. The idea of self-reliance and the People's Commune system were linked, with people's communes having their own town factories and rural industries, and the automotive industry developed into a system of small units. The principles of self-reliance were emphasized in the No.1 Automaker Factory in Changchun and other large factories, and the aim was to develop technologies independently. Automotive production was considered to have a deep connection with combat vehicles and airplanes, so factories were moved to remote areas in preparation for war against the Soviet Union. This is why the No.2 Automaker Factory, later called Dongfeng Automotive Company, appeared in the mountains, in areas like Shi Yan in Hubei. Though automotive production was still conducted in major cities like Beijing, Nanjing, and Chongqing, and in rural provinces, the scale was small.

The Chinese automotive industry thus had three periods: the period of establishment, in which China depended on technical assistance from the former Soviet Union; the period of generation, in which large trucks and buses were produced under the planned economy; and the period of self-reliance. In the self-reliance period, though it was still tied to the legacy of the previous period, dual structures existed. One was closely related to the rural industry, in which two-wheelers, three-wheelers, and vehicles were used both as cars and agricultural machines, and the other structure was the existence of the state-owned large enterprises, which had started in the period of generation.[3]

The Cultural Revolution ended in 1977. China shifted to reform and opening up under Deng Xiaoping, and a socialist market economy was called for. However, the automotive industry, which was combined with the defense industry, was put under the control of both the central government and provincial governments in the country's planned economy. Being under the control of the government meant that the production models and the number of state-owned automotive enterprises were decided by government plans, and as a result, the automobiles produced were bought up by state organizations or similar corporate organizations. This trade practice from the period of the national enterprises remains in China, and was why China's demand for automobiles at that time came mainly from corporations. As long as this practice existed, the national enterprises did not need to find their own sales, knowing that all of the automobiles in their production quota would be bought. There was no competitive pressure, so models were not renewed or changed very often, and progress in quality was slow.[4]

China's route to reform and opening up was well established by the 1980s, and the Chinese government naturally tried to fix China's lag in technology and quality in the automotive industry. The technology imported from the former Soviet Union was deteriorating, and the Chinese government realized that its tradition of technology carried out under self-reliance, which later was linked to problematic imitation technology, could not foster an automotive industry suitable for the world market. As a result, the Chinese government promoted a technical shift by approaching the automobile makers of Europe, the US, and Japan. They also tried to operate businesses by joint venture with foreign enterprises which were willing to make a serious investment in China under carefully considered conditions and which could be operated without losing independence – in other words, within such a business range that China would not lose control over the majority of shares.

The transfer of technologies was conducted with technical support from European, US, and Japanese automobile makers. Technical cooperation and transfer were established in various areas under license, including diesel engines, power trains, casting, forging, machine processing, and electronic parts. At the same time, licensed production of commercial vehicles, especially middle and small trucks, was conducted. Japanese automotive makers and parts makers cooperated in various aspects, believing in the potential of the Chinese market.[5] However, any technological cooperation during the 1980s and 1990s had to pass strict examination and receive permission from China's central government. At that time, since China was extremely lacking in foreign currencies, big projects were difficult to establish. Therefore, technology was licensed in exchange for permission to import certain trucks and buses to China, as a way of combining trade and technology, and other barter trades were conducted.[6]

China's second full-scale joint venture with a foreign company was that set up between the Shanghai Automotive Company and Volkswagen of the former West Germany. This project started as a small joint venture between the Shanghai, a small company, and VW.[7] However, direct negotiations between Helmut Kohl, Chancellor of the former West Germany, and Deng Xiaoping, General Secretary of China's communist party at that time, took place when Kohl visited China and the project acquired "national" status. It was begun in 1985, and the government of the former West Germany guaranteed the investment made by VW. The biggest feature of this project was the launch of the full-scale production of passenger cars. Until then, most of China's automotive production was limited to trucks and buses, and there were no passenger cars except those for the use of some party and government leaders, like the "Red Flag." The Shanghai Automotive Company was started with 50–50 co-funding with VW, and the company grew as an automobile maker specializing in passenger cars, for which demand was increasing in China, without losing its current status as a state-owned enterprise. For VW, this project was like killing two birds with one stone. VW utilized Santana's old model from 1983 as well as the Santana model, which was developed and produced by a VW subsidiary company, Brazil VW.[8] VW also shifted plant and equipment to China which had become useless after stopping local production at Westmoreland, in North America, in order to concentrate production in Mexico. By 2001, Shanghai VW could produce more than 200,000 Santana cars annually. From the latter 1980s to the 1990s, Shanghai VW almost monopolized the increasing number of taxis and other demand for corporate cars, and the company became number one in the profit ranking for foreign companies investing in China.

However, the success of Shanghai VW did not last. By 2000, foreign investors and private companies were permitted to start producing passenger cars, and Shanghai VW's market share has been decreasing ever since. This is because old models, even for popular cars, are no longer desirable in modern China; new and luxury models have become popular. Because of this, Shanghai VW built a second factory and began producing the more upmarket Passat.[9]

China's reform has had several effects on the Chinese automotive industry. One of these is that automobile makers shot up everywhere in response to inconsistent adoption of policies to nurture the automotive industry at national and local levels; another is that market mechanisms have been introduced into state-owned enterprises. Local government protection of the automotive industry resulted in as many

as 118 companies across the country and problems caused by overlapping investment. The introduction of market mechanisms can be seen
in the example of the First Auto Works and Dongfeng Automotive
Company. This group conducted its own product development and
started a kind of development competition in order to renovate obsolete models for trucks. It also moved away from following its production allocation and began to compete for sales by setting up a division
for sales and services by the end of the 1980s.[10]

Consequently, in 1987 the Chinese government came up with a
policy of limiting and combining the existing production bases for
passenger cars. The aim was to achieve economy of scale as soon as
possible. A policy known as "Three Big and Three Small" called for
three makers for large cars and three makers for small cars. This
policy aimed to concentrate the production of large and small passenger cars into a total of six auto makers: First Auto Mobile Works,
Second Automobile Works (currently called the Dongfeng Motor
Company), and Shanghai Automotive Company for large cars; and
Beijing Automotive, Tianjin Automotive, and Guangzhou, for small
passenger cars. The latter three collaborate with foreign makers, under
local government initiatives. This policy of "Three Big and Three
Small" soon became "Three Big and Three Small with two smallest"
as two makers for light, or smallest, cars were included, but it failed
to halt the appearance of local automotive enterprises; more comprehensive polices for the automotive industry were needed. In the
same year, the Chinese government hammered out a policy to localize
parts production for passenger cars in parallel with the policy of
"Three Big and Three Small," which aimed to limit the number of
production bases for passenger cars. In 1996, a policy of "the strategy
for developing China's automotive parts" was established. This policy
was to adopt a preferential tariff complying with a localization ratio
of sixty kinds of major parts, which were chosen for localizing first
in order to stimulate the domestic parts industry.[11]

In 1994, the "policy for the automotive industry" was decided on,
on the basis of the ninth-term five-year plan (9–5 plan) instituted by
the State Planning Commission. The outline of this policy was (1) to
group and intensify the automotive industry (reduce the 120 makers
to 8–10 groups by 2000), (2) to promote the personal purchasing of
cars in order to make passenger cars the pillar of the automotive
industry, (3) to limit production of passenger cars to 0.15 million

units and institute minimum production of small commercial vehicles
at 0.1 million units annually, (4) to allow foreign capital investment
up to 50 percent, and (5) to institute an incentive measure for localization which reduces the import tariff of parts depending on the
localization index.[12]

The "policy for the automotive industry" based on the 9–5 plan is
epoch-making in the following ways. With this plan, the personal
ownership of cars was promoted for the first time and, in order to
achieve this, a positive effort was made to have the production of
passenger cars act as the pillar for development of the automotive
industry. Furthermore, in order to promote the production of passenger cars, capital import was allowed to a large extent. The acceptance
of individual car ownership meant that the governmental attitude
toward individual car ownership had been revised. Until then, car
ownership was considered too luxurious and too early from the
point of view of China's economic development level and the international trade balance. In China, crude oil was an important export
product even around the time when reform and opening up was in
progress in the 1980s, but as China's industrialization developed,
China became an importer of crude oil, and it has become a main
importing country for crude oil since then. However, at least until the
first half of the 1990s, there was no way to allow personal ownership
of cars in view of the trade balance, since such personal ownership
would increase the consumption of oil dramatically. Furthermore,
since the roads, traffic control, and other transportation infrastructure
were not ready in urban locations, there was a concern that traffic
accidents and other social confusion would increase if the personal
ownership of cars rose significantly. This was one of the reasons why
the Chinese government hesitated to promote ownership. However,
because of industrialization and the economic development of China,
the trade balance largely improved and the government judged that it
could see daylight even if the import of crude oil increased. There was
also a prospect for further investment in the transportation infrastructure. The government officially recognized that it was important to
emphasize the production of passenger cars for individual use in order
to promote personal ownership of cars, and to achieve this a wide
range of foreign investment was required. Table 9.1 shows a summary
of China's leading automotive enterprises in 1993, and the main data
for the automotive industry before 2001.

Table 9.1 *China's leading groups of companies around 1993 – the main data of the automotive industry and the data after that*

Summary of the leading groups of companies

	Number of companies (factories)	Number of workers	Production units (passenger cars)	Main business partners
First Auto Works	12 (3)	118,187	177,769 (29,924)	Nissan, Mitsubishi, Hino, VW
Dongfeng Automotive Company	11 (5)	128,260	231,155 (5,062)	Nissan Diesel, Citroen
Chongqing auto maker	16 (6)	71,866	18,240 (0)	Steyr, Daimler, Puch
Nanjing auto maker	10 (2)	27,425	71,286 (0)	Iveco
Beijing auto maker	22 (5)	43,166	125,084 (13,809)	Chrysler
Tianjin auto maker	59 (5)	43,977	107,652 (47,550)	Daihatsu
Shanghai auto maker	28 (2)	44,814	102,342 (100,001)	VW

Table 9.1 (*cont.*)

Main data

	Production		Newly registered		Imports		Holding	
	Passenger car	Business car	Passenger car	Business car	Passenger car	Business and other cars	Passenger car	Business car
1960	98	22,476	–	–	76	22	–	–
1970	196	86,970	–	–	–	–	133,000	480,000
1980	5,418	216,870	60,000	238,131	1,459	25,087	60,000	900,000
1992	161,745	904,997	160,000	837,000	106,000	30,700	1,839,303	5,177,378
1993	229,661	1,081,800	223,000	948,000	199,765	111,944	2,859,800	5,316,000
1994	247,631	1,090,900	248,000	1,073,000	178,210	102,865	n.a.	n.a.
1997	481,611	1,096,287	481,611	1,096,287	33,305	15,162	5,319,074	6,871,828
1998	465,139	1,142,572	418,917	1,064,863	24,331	14,933	6,548,324	6,644,710
1999	570,000	1,234,500	570,410	1,181,184	19,953	15,239	7,402,307	7,127,106
2000	604,677	1,464,392	721,463	1,476,205	21,620	21,620	7,508,000	11,817,900
2001	717,190	1,641,352	701,602	1,629,581	n.a.	n.a.	8,537,333	6,355,000
2002	1,101,696	2,185,108	1,126,029	2,122,029	70,520	55,828	12,023,679	8,507,998
2003	2,018,875	2,424,811	1,971,601	2,419,205	103,110	66,228	n.a.	n.a.
2004	2,316,262	2,754,265	2,326,492	2,744,569	116,259	57,376	n.a.	n.a.
2005	3,078,153	2,629,535	n.a.	n.a.	n.a.	n.a.	n.a.	n.a.

Source: Nikkan Jidousha Shimbun-Sha, *Handbook for the Automotive Industry*, Bulletins of 1996, 2001, 2002

In the 9–5 plan, the acceptance of personal ownership of cars, the promotion of passenger car production, and capital import had a significant meaning in the history of Chinese automotive industrial policy. But these measures were not sufficient in themselves to trigger a drastic increase in car ownership in China. The basic infrastructure was needed, including tax and registration systems, sales finance, a service system, and sales networks, and until it was ready, personal ownership of cars increased only slowly. Even several years ago, more than 60 percent of the total demand for automobiles in China was not for personal use. Though new projects with imported capital have been approved since 1997, this has not spurred the production of passenger cars. Therefore, although the 9–5 plan brought political changes, the original aim to concentrate the automotive industry after it had been stimulated by the full-scale production of passenger cars was not achieved.[13]

China's entry into the WTO in 2001 was not taken into account when the 9–5 plan was proposed. The 10–5 plan (the tenth-term five-year plan), which was proposed in 2001, was the first five-year plan since opening up that considered participation in the WTO. This 10–5 plan adhered to conventional policy for the automotive industry, but at the same time it clearly reflected the promotion of competition and policies for opening up China to the outside. This 10–5 plan set five agendas as its political goals:[14]

(1) To actively import capital, while trying to increase technology and to accelerate market reorganization.
(2) To switch policies from the protection of domestic industry to the promotion of competition by abolishing the regulations on nationalization and by bringing down tariffs.
(3) To reduce the existing 116 companies to 2 or 3 "big-enterprise groups."
(4) To promote and develop economical passenger cars with emission of 1300cc or under.
(5) To implement new technology, mainly technology for the environment, electronics, and safety.

With the 10–5 plan, the aim was to rearrange the organizational structure of the industry with the big enterprise groups as its core, while adopting guiding principles of maintaining the opening-up policy in collaboration with foreign capital and accelerating independent development and expansion. The aim was also to develop the automotive industry as a pillar industry (strategic industry for the Chinese national economy before 2010). Its first step was to take the production of passenger cars to 1.1 million units out of the total production number of 3.2 million units, and to aim for demand of 1.1–1.2 million units of passenger cars out of the total of 3.1–3.2 million cars by 2005. If the goals were achieved, the total production of the automotive industry would account for 600 billion Yuan, and 1 percent of GDP.[15] However, this numerical goal was upwardly and drastically revised in 2003, with the production of passenger cars to be 2–2.2 million units out of a total production of 4.8–5.2 million units in 2005, and 1.6–1.9 percent of GDP.[16] This shows how fast China's automotive industry had been growing in the two years after the 10–5 plan was proposed. The 10–5 plan advocates that two or three big enterprises with relatively strong international competitive power will initially construct an automotive sales and service system suited to international standards, and that the domestic market share of the product will be over 70 percent and some of them will be exported.

In May 2001, a new plan for the automotive parts industry was laid down in relation to the 10–5 plan. The main points were:[17]

(1) To achieve a situation where the gross product component ratio of the automotive parts industry is 25 percent of the entire automotive industry in 2005. This means that the component ratio of the parts industry will be 0.25 percent of GDP.

(2) To form 5–10 parts groups, which can participate in international division of labor, and to make the groups achieve more than 60 percent of domestic share.

(3) To reduce the companies to the top three enterprises in parts (the share for the three enterprises being 70 percent), and to achieve a situation where the exporting ratio of these parts makers is more than 20 percent.

(4) To nurture system-module suppliers and to strengthen the module delivery system.

(5) To establish 6–8 development centers for key parts at the national level among the substantial enterprise group of automotive parts, and to nurture them so that they can develop key parts and automobiles at the same time, with a view to strengthening international competitiveness.

Table 9.2 *Automotive-related parts of investment incentive*

- Brake arrangement, drive-train arrangement, transmission, combustion pump of diesel engines, diesel engine turbo charger, emission control device for diesel cars, clarifier (triple filtration), asynchronous universal joint, shock-absorber damper, meter unit, fixed parts especially for high speed
- Electronic fuel injection system, electronic control system to prevent fatal accidents caused by wringing up, manufacturing of air bags and other electronic equipment for cars
- Die for cars and motor bikes (press mould, moulding), designing and manufacturing of jig (welding jig, jig for inspection, and others)
- Precision press mould, precision chamber mould, production of standardized parts for mould
- Manufacturing of precision bearings and bearings specially for body equipment
- Casing for cars and motor bikes, manufacturing of casing parts

Source: "Guidance for foreign investment industry," *Medium and Small Public Loan Report*, January 2003, p. 6

This restructuring and consolidation of China's parts industry focuses on areas with high growth potential. The field covers a lot of ground, including EFI (electronic fuel injection) devices, brake systems, steering systems, car air conditioning, high-tech air bags, automatic transmission, three-dimensional catalytic converters, die, jigs, and precision bearings (see Table 9.2). Importing foreign capital and participating in the international division of labor is being used to hasten development.

The policy to restructure, combine, and narrow down the parts industry is an ambitious approach aimed at overcoming the weakest points of China's automotive industry through using WTO membership as an opportunity to take part in global activities. Thus, the success of this policy depends not only on China's efforts at reforming the parts industry but also on how much cooperation the Japanese and Western parts makers, with their excellent technology, will give. By taking a big step toward an open automotive industry and following the route of opening up, China is trying to make up for its late start in technology and to bring forward the restructuring of its industrial organization.

However, a true opening-up policy, suited to the WTO era, does not mean only a policy that is open to foreign capital, but also that

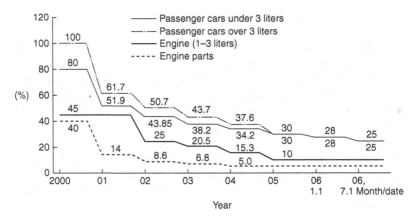

Figure 9.1 Schedule for decreasing tariffs for China's automobiles and their parts

China's automotive industry must be exposed to global competition through reduced custom tariffs on finished cars and parts. The Chinese government planned to gradually reduce custom tariffs for passenger cars, from 100 percent for greater or equal to 3000cc and from 80 percent for less than 3000cc in 2000, to 25 percent by July 2006. As for engines, it was planned to reduce tariffs from 45 percent in 2000 to 10 percent in 2006, and engine parts were also the subject of reduction of 40 percent to 5 percent (see Figure 9.1). This means that the Chinese government was essentially ordering the automotive industry to increase its cost competitiveness within six years and to try to make the price difference less than 25 percent for finished cars. By 2006, import quotas would be abolished, and a shakeout of small makers and price reductions for new cars would be advanced by complete open competition. The custom tariffs for engines, the heart of a passenger car, and the engine parts had been set extremely low to make importing easier, and at the same time aimed to hasten the introduction and development of advanced engine technology.

3. Japanese automobile and parts makers' China strategies

China is becoming a country with an annual production of more than 5 million cars. Japanese automobile and parts makers had advanced in various parts of China through technical collaboration and with a limited amount of knockdown production, but came to a temporary standstill. Recognizing that they needed to make further and larger-scale investments in China, something had to be done.

Toyota began preparing to produce small cars by building an engine production line near Daihatsu in Tianjin, where Daihatsu was licensing the technology of the Charade and conducting CKD production. Nissan avoided big projects for a period of time while still conducting technical collaborations in China. Honda, too, was running research but was wary of big four-wheel car projects, and kept its technology licensing to producing bases for two-wheelers in more than forty places in China.

Mitsubishi Motors began by licensing technology for large-size trucks, but has been seeking a way toward bigger projects since 1997, when it built a factory to build engines for passenger cars and small trucks and announced a project for technology licensing. Isuzu had a deep and long relationship with China to license technology for large trucks and diesel engines, but recently decided that the next step was to collaborate with business partner GM and its own strategies toward China.

Why were Japan's automotive makers cautious about making large-scale investments in China, in spite of their interest in China's future? There were a number of problems.

First of all, China's policies for the automotive industry had changed vertiginously and in an unorthodox way along the route from socialist economy to reform and opening up, and as the market economy progressed. Under the new principles of a socialist market economy, state-owned enterprises began competing for customers. But because the government's industrial policies still carried the echoes of the socialist state, reforming principles lacked consistency and the position of the automotive industry in the industrial structure was difficult to determine. China, for instance, tried to promote the importing of trucks and buses from Japan as a way to introduce new technologies, but suddenly stopped this – partly because of the foreign currency situation – showing how, on the one hand, it welcomed and promoted investment from foreign makers, but on the other hand tried to limit it.

The second problem was the policy differences between China's central and local governments on how best to nurture the automotive industry. Historically, all over China there were more than 100 small automotive factories, ranging from repair to building, and more than 2,000 farm-equipment manufacturers in addition to the three giant automotive manufacturers, the First Auto Works (Changchun), Second Auto Works (Dongfeng), and the Shanghai Automotive Company.

Though small, the local governments cannot ignore the existence of these factories and their impact on local industrialization, and want such factories to bring in foreign capital and technology. This tendency was particularly strong in the southern part of China, including Fujian, Guangdong, Yunnan, and Sichuan, which depend for their supply of automobiles on the north-east and the northern half of China. Feuding and differences in opinion between the central and local governments made it difficult for foreign companies to deal with them in order to promote themselves in China.

Since the central government can halt foreign investment unexpectedly, even though local governments may be positive and welcoming, foreign companies cannot easily start investing. However, since the government's policy of "Sanda Sanxiao liangwei" (three makers for large-size cars, three makers for small-size cars, two makers for light-size cars) was established at the beginning of the 1990s, a window has been opened for dealing with technical and capital tie-ups. Officially, policy dictates that a tie-up is not allowed without approval by central government, in spite of how enthusiastic local government may be, but in reality, the situation of "the central government with some policy, and the local governments with some countermeasures" still exists, preventing Japan and other foreign countries from taking an aggressive investment approach toward China.

The third problem was that China's basic policy of "Sanda Sanxiao liangwei" was established only in the 1990s. Since then, competitiveness among the three large state-owned makers has been stimulated in order to raise the independence of each maker. However, these companies are still nationally owned, and they have not detached themselves from government operations. Factories are a commune containing a school or a nursery center, and the number of employees remains much greater than the scale of production would suggest. If foreign companies attempt to form mergers in China, they have to be conducted with state-owned companies, and this means various kinds of regulations. Unless state-owned companies are reformed through demutualization, tie-ups are not easily made. Recently, the Chinese government hammered out the demutualization of the state-owned companies, and it will be interesting to see how this policy percolates down through the automobile makers.

The fourth problem was government reluctance to approve new projects like VW's Shanghai project, even without the demutualization of state-owned companies. This project established the joint venture separately from the main body of the state-owned Shanghai Automotive Company, and the model being produced was not being made by China's other state-owned makers, making it easier for VW to take the decision to invest. However, China approved few such projects until the 1990s, and tried to stick to the policy of "Sanda Sanxiao."

The fifth problem was that China wanted access to parts makers rather than assemblers. But without having an entrance into assemblers from Japan, with which Japanese parts makers can make safe transactions, it is difficult for parts makers to make an independent move. Also, the infrastructure needed for parts makers to become established is not yet completed in some parts of China. Some parts makers, which were attracted to China's cheap labor, withdrew from China because they could not bear the cost burden from building infrastructure, including roads and water, as well as housing for employees. Another problem for parts makers is standardization, which is hindered because parts makers, including small automotive makers which are scattered everywhere in China, tend to build parts by copying others. Though standardization and high machining accuracy are essential for parts and components, conditions were not ideal, and this also limited entry of parts makers into China.

Since China has been admitted to the WTO, progress in policies for the automotive industry can be expected. What China really needs is the demutualization and privatization of state-owned automotive companies. The basic policy of "Sanda Sanxiao" and strict controls on foreign capital and technology mergers by the central government will continue for a while. But once the prospect for demutualization of the state-owned enterprises becomes brighter, the likelihood of receiving central government approval for foreign capital participation will improve.

The Shanghai-VW project is considered to be a success story, and Shanghai-VW made the highest profits among foreign enterprises in China. Because this project received little interference from state-owned companies and the government in business politics, it became easier to select suppliers and to demand that Japanese suppliers like Koito Manufacturing Co. be permitted to enter the Chinese market. There were also benefits on tariffs for importing KD components from Germany. Though US automotive companies like GM and Ford targeted Shanghai with VW-type cars, Chrysler found a way into China with the Beijing Jeep. Behind all of this, the power diplomacy of the two great countries of the US and China could be detected.[18]

GM and Ford began their full-scale entrance into Shanghai and Changan between 1997 and 2001, in response to China's efforts to join the WTO and its 10–5 plan of 2001. The 10–5 plan meant that regulations on the entry of foreign capital were largely relaxed, prospects for abolishing regulations on nationalization and tariffs rose, a passenger car market would be developed, and state control would be relaxed in favor of competition. Figure 9.2 shows the expansion of the leading foreign makers into China, and Table 9.3 shows the production models and numbers of the leading foreign makers.

Japanese automobile makers and parts makers, which had been cautious about entering China's market, were now serious about advancing into China. Toyota at last set up business in China as its most important strategic project, starting by taking over the plant of a light car, the Charade (called Xiali in China), from its affiliate company, Daihatsu, in Tianjin. In 2000, Toyota began producing the small car, Xiali 2000 (its base is Plats), and in June of the same year Toyota started to produce 30,000 units annually of the four-door sedan VIOS, of which the base is the platform of a small passenger car, Vitz. However, Toyota's business in China reached full scale only after a complete affiliation with China's top maker, the First Auto Works, which drew the ailing Tianjin automobile maker into its orbit in June 2002.[19] After this fully fledged affiliation, Toyota started a new factory with an annual production scale of 50,000–60,000 cars in Tianjin, and began full-scale production of a mid-size passenger car, the Crown. Toyota aimed to introduce successor models of the Hongqi, one of the luxury models of the First Auto Works, as well as other types of models, and aimed to have production running with full lines. However, the First Auto Works had already started production of various kinds of models after making a tie-up with VW and Audi in Changchun, so one of the biggest problems for Toyota was how to adjust and compete with them. According to press reports in July 2003, Toyota was negotiating a tie-up with Guangzhou auto maker in order to establish another collaboration in Guangzhou. Guangzhou auto maker already had a fully fledged tie-up with Honda. By doing this, Toyota's narrow production bases, which were concentrated in northern and eastern China, would expand to southern China and increase production of the mid-size Camry model to 200,000 units.[20]

A company which was as cautious as Toyota over its entry into China at the beginning, but then made a similar leap and achieved clear results, is Honda. The company's two-wheeler business started with a technical

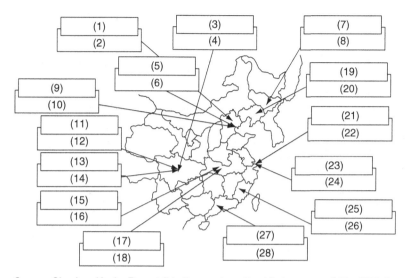

Source: Chushou Kouko Report (Medium and small public loan report) No. 2002-2 (January 2003)

(1) DaimlerChrysler: Beijing Automaker

Beijing Jeep (in operation in 1985)

(2) DaimlerChrysler 42.1% Beijing Automaker 57.6%

Cherokee, Grand Cherokee, BJ2020 Ability 100,000 units

(3) Isuzu: Qing Automaker (in operation in 1985)

(4) Isuzu 7.4%, Luling 51%

ELF, Wizard, Forward, Ability 100,000 units

(5) Toyota; the No.1 Auto maker

Tianjin (in operation: expected in 2005)

(6) High-class passenger car (expected) Ability 150,000 units

(7) Volkswagen: the No.1 Auto maker

First Auto Works VW (in operation in 1991)

(8) VW 30%, Audi 10%, First Auto Works 60%

Jetta, Audi A6, Bora Ability 150,000 units

(9) Toyota: Tianjin Auto maker

Tianjin Toyota (in operation in 2002)

(10) Toyota 50%, Tianjin Automaker 50%

VIOS Ability 30,000 units

(11) Ford: Changan Automaker

Changan Ford (expected to operate in 2003)

(12) Ford 50%, Changan Automaker 50%

Fiesta (expected) Ability 50,000 units

(13) Suzuki: Changan Automaker

Chongqing Changan Suzuki (in operation in 1995)

(14) Suzuki 35%, Changan Automaker 50%

Alto, Cultus Ability 150,000 units

(15) Peugeot Citroën; Dongfeng Automaker

Fengshen Automaker (in operation in 1996)

(16) Citroën 25%, Dongfeng Automaker 70%

CitroenZX, Picasso Ability 150,000 units

(17) Nissan: Dongfeng Automaker

(expected to operate in 2003)

(18) Nissan 50%, Dongfeng Automaker 50%

Cefiro, Sunny, March, small-size bus and other assembly types

(19) GM: Jinbei Automaker

Jinbei GM (in operation in 2001)

(20) GM 50%, Audi 10%, Jinbei Automaker 50%

Blazer, S-10 Ability 30,000 units

(21) Volkswagen: Shanghai Automaker

Shanghai VW (in operation in 1985)

(22) VW 50%, Shanghai Automaker 50%

Santana, Santana2000, Passat Ability 300,000 units

It has become the largest production region for cars in China.

(23) GM: Shanghai Automaker

Shanghai GM (in operation in 1998)

(24) GM 50%, Shanghai Automaker 50%

Buick, GL8, Sail Ability 100,000 units

It has become the largest production region for cars in China.

(25) Zhonghua Automaker (Taiwan): Fuzhou Automaker

Dongnan Automaker (in operation in 1999)

(26) Zhonghua Automaker 50%, Fuzhou Automaker 50%

Freeca, Delica Ability 60,000 units

(27) Honda, Guangzhou Automaker

Guangzhou Honda (in operation in 1999)

(28) Honda 50%, Guangzhou Automaker 50%

Accord, Odyssey Ability 60,000 units

The production ability of Honda is expanding to 120,000 units.

Figure 9.2 Expansion of the leading foreign-affiliated automobile makers in China

Table 9.3 *Production models and number of the leading foreign-affiliated automobile makers*

Group	Local name	Place	Registration of new model			Production models
			2000	2001	2002	
Toyota Group	*Tianjin auto maker Xiali	Tianjin city	81,951	51,019	89,720	Sharade TS710, 713
					2,147	Sharade2000 (Platz) Vios
	*Tianjin Toyota	Tianjin city	–	–	–	
	* Jinbei	Shenyang city	61,220	63,588	68,400	Hiace (licensing)
	*Sichuan Toyota	Chengdu city	0	2,179	2,842	Coaster (bus)
Honda	*Guangzhou Honda	Guanzhou city in Guangdong	32,228	51,146	59,024	Accord
Renault–Nissan Group	*Zhengzhou Nissan	Zhengzhou city in Henan	7,360	7,189	10,734	1 ton pickup
	*Sanjin Renault		557	347	497	Bus
	*Fengshen auto maker	Huadtu, in Guangdong, Shenzhen	–	18,501	38,897	Bluebird
GM Group	*Shanghai GM	Shanghai city	30,024	58,543	111,623	Buick, BuickGL8, Sail
	*Jinpei GM	Shenyang city	–	–	–	Chevrolet, Blazer, S-10
	*Changan auto maker (Suzuki)	Chongqing city	48,235	43,123	3,751	Alto, Cultus
	*Changhe Feiji (Suzuki technical aid)	Jingxi	–	5,223	67,846	Wagon R
	*Liuzhou Wuling	Guangxi province	111,908	120,128	20,564	Mini-size truck, bus
	*Guizhou (Fuji Heavy Industry technical aid)	Guizhou	555	1,253	149,368	Rex

Table 9.3 (*cont.*)

Group	Local name	Place	Registration of new model			Production models
			2000	2001	2002	
	*Qingling auto maker (Isuzu)	Chongqing	34,862	21,396	1,831	Forward, ELF, and other
	*Jiangling Wushilin	Nanchang city in Jianxi			31,893	Middle-size truck
			21,284	29,651	40,719	ELF
Daimler–Chrysler Group	*Beijing Jeep (DC)	Beijing	4,867	4,258	5,965	Cherokee
	*Dongnan auto maker (Chonghua auto maker)	Fujian	–	15,749	16,808	Freeca (licensing by Mitsubishi, multi-purpose cars of Asia Dongfeng)
	*Changfeng auto maker (Mitsubishi)	Hunan	1,188	10,477	15,067	Pajero
	*Beifang Benz	Baotou in Neimengga	623	763	1,040	Heavy truck
Peugeot–Citroën Group	*Shenlong auto maker	Wuhan city Hubei	53,900	53,680	84,378	CitroenZX, Picasso
Ford Group	*Jiangling auto maker (Ford)	Nanchang city in Jiangxi	5,526	7,197	10,667	Transit (light bus)
	FAW Hainan	Hainan	3,059	4,710	17,912	Premacy, 323
	*Shanghai Volvo	Shanghai city	355	878	829	Bus
	*Xian Volvo	Xian city in Xiaxi	365	252	428	Bus
VW	*Shangai VW	Shanghai	22,524	230,281	278,890	Santana, Santana2000, Passat (Bb)
	Changchun FAW VW	Changchun city in Jilin	110,005	133,896	191,695	Jetta, Bora, Audi

Source: "Chushou kouko report," *Medium and Small Public Loan Report*, no. 2002–2 (January 2003) and the documents given by Fourin

collaboration in 1981, and Honda established manufacturing bases in Guangzhou and Tianjin in 1992, already a significant achievement. However, Honda faced a price offensive from more than 1,000 of China's local makers, which assemble two-wheelers with open-architecture type imitation parts, and its market share dropped from 60 percent in 1984 to 9 percent in 2006. Honda was trying to work out how to tackle this price offensive while maintaining its brand value as Honda.[21]

Honda's four-wheel operations in China started when it merged with Dongfeng Automotive Company and entered the market for engines and parts for the under body that met nationalization regulations. In 1998, Honda expanded to Guangzhou after the dissolution of a tie-up between Guangzhou auto maker and PSA Peugeot, and established Guangzhou–Honda Co. Ltd. Unlike other foreign makers in China, Honda undertook the drastic strategy of sending the newest model Accord to the market. Honda sold the 2300cc US-specification Accord as a high-class model with an aggressive price setting of 290,000–348,000 Chinese yuan (approximately 2.4–2.9 yen). Since many cars produced by other makers in China were 1980s' models and obsolete, Honda's strategy captured the needs of the wealthy class which began appearing around this time. The production number increased over three years, from 10,000 units to 50,000 units in 2001. As soon as the minivan Odyssey was put on the market in 2002, it reached full production. By 2003, production had reached 120,000 cars annually and was still increasing.[22]

Honda's success had a big impact on other makers, especially on the biggest maker, VW, and led to VW introducing new models and setting up a second factory for the high-class Passat. But success happened unexpectedly even for Honda, and the company made a surplus continuously since 2000; the profit in 2002, for example, accounted for 60 billion yen.[23] This happened mainly because Honda's strategies for selecting models proved to be correct, but also because Honda minimized new capital investment by using press and other equipment effectively when it took over the factory from Peugeot, and maintaining its style of establishing factories that produced profits from small lots. Honda planned to build a factory specializing in exporting cars, with an annual production in the scale of 50,000 units, and to export the small-size Fit to Europe.

Since the mid 1990s, Nissan had given up on the idea of entering China because of poor business performance and the need for management reconstruction. But the reconstruction plan under Carlos Ghosn began taking off, and Nissan decided to enter China, starting a collaboration with the Dongfeng Motor Company in September 2002. According to Ghosn, in 2003 Nissan had already invested $1 billion in this project.[24] Nissan had also set up consignment production of the Bluebird passenger car model with Fengshen auto maker, which is an amalgamated company of Dongfeng auto maker and its Taiwanese partner, Yulong auto maker. As this full-scale collaboration business was starting, Nissan began producing its Sunny and Cefiro in addition to the Bluebird in Guangdong, and was likely to begin production of a litre-car, March, and other small business cars at the factory in Hubei. In June 2003, Nissan established an amalgamated company, New Dongfeng auto maker, with Dongfeng auto maker, and began production of mainly commercial vehicles and the Sunny-class passenger car. Nissan's ambitious goal was to expand the number of passenger models (with more than 2000cc displacement) to six by 2006, and its sales target was 220,000 passenger cars and 550,000 trucks, commercial vehicles, and cars in the same year.[25] Because Nissan was the last company to join the Chinese market, it increased the number of models at once. But one of the key issues was whether Nissan could establish a sales network suitable to the situation quickly enough.

The China strategies of the three leading auto makers in Japan have been developing rapidly since the turn of the century, and other makers are also making a gradual entrance into the Chinese market. Almost all of these makers are establishing tie-ups with other foreign enterprises and their strategies for China are strongly related to the strategies of the allied foreign enterprises. Mitsubishi Motors, for example, had already been operating engine factories in Harbin and Shenyang before it entered DaimlerChrysler AG, but did not have a license to produce passenger cars. It became a member of DaimlerChrysler AG and attempted to add the Pajero Sports as a second model (in addition to the Jeep Grand Cherokee of Beijing Jeep, which had been taken over by Chrysler after it allied with AMC), but this and other strategies in China were to be reconsidered after aid from DaimlerChrysler AG was stopped.

Mazda, a member of the Ford Group, was conducting consignment production of the small-RV models Premacy and Familia at First Hainan auto maker of Hainan, but started to produce the minivan Atenza at First Auto Works Group. In parallel with this project, Ford was planning to produce a small-size passenger car, Fiesta, through a tie-up with Chanan auto maker.[26]

How are Japanese parts suppliers responding to the China strategies of Japan's leading auto makers?[27] Because of the differences among suppliers in the technical fields, labor intensity, the degree of *keiretsu* transactions with specified auto makers, and the decision-making processes, their strategies vary.

Among Japanese suppliers, those in relationships with Toyota and Honda have entered China in a relatively orthodox way. Many of the suppliers in this group have established near their assemblers, and many started appearing on the Chinese market after the mid 1990s. However, given their excellent technology, they will use their China operations to produce parts not only for Japan's OEM assemblers, with which they have long-standing business relationships, but also for VW, GM, and other Chinese automotive makers connected to European companies, in order to assure delivery partners of multiple countries. For example, Koito Manufacturing Co., a headlamp maker, entered the market in Shanghai in 1989 following a request by Shanghai VW, but because the company is a member of Toyota's cooperative organization, Kyohokai, Koito Manufacturing Co. was also making full-scale deliveries to Toyota. In another example, Yazaki, which is famous for its wire-harness, set up in Tianjin in 1988 under joint management with a foreign company. Since then it has expanded its production bases to Shantou city and Chungchin city in Guangdong prefecture and Chengdu city in Sichuan prefecture, and aims to increase its delivery partners not only among Japanese companies but also among foreign companies.[28] Since Yazaki has many labor-intensive processes, it can benefit greatly from manufacturing in China. Yazaki's role will not be limited to China's domestic markets since it will also have a role as an exporting base working closely with ASEAN production sites.

Suppliers are divided into tier one, which produce unit parts and other functional parts, and secondary suppliers, with their own technology and know-how in the field of gadget parts and die assembly by press, as well as machine work. It is possible for some of these suppliers to partner with local suppliers under joint management, or to have a business relationship with Bosch, Delphi, Vestion, Dana, Lear, TRW, GKN, and other European and US mega-suppliers. Many European and US mega-suppliers are doing business under the significant strategic concept of expanding their production sites not only in China but also in the rest of Asia, including ASEAN, Korea, India, Australia, and Japan, by taking over suppliers of Japanese origin to build a complementary local network system and support the relatively new Chinese bases.

In addition to this, China will use international competitiveness to drive the reorganization and integration of the local parts industry. China has growth potential in the parts industry, and technology transfer is urgently needed in the weak areas of electronic parts, high system parts, functional parts, engine power-trains, environmental purification, precision die assembly, high-level jigs, and the production of material for, for example, die cast and its process technology. Foreign investors are expected to set up joint management with local companies, or to enter as independent capital, though the risk is very high. As for module suppliers, which have a strong orientation toward open architecture and which are the main focus of the reorganization of the parts industry, possibilities may exist for collaborations in the multi-module field, which requires not only a simple open module but also a higher level of design ability. However, it is worth remembering that there are various design concepts and the success and failure of the suppliers will largely rest upon their ability to provide some consistency of concept.

4. Conclusion

The final goals for the globalization of the automotive industry are the globalization of the Chinese market and China's automotive industry, and the establishment and implementation of a road map toward solving global environmental issues, and these two goals are closely linked. It is reported that Toyota engineers have for a long time believed that it is essential to establish environmental technology, especially for the issue of global warming, in order to succeed in the automotive business in China. That sums up the issue and I would like to show approval.

China's development and participation in the global economy has happened more rapidly than expected, and automotive pollution is now extremely severe in some parts of the country. The problem with environmentally harmful emissions in Chungchin city, a great basin in the outer country, is rapidly getting worse, and in Beijing and other big cities traffic with two-wheelers is completely prohibited. One of the reasons for this situation is traffic accidents; another is that there are no exhaust emission controls for two-wheelers.

The environmental issue China is facing is not simply regional but is also related to global warming, and this is directly linked to the desertification of agricultural land and the depletion of water resources.[29] If this situation is sustained, with China's automobile pollution – and especially with global warming caused by CO_2 emissions – things will deteriorate continuously. Contaminated materials from China are likely to hit Japan and Korea directly, carried onto the yellow sands by westerly winds. Of course, the Chinese government is not neglecting these issues. Technology for environmental measures and energy efficiency are listed as important issues in the reorganization of the parts industry and the high level of technology transfer. New technologies for CO_2 reduction and energy efficiency will be helpful in stopping global warming and for air-quality control in China. Since China is becoming a major crude oil importer, and crude oil must be paid for with large amounts of foreign currency, technologies that will bring energy reduction will be a national benefit. Shanghai implemented Euro 2, the European emission controls, in March 2003, and it was said that Beijing would implement Euro 3, a tougher emission control, in 2005.[30]

However, China is putting its growth ahead of solving environmental issues. Originally, and especially before the 9–5 plan in 1993, China tried to restrain the development of the automotive industry under the "Sanda Sanxiao" policy. As long as China was choosing a realistic route, which tried to develop the automotive industry as a public industry and for company demands, environmental issues were unlikely to be significant in comparison with other heavy industries. However, a new situation developed after the 10–5 plan, and China's entry to the WTO means that China has set up the automotive industry as a growth industry and has started toward expanding individual demand and drastic liberalization. As a result, production numbers are increasing much faster than the Chinese government expected, and the rapid growth is unlikely to stop now, even when China's economy faces temporary problems, such as the SARS scare in 2003. It is said that China needs to have at least 7 percent annual economic growth in order to feed its nearly 1.3 billion population. Though China is trying to have the automotive industry contribute to this 7 percent growth, there is still no clear scenario to establish how and by whom environmental problems are going to be solved. Assistance from the Japanese government's ODA has to be shifted to this field promptly, but it is a drop in the ocean. Japanese automotive makers must develop new environmental technologies and shift everything toward being involved with environmental issues in the future, even if this will determine the future of their companies. Believing that China is the last giant market available for the twenty-first century and the biggest market in the world, and simply being optimistic about increasing production numbers and riding on the growth – all this might end with a pitfall. Thus, the rapid growth of China's automotive industry and environmental issues will always be a kind of rat race, and the time of integration, rather than alternation, of growth and environment might come soon. It is no exaggeration to say that whoever conquers the environmental issues in the Chinese market will conquer China. However, even the Chinese government has to go through twists and turns before this is achieved, and it is obvious that there are a lot of unsolved problems and risks remaining.

What kinds of risks do Japanese automotive makers deploying in China have to consider for now? The first big risk is related to the success or failure of the plan to restructure and integrate the 116 auto makers into 2–3 groups of leading companies. This idea was hammered out in the 10–5 plan. The core companies of the groups are naturally the state-owned companies, including First Auto Works, the Dongfeng Motor Company, Shanghai Automotive, and Guangzhou auto maker, and the companies targeted for restructuring are local companies which receive assistance from local governments and private companies, like Futian auto maker in Beijing or Geely auto maker in Zhejiang. The issue here is whether this far-reaching restructuring and integration will go smoothly, according to schedule, under the leadership of the state-owned companies, which are still under pressure for their own, internal reforms. The current situation is not as simple as the era of "Sanda Sanxiao," when everything was carried out by the central government. Private enterprises in local areas have emerged by taking advantage of the reforms, and it is impossible to conduct restructuring and integration with the initiative of the government while ignoring their existence. It is also possible to conduct restructuring and integration through free competition, which respects entrepreneurship growing in private companies.

On this point, I conducted a survey of automotive and two-wheeler makers in the middle and southern part of China in August 2002 with Professor Fujimoto of Tokyo University. Almost all of the makers were local, private companies. I had heard about the speed of development of the local economy in Shanghai, Zhejiang, and Guangdong, but it was far beyond my imagination, and I was stunned.

Until around ten years ago, China's automotive industry was concentrated in the area further to the north of Changjiang and to the north-east, and it was thought that the southern part was for light industry and the automotive industry would not develop there so easily. This was considered natural, since the core companies under the government's "Sanda Sanxiao" policy of nurturing the automotive industry were state-owned companies relying on coal energy. However, after Deng Xiaoping's famous tour in the southern part of China, that area began to develop dramatically. Shenzhen and other areas along the sea coast in the south used their experience and took a lead in the economic development of the south. As the industrial base expanded to Dongguan and Shunde, this area moved into full-scale production for two-wheelers and cars as well as consumer electronics. I was also surprised to see significant development in Hangzhou, Ningbo, and Taizhou and other parts, and die-cast industries in Huangyan, which appeared to be hidden under the shadow of the glorious development of Shanghai and southern China.

The places I visited then were Shanghai's VW factory, specializing in the Passat, a Taiwan-origin bicycle maker named Giant, the Zhejiang Die Factory for plastic dies, Wanxiang in Hangzhou for constant velocity joints, a two-wheeler and passenger-car maker named Geely in Hangzhou, an air-conditioner maker the Media Group in Shunde, a microwave oven maker named Galanz, and a TV maker named TCL, which is getting worldwide branding. Most of these companies have become leading enterprises in only ten years, and they are likely to develop much faster.

It is impossible to introduce all of these companies, but what they share is their entrepreneurship, which supports the boom of reform and the opening up of China. This was emphasized by China's entry into the WTO. What was especially impressive was the fact that many of the enterprises, which appeared as township and village enterprises, grew into big companies in a short period of time. In exhibition halls for introducing companies, pictures of their establishment around 1980 were displayed, with most starting from a shed or shanty rather than a factory. Villagers who were *wanyuanhu*, regarded as rich with an annual revenue over 10,000 yuan, started by investing money together and achieved success by changing and expanding their businesses, and by taking advantage of increasing domestic demand. As a result, a public company started with 4,000 yuan in 1979, for example, grew into a big enterprise with assets of 10 billion yuan.

Rapid growth was possible because of a system that promoted business through the integration of local governments, universities, and enterprises, and supported aggressive entrepreneurship. Local governments have been trying to address the privatization of state-owned companies, and are not only stimulating privatization but are also to create a

Chinese style of M&A by combining both. In response to this movement, universities are changing to introduce practical education, and some universities teach the reverse engineering of cars and two-wheelers. Currently, engineers and business people with university degrees, including PhDs, are in great demand, and their number is small. Thus, enterprises are working on building universities themselves and establishing a support system.

This aggressive entrepreneurship among China's local enterprises is supported by employing young university graduates, aged in their thirties to early forties, as executives in addition to the founders, and they are succeeding in conducting strategic management and business deployment by getting the most out of opportunities. The existence of many diligent workers, who are good with their hands and who work under a contract of around yen 12,000 monthly, is perfect for businesses with labor-intensive processes and mass production line work. China has become the world's biggest production country for two-wheelers, with 12 million units annually, and this is helped by the local development of a distinctive parts industry and industrial accumulation. For example, there are makers which specialize in constant velocity joints or pistons and produce parts of the unit, several millions to 10 million, for domestic and overseas makers. We also can see industrial accumulation with several hundred plastic die makers, such as around Huangyan in Zhejiang. In this kind of circumstance, budding companies are emerging in the southern part of China. Geely, which started by producing two-wheelers, for example, invested the profits from two-wheelers into producing cars. Geely has produced a small model, the Meiri, which is close to the class of the Entry level. Geely is also planning to produce a sports car model, with an annual production of 300,000 units.

However, though new business is emerging, excess production of consumer electronics and two-wheelers has become perceptible, so companies are restructuring. The automobile industry has at last freed itself from the constraints of the "Sanda Sanxiao" policy and the most honest impression is that a restructuring/selection era might come sooner than expected in spite of the opportunities for growth.[31]

The entrepreneurship which is everywhere in south-central China and the dynamism of private auto makers in local areas, which was stimulated by that entrepreneurship, should be utilized fully. However, simply depending on the dynamism of local enterprises and restructuring/selection will not necessarily lead to success. In order to maximize the dynamism of local enterprises, the most important thing is for national automotive companies to reform themselves, and this reform has to be better than that of private enterprises. In other words, it is essential to use the dynamism of local private enterprises as an accelerator for the reform of state-owned companies. It is also essential for central government to introduce policies that will promote drastic restructuring and integration, but whether this type of restructuring and integration would lead immediately to forming strong auto makers which can compete in global competition is a different issue. Another challenge is how to position the role of foreign capital in this restructuring, whether it should be left out of the restructuring and integration process completely or used as a source of technology transfer and capital, and whether strategic behavior by foreign companies can be identified and maximized.

Foreign companies – whether of Japanese, European, or US origin – entering China have to be prepared for the risk that they might not be able to conduct their own strategies, being in danger of being caught between the reform of the leading state-owned automotive makers and freewheeling local private enterprises on the wave of restructuring and integration. A recent significant trend has been for the major state-owned makers to tie up with plural forms of foreign capital under joint management, such as First Auto Works with VW and Toyota, Shanghai Automotive with VW and GM, and Guangzhou auto maker with Honda and Toyota. Though these have been conducted as separate tie-ups, there is a risk that this sort of two-pronged tie-up will restrict individual strategies.

The restructuring and integration of parts makers, which was announced just after the 10–5 plan, also face much risk and difficulty. The proposal to make the gross product of the parts industry 25 percent of the entire automotive industry by 2005, was possible, and we can expect it to go beyond that goal. However, the issue of the structure and quality of parts production will still exist, and it is not easy to resolve the situation in which excellent parts makers with a high level of technology coexist with parts makers with a low level of technology and quality, in spite of the ability to produce high quantity. The issues are how to establish a group with 5–10 parts makers which can join the international system, and to consolidate the top five main-parts companies. Table 9.4 lists the automotive parts that the Chinese government supports mainly, divided into two levels.

One of the most important points when we talk about China's automotive parts industry is regional accumulation. Tomoo Marukawa of

Table 9.4 *List of auto parts which are mainly supported*

Power-unified type	Auto parts EFI, ABS, ASR(device for stopping slippage), air bag
Tier 1 parts	AT, clutch, brake system, steering system, mission system, suspension system, air conditioning, sheet, interior system, lamp/light system, lock, anti-theft device, wiper, window regulator, combination meter, 3D catalytic converter
Tier2/3 parts	Piston, piston ring, engine bearing, valve lift, turbo charger, filter, radiator, spark plug, wire harness, small-size motor, fastener, wheel bearing, friction material, sintered metal parts, brake disc, universal joint, (iron, aluminium), casting parts, low-pollution special auto device

Source: Speech material of Mr. Huang Yonghe, China's automotive technology research center at the forum for Fourin China's automotive industry, April 21, 2003

Tokyo University commented about this in a recent study. One point he makes is that, as the products markets have accumulated in one region and competition has become more intense since 1992, this is affecting the accumulation of suppliers. This situation is more significant from the Shanghai region to Jiangsu and Zhejiang, where the production of passenger cars is increasing. This tendency can also be seen in Changchun and Jilin, where the production of passenger cars is expanding. The biggest reason for this accumulation is considerations of transportation cost rather than closed trade practice. Marukawa points out that the accumulation will not be limited to these two areas; in the future it is likely to expand to Hubei, Guangzhou, Tianjin, Beijing, and Chongqing. [32]

The parts industry has various fields, some easily copied and some not so easily because they require particular skills and technology. The Chinese government had been thinking of taking a lead in restructuring the parts industry by strengthening advanced areas and by emphasizing high technology. But more realistically, if modern equipment or metal molds are brought into China at cheap prices, the small press, plastic products, and other parts, which easily fit into open-style architecture and quickly expand in production, can compete straight away, especially if standardized parts which are suited to imitation parts are manufactured. Some of the parts makers for two-wheelers, of which China has the world's highest production, have fully entered the area of automotive parts as makers of open modular-oriented parts for general purposes.[33] Some of these parts makers are expected to act as a core as production accumulates.

In comparison with open modular-oriented parts, China is still behind in the technology for more complicated and high-level integral architecture-oriented function parts and system parts, including engine power trains, suspension, transmissions, and other parts related to vehicle control, and for which they still largely depend on capital import. The parts makers of Japan, Europe, and the US could easily participate, especially in their areas of skill: design and development, high-precision processing, and software for using electronics. The national parts development center is also expected to support China's parts makers in skills development, but this development center has a tendency to overemphasize the design and development ability of fundamental parts when open-modular oriented. Support for design and development skills in parts makers has depended largely on what ideas China's automotive makers have for architecture, and this depends on what kind of concept the Chinese consumers choose for their cars. If many consumers prefer cheaper cars with better quality rather than focussing on looks, the basic, multipurpose and open modular parts will be the center of attention. However, it is unlikely that Chinese consumers who have seen imported cars will be satisfied with low-level cars for long.

There is a strong possibility, therefore, that the restructuring and accumulation of China's parts industry will not make much progress under government initiatives. Rather, it is likely to move forwards under initiatives that combine private enterprises with foreign capital. There is an issue of whether China's parts industry will be organized in a pyramid-shaped, vertical, and horizontal division of labor, similar to that of Japan. It is likely that China's parts industry will nurture large-scale module suppliers and create a supply chain-like and unified supplier system without having a complicated trade structure, instead of developing the small and medium-size infrastructure of subcontracting suppliers as a supporting industry. Since China's policy officials are advertising the effectiveness of the supply-chain system, this direction is likely to be pursued in policies. However, how the initiative will be taken, and by whom, is not yet clear.

When we consider the future of China's automotive industry, the most important matter is the direction of economy cars of under 1300cc displacement, which are advocated in the 10–5 plan. Though the center

Table 9.5 *Demand forecast for China's automotive market in 2015
(10,000)*

	2001	2002	2003	2004	2005	2010	2015
Truck	82	107	125–131	144–151	163–169	184–203	174–200
Bus	85	106	116–121	131–137	141–147	174–187	185–206
Car	77	120	144–156	180–188	221–230	397–424	660–723
Total	243	333	385–408	455–475	525–546	755–814	1020–1128

Notes:

(1) Actual data are used for 2001–2002.
(2) China's automotive technology research center, WTO, and APEC policy research
department
Source: Speech material, p. 5, of China's automotive technology research center at the
forum for Fourin China's automotive industry

for China's automotive market is its growing wealthy class, and though
the market is expanding with the consumption of high-class mid-sized
cars or RV cars, rather than economy cars, the demand for small
economy cars shows outward signs of increase. It is essential to stimulate and expand the demand of this bottom class with the consumption
of small economy cars in order for China to become a motorized
country. VW with Polo, Jetta, and Bora, and Toyota with Vitz and
Vios, have already started to produce small economy cars, and this
segment will eventually decide the hegemony of China's automotive
market. Geely auto maker in Zhejiang and other private enterprises
produce low-priced cars which closely imitate the abovementioned
small cars, and the time when imported and domestic cars compete
fiercely is close. It is not an exaggeration to say that the key for China
becoming the world's largest market depends on the future of small
economy cars. But when small cars are produced in millions of units,
China will have to face environmental issues as we have seen. The
production of super low-fuel consumption cars and zero-emission cars
will soon be the top priority in the world.

Though China has a huge population and nobody would deny the
idea that it will be the largest market in the world, it does not follow that
China will reach that sort of level without experiencing any problems.
Table 9.5 shows predictions for China's automotive demands before
2015. This table reflects earlier forecast figures, but real demand

reached almost 6 million cars, which is beyond Japanese domestic demand. The reform of state-owned companies and the rise of energetic private enterprises, conflicts between central and local policy authorities, participation in the WTO, using global markets as a driver for reform and opening up, and other challenges will all continue to drive change in China's automotive industry.

Notes

1. For further information, please refer to M. Shinomiya, "Nihonno Jidosha Sangyo" (The automotive industry in Japan), *Nihon Keizai-hyoron sha*, 1998, pp. 61–120. Incidentally, as I recall, one of my classmates at junior high school used to go to work as an industrial recruit at an automotive factory in Manchuria.
2. C. Li, "Gendaichugoku no jidoushasangyo" (The automotive industry in modern China), *Shinzansha*, 1997, pp. 340–341.
3. N. Shiomi, "Ikouki no Chugoku Jidoushasangyo" (China's automotive industry in transition), *Nihon Keizai Hyoronnsha,* 2007.
4. In the 1980s, the No. 1 Factory conducted a full model-change as a response to the challenge made by the No. 2 Factory for the first time in thirty years. The passage is in Li, ibid., p. 64.
5. K. Shimokawa, "Chugoku kindaika to jidousha shijyo" (Modernization of China and China's automotive industry), *Nikkan Jidosha Shinbun*, December 8, 1984.
6. J. Chen, "Chugoku jyoyosha kigyou no Seichou sennrayku" (The strategies for the development of China's enterprises for passenger cars), *Shinzansha*, 2000, p. 58.
7. Talk given by Mitsuhiro Seki at Tokyo University Gendaikigyo Workshop on July 30, 2003. H. Seki and Y. Iketani, "Chugoku jidousha sangyo to nihon kigyou" (China's automotive industry and Japanese companies), *Shinpyouron*, 1997, p. 127.
8. Li, ibid., pp. 226–227.
9. Chushokigyo kinyukouko chousabu (Research department for public loan corporation for medium and small sized enterprises); "Ootejidousha meka no chugoku shinshutsu to chushou buhinn sangyo heno eikyou to taiou" (The presence of the major automotive makers in China, and its impact for and tackling by the medium and small parts industry), *Chushou kouko report* (Medium and Small Public Loan Report), January 2003, p. 22.
10. Li, ibid., pp. 69–72.
11. *Chushou kouko report*, p. 4.
12. Ibid.
13. Ibid.

14. Ibid., p. 5.
15. Ibid.
16. Information packet, Fourin "Chugoku Jidoshasangyo Foramu" (Forum for China's automotive industry), held on April 21, 2003. Speech material by China's Automotive Technology Research and Huang Yonghe "Chugoku jidoushasanngyo hattennseisaku no shouraitennbo" (Future views for policies for the development of China's automotive industry), p. 9.
17. *Chushou kouko report*, p. 6.
18. K. Shimokawa, "Nichi-bei jidoshasangyou koubou no yukue" (The future of the offense and defense of the Japan–US automotive industry), *Jijitsushinsha*, 1997, pp. 233–238.
19. *Chushou kouko report*, p. 6.
20. *Nihon Keizai Shinbun*, July 7, 2003; *Sankei Shinbun*, July 7, 2003.
21. In the big cities in the coastal area, regulations on two-wheelers were put into place and this triggered a sales slump of high-class brands of two-wheelers. In order to tackle the bargain offensive, Honda began production of low-price scooters and motorbikes through a business merger of Xin Dazhou Honda (according to Honda PR accounts).
22. *Chushou kouko report*, p. 18.
23. Guangzhou-Honda made a surplus in the first year, and the cumulative deficits were eliminated in the first three years (interview with the executives of Guangzhou-Honda at Shanghai in August, 2002).
24. K. Shimokawa, from the record of an interview with Mr. Ghosn on July 17, 2003.
25. *Chushou kouko report*, pp. 16–17.
26. Ibid.
27. Ibid., pp. 37–63.
28. Ibid., p. 36.
29. T. Watanabe, "Kankyoosen taikoku no yomei" (The expected life of a great country with environmental pollution), *VOICE*, July 2003, p. 63.
30. *Nihon Keizai Shinbun*, July 9, 2003.
31. K. Shimokawa, "Chugoku chunannbu niokeru jidosha, nirin meika no kinkyo" (The recent history of makers of automobiles and two-wheelers in south-central China), *Nikkan Jidosha Shinbun*, October 12, 2002.
32. T. Marukawa, "Chugoku jidosha sangyo no sapuraiya network" (The supplier network of China's automotive industry), *Tokyo daigaku sha-kaikagaku kenkyu 2* (Tokyo University Social Studies), vol. 54, no. 33, 2003, pp. 149–151.
33. T. Fujimoto and Y. Sugiyama, "Chugoku nirinnsha-sangyo ni okeru mojuura aakitekucha ni tsuite" (Concerning modular architecture in China's two-wheeler industry), in A. Masahiko and J. Teranishi (eds.), *Transformation of East Asia and Japanese Companies*, March 2000, pp. 405–454.

10 | Conclusion – the global automotive industry's perspective on the twenty-first century and tasks for the Japanese automotive industry

In the past quarter century, dynamic and dramatic changes, unimaginable twenty-five years ago, have occurred in the world's automotive industry. This industry started in Europe as car assembly by craftsmen, and then developed dramatically in the US, where a manufacturing system based on mass production was established. The automotive industry in Europe and the US developed along mass-production lines, but in Japan it lagged behind for more than forty years, and nobody would have predicted that Japan would become a world leader. There was a time when the automotive industry was expected to be mature once it entered a certain growth stage, and a kinked growth curve was also much discussed.[1] Almost all of these predictions were completely wrong, and the automotive industry has shown a more dynamic development. Japan's automotive industry took the lead, adding vitality to the whole industry, and contributing a dynamic industrial model.

If the world's automotive industry had not departed from Fordism's mass-production system, and, as W. J. Abernathy pointed out, had stayed an industry, which settled for economy of scale, moving from a learning curve to a mature curve, then it would certainly have become a mature industry, and technology for production, development, and parts might have stagnated.[2] Maturation would not be simply because automobile demand was saturating, but because the industry had lost its dynamism. Certainly, the Japanese and other automobile markets in advanced countries have experienced several periods of growth stagnation caused by saturation.

However, the technical environment behind developing automobiles has changed dramatically. The weight of the materials used for automobiles sold in advanced markets has been reduced. The automobiles themselves are equipped with electronic devices, which are compilations

294

of engine controls and semiconductors that electronics are applied to. In recent years, many micro-computers have been built into automobiles, and information and communications technologies, such as navigation systems and cruise control, are becoming more common. The automotive industry also has to be responsible for developing green technologies in order to address the universal issue of global warming. The commercial viability of hybrid cars and the development of fuel-cell vehicles, which were once only dreams, exist now in a range of practical applications in the technological sense. Traffic accidents, especially on highways, have been a negative heritage of the convenience of a motorized society. The establishment of a fail-safe traffic system to eradicate these accidents is about to come into being in a range of applications known as ITS (Intelligent Transportation System). So while automobile demand has begun to look saturated, this situation is a driving force for dynamic evolution and development.

However, the advanced technical environment would not have happened without dynamic competition in the industry, which stimulated and promoted technology. This state also could not have developed without the strategic behavior of companies in promoting this situation, as well as a positive lead in management systems – especially in close linkages between the development system and the production system, and parts supplier and sales distribution systems. Despite being late joining the industry, it was Japan's automobile industry that provoked the industry to shrug off its tendency to maturation and triggered the promotion of advanced technology.

In the 1970s, in my previous book, *A Business History of the US Automotive Industry*, I titled the final chapter "Change of the Social Environment and the US's Automotive Industry."[3] Around that time, the US's automotive industry was about to begin fuel-efficiency control for automobiles, under the influence of the energy-conservation measures established in 1975. The air clean-up under the Muskie Law and the first oil shock in 1973 added momentum to these measures. In the final chapter, I suggested, if the US automotive industry continued to suffer technical stagnation because of the circumstances described and because of the oligopoly of the Big Three, and if the industry continued to go against changes in the social environment, then even the Big Three, which held sway over the world, would eventually fall. This was a warning directed not just at the US's automotive industry but rather at the entire automotive industry, including Japan. At the time, I was inspired by Emma Rothschild's great book, published in the autumn of 1973, and so in the same chapter I introduced some extracts from her book, while giving warnings to the future automotive industry.

Rothschild's book, *Paradise Lost: The Decline of the Auto-Industrial Age*, acutely pointed out that the US's automotive industry, having established the mass-production system by applying Fordism, kept to the framework of Fordism while making further development by applying the Variety Marketing of A. P. Sloan and Sloanism – an autotelic pursuit only for the purpose of obsolescence and the replacement of products.[4] But, as the book pointed out, the industry's system itself ended up obsolescent, because the US's automotive industry forgot that it needed to adapt to changes in both the social environment and the philosophy behind what automotive civilization should give to human society. For this book, Rothschild conducted field surveys at the state-of-the-art robotic plant, Lordstown, owned by GM, the company that had the majority (60 percent) share of the US market. (The US was the biggest market in the world at that time.) She also made her observations so deeply that she observed the troubles of the organizational operations at GMAD (GM Assembly Division), which were part of an ambitious organizational reform by GM. (In the late 1960s, the functions of Fisher Body, which was operating almost as an independent body in spite of being a division of GM, were restructured under the management of the GM Assembly Division. This organizational restructuring was made under an ambitious overall concept, and the target was to standardize chassis among GM divisions through the integration and restructuring of design and the development of chassis and bodies. Until then, design and development were handled among automotive divisions and Fisher Body. However, it is thought that in-house troubles over product development and preparation occurred frequently in the process of bureaucratizing GM's organizations.) The author vividly described GM's overconfidence in its computer system and robot automation, which caused the famous strike at the Lordstown plant, and pointed out how much these troubles were caused by organizational operations based on desk plans that were detached from the production and development sites.[5] The book's bottom line was that the reason for the stagnation of the automotive industry was because GM and other makers in the US's automotive industry adhered only to the two principles of Fordism and Sloanism and they lost perspective on how to evolve and renovate by outgrowing that framework. Simultaneously, Rothschild pointed out that the cause of the stagnation of the automotive industry was the changes that happened in the social environment. For instance, Rothschild emphasized that society, which had supported the automotive industry as a growing and giant sector, was not necessarily giving a high evaluation and sense of support to the industry any more, because personal mobility in society changed due to the development of telecommunications. This book was published just before the oil shock (1973), so it does not directly cite either the energy-resource issue or the air-pollution control issues of the Muskie Law, since the establishment of the act was postponed.

In spite of this, Rothschild had already understood more than thirty years ago that the US automotive industry, which relied on the obsolete paradigms of Fordism and Sloanism and which had lost the ability to evolve and innovate, would be a stagnant industry and would lose the support of a society where people were detaching themselves from the Ptolemaic environment around the automotive industry.[6] While introducing her points of view in the previous book, I introduced the energy issue as well as the air-pollution control issue. In the book, I also emphasized the point of view that the social–environmental issue was becoming a matter of burning concern, not only for the US but also for the worldwide automotive industry, and that the future automotive industry should be responsible for traffic and environmental issues, especially the issues of natural resources and energy.

In a batch review of my previous book, Mr. Hiromi Arisawa, a chairman of the audition for the Nikkei-tosho Bunka-Award, made some comments on the social environment issue in the last chapter, and said that I needed to explore these issues more. These comments are absolutely appropriate. However, the direction of the development of automotive technology was still obscure, and it could have been possible for futurologists like Alvin Toffler to have a perspective of how the automotive industry might develop into an industry that could be responsible for coexistence and harmony between self-innovation and society, but it was almost impossible for a business historian such as myself to do so.

The automotive industry has created vehicles equipped with cutting-edge electronic and materials technologies, and it has adopted the products of information technology. A system for emission control and fuel efficiency has been prepared, and the practical application of environmentally conscious hybrid cars is in progress. And now, fuel-cell automobiles are at the final stage of developing practical applications. Under these circumstances, and by considering global innovations in product development, production systems, and parts-supplier systems over the past quarter of a century, we can observe clearly that the current automobile industry is beginning to gain the ability to evolve and innovate by detaching itself from stagnating, the path the US automotive industry took.

The past thirty years have seen the global automotive industry experience a lot of twists and turns in the process of creating dynamic evolution and innovation. It is worth remembering that Japan's automotive industry started this situation. Of course, this does not mean that Japan's automotive industry always took the lead in all aspects of shaking off maturation. During the development of the information revolution in recent years, there was a tendency to call the service economy (which was growing by making full use of IT) and the IT information network "the New Economy," while referring to industries that created goods using hardware as "the Old Economy." According to this categorization, the automotive industry was part of "the Old Economy". Is it really so? As has already been described, the automotive industry is applying high-level technology to all areas. The industry is using new materials, and is nurturing and using cutting-edge products for processes as well as for design and development. The automotive industry is also applying electronics to making parts and other products, while introducing high-level technology to fine-processing, casting, and the speeding up/raising pressure of die-casting and cast-forging. In addition, the automotive industry is making full use of IT technologies such as the development of digital design by CAD, CAM, and CAE, the introduction of LAN systems in manufacturing plants for processes, and also for central control for robot automation. There is no other industry which utilizes IT technology as much as the automotive industry. It is also striking to see the global spread of in-car navigation systems, telematics, and other IT products.

These various and dynamic technological revolutions could not possibly be achieved overnight, nor have they emerged because of a breakthrough in technology made by some genius inventor. Certainly, some technologies, such as semiconductors, computer software, and IT, developed through a technical breakthrough. Nevertheless, the skills of automobile makers in design and development and in production and parts technology make it possible for them to adopt advanced technology and apply and evolve it to mass-production technology in a process of incremental and accumulative technological innovation. This incremental innovation shows the expertise of Japanese automotive and parts makers, in other words, of Japan's automotive industry as a whole.

What made the adoption, evolution, and application of advanced technologies possible has been dynamic competition in the automobile industry – the strategic behavior and the business systems of corporations that promote this competition as well as the progress of the technology itself. In this, Japan's automotive industry played a leading role in the 1980s.

Japan's automotive industry began its challenge by shrugging off maturation. In an extreme sense, it challenged the eroding paradigms of Fordism and Sloanism, as pointed out by Rothschild. These paradigms are generally separated into mass production and mass sales systems of variety marketing, but they are, in fact, from the same root. Basically they are variety marketing based on possible mass production. Once the Japanese and just-in-time production systems emerged, Fordism and Sloanism – which had become synonymous with rigid mass sales and an inability to adapt to consumer and social needs – were exposed as deadlocked. We can see this situation vividly in a famous historical event which happened around the time of the coup in Iran in 1979 and just after the second oil crisis. This was the dramatic decline of the US automobile industry in Detroit. As discussed in Chapter 1 of this book, at that time, the US automotive industry could not cope with the sudden changes in the US's consumer needs, from large vehicles to smaller vehicles that met the fuel-efficiency requirements for automobiles introduced by the US government. The drastic drop in demand for large automobiles caused the US automobile industry to suffer from massive amounts of dead inventory, excessive plant and equipment, and a slump in market share, while the market share of Japanese automobiles increased from 13 percent to nearly 15 percent. This caused friction between Japan and the US and eventually developed into Japan's voluntary restrictions on exports of automobiles. The reversed situation between the US and Japan that occurred at this point happened neither accidentally nor temporarily, as was proved by later history. The maturation of the automotive industry and Fordism and Sloanism, industrial paradigms symbolizing the stagnation of the industry, ended their historical missions. Around this time, many researchers sought to understand the competitiveness of the Japanese automotive industry. Among these was the well-known MIT International Motor Vehicle Program, in which I was involved for about twenty years, and which was the study that most vividly and clearly interpreted the Japanese automotive industry's competitiveness and new industrial paradigm, called the lean production system.[7] Though this research will not be described in detail here, in short it tried to analyze and compare internationally the characteristics of plant production systems, supplier systems, and R&D systems in Japan's automotive industry, and made it clear that the mass-production paradigm that places economies of scale ahead of all else had reached obsolescence, and that therefore the new industrial paradigm had to be the lean paradigm.

The changeover of industrial paradigm produced a great impact not only on the US's Big Three but also on Europe's automobile makers, especially Europe's mass-production manufacturers, and this was seen in how the automotive industries of the US and Europe reformed and learned about lean production. This learning and reform were promoted by the globalization of Japan's automobile makers, which had begun to enter into local production overseas. For Japanese automobile makers, local production overseas was a way of avoiding trade friction and the risk of a hike in the yen. The risk was so high that it could decide the fate of companies. Lean production developed, and what was thought to work only in Japan was shifted overseas. Eventually lean production was adopted overseas, after a period of adapting to local cultures and business customs. MIT's research results had already pointed out, as early as the end of the 1980s, that Japan's local plants were better than the US and European makers in terms of quality, productivity, factory stock, and delivery dates.[8] Without waiting for the points made by MIT, local plants of Japanese makers cropped up relatively close by, some being joint factories between the Big Three and Japanese partners. This hastened the learning opportunities for European and US makers.

The process of learning and introducing lean production was different among European and US automobile makers. The process was related to the business strategies and climate of each manufacturer, therefore it is hard to generalize about the process each manufacturer took. However, on the whole, the European and US makers began by improving the efficiency of product development or by shortening lead-times. They also worked on introducing a cross-functional development system and concurrent development systems, where the development sections overlapped. As to the supplier system, the rate of subcontracting increased while the rate of in-house manufacturing decreased, because parts divisions were spun out. At the same time, the number of suppliers with which the makers had a direct business relationship was reduced in order to cultivate the system suppliers and module suppliers. Though the system of module suppliers began among the European rather than Japanese makers, even this was created from the large stream of innovative changes to the entire supplier system.

Chapters 2 and 3 described how these innovative changes and the introduction of the factory production system are lagging behind in comparison with how quickly lean production was introduced to product development and supplier systems. There was a tendency to retain the process-designed factory system, which placed economy of scale above everything else, and certain merits existed in this. Innovative change to the factory system would probably produce a great change in labor and employment practices, while it would have a great impact on industrial relations. Therefore, introduction of QC circles, the *kanban*, the fail-safe device, and the andon-system was happening in automobile factories in Europe and the US, though it was not quite a full reformation. As a condition for retaining mass-production factories that could not escape from economy-of-scale considerations in the Big Three, even if old models were continuously produced, they had to achieve cost competitiveness, fleet sales (where cars are stocked because of speculative production, and makers sell the cars to rental car companies at a cheaper price then the makers buy back these cars in about six months and sell the cars in the used-car market), rebate sales, and other forced sales. The Big Three could also counter Japanese cars with lightweight trucks and SUVs, which did not require model changes as frequently as passenger cars. Industrial relations were like a historical Achilles' heel. In order for labor and management to realize industrial harmony through job security, there was no option but to postpone problems. However, at last Ford and GM started to bring out strategies aimed at thorough reform.

There are some common features in how lean production was introduced by European and US automobile makers. The main part of the Japanese production system was born from a belief in local production, and included the movements for improvement, the QC circle, the *keiretsu* transaction, and simultaneous product development. European and US makers introduced the lean production system in an effort to make progress by systematization and integration. Therefore, using Japan's simultaneous methods for product development under project general managers, they introduced a systematization of the method as a piece of concurrent engineering, the computation of QCDE, which is the outcome of a partnership between suppliers and assemblers that is at the core of the *keiretsu* transaction, and the adoption of a systematic method for benchmarking suppliers. This is an integration of extremely complicated elements, and systematizing the reform of a factory production system which has strong personal elements is difficult, which is partly why such factory reform has been postponed until today. However, it is important to note that European and US automotive makers studied and learned about lean production in an extremely strategic way, and their quick decisions on which elements were easily systematized and introduced, along with their quick decisions on what should be accorded priority, hastened and increased the outcomes from this learning process much faster than their Japanese counterparts had expected.

A new era emerged in the global automotive industry in the 1990s. The flows of human resources, goods, and capital became borderless, freer, and rapid, and IT innovation improved information speed and the quantity of the data-processing reservoir. As a result, business and the exchange of data and information, which until then could be processed only manually by analog technology, could soon be processed by means of digital technology. In the case of the automotive industry, IT innovation improved efficiency and the speed of processes dramatically, from designing to conducting trials, through the introduction of three-dimensional CAD/CAM and CAE for design development. IT innovation also improved networking of LAN systems and other production information in factories, and, as a result, fast discovery of problems and fast production became possible. IT is also playing an important role in the internet procurement of parts which are easily standardized, and in building supply chains for the distribution of parts and materials. IT helps simplify the bloated services of white-collar employees and streamlines the complicated administrative stratum, and in the distribution and sales of automobiles it also helps with internet sales, and support for dealers and sales people in communicating with customers over built-to-order cars. The Big Three implemented this outcome from IT innovation immediately, and this had an impact on the European makers.

As pointed out in Chapter 3, changes through systematizing lean production were rapidly promoted in European and US makers, especially in design and development systems and in supplier systems. Japan's automotive makers, which place importance on experimental knowledge and real places and things, lagged behind in adopting IT innovation because they lacked strategies for corporate behavior. However, it should be emphasized here that IT is merely a tool for corporate behavior, and though it can offer a technology advantage, this advantage cannot be maintained forever. So while Japan's automotive makers originally lagged behind in IT, they are now on the way to a quick recovery, and the gap is not as big as it was before. Digitalization of design and development and the reduction of the number of trials by virtual engineering are in progress,[9] as is the building of benchmarking and information networks for suppliers. Trials for digital information networks and Toyota's electronic *kanban*, which are distinctive characteristics of Japan's automotive makers, are also penetrating into the industry. You can see this in Toyota's V-Com (Virtual Communication) or Mazda's MDI (Mazda Digital Innovation), which aim to connect the factory production system and digital design.[10] As a result, Japan's inferiority complex over IT, which was seen often in the past, seems to be disappearing.

So how do we understand the globalization and global restructuring of the world automotive industry in the 1990s? This is the most important part of the conclusion to this book, and any perspective on the global automotive industry in the twenty-first century should stem from this. The 1990s was an era when European and US automotive makers made great profits and succeeded in making a comeback. The profits made by the Big Three, especially Ford and GM, were said to be unprecedented in some years. Japan's automotive makers, which had previously seemed to be sweeping the world with their lean production system, suffered from a sharp drop in profits – some makers produced unprecedented deficits due to bad conditions, including the end of the bubble economy in 1991, the functional failure of the main banking system, stagnation of the domestic market, the extreme deterioration of export profits caused by the high yen, a burden from investing in local factories, and an increase in the cost burden caused by the support of local industry. As we all remember, restructurings were conducted even in the automotive industry, which had been a symbol of steady industrial growth, and some makers had to close their factories and had to cut back on personnel. In this situation, Ford, followed by GM, launched bold global strategies, and this eventually developed into the global restructuring of the world automotive industry after 1998.

What we have to observe coolly now are the main conditions which made possible the global strategies carried out by Ford and GM, and the problems of the industrial paradigm in global restructuring. What made the global strategies of Ford and GM possible was the business boom in North America, not any success in overseas business. The business boom in North America happened mainly because of the temporary success of a product strategy that concentrated on light trucks and SUVs, which produced high profits through the expansion of the automotive industry in North America. This happened partly because of the IT boom that was played up by the Clinton administration. Another reason was because the optimum factory operating rate was somehow maintained, while retaining mass-production, high-volume factories. In addition, the number of cars produced per platform increased, due to the stretching of the products' life cycle, and GMAC, a form of automotive sales finance, and Ford Credit helped profits and the cash flows of GM and Ford increase. In addition to these conditions, efforts at reforming design and development and supplier systems as they learned lean systems and promoting the adoption of IT technology and its use in various fields helped the business boom in North America.

However, if we look back now, we realize that many falsities were hidden behind the unprecedented profit and prosperity of the US's automobile makers. The biggest problem was that, because the reform of mass-production factories was postponed due to the temporary business boom, the rigid mass and high-volume production system was consistently retained, and lacked what was the keyword for progress among automotive factories: flexibility. As a result, model changes that responded quickly to changes in market needs, responses to variations among the same-model cars, and mixed production were postponed. Because of this, the factories of the Big Three in North America developed characteristics whereby they could not make up for the high break-even point without making their operating rate appear increased.[11] Essentially, the US's automotive industry, despite its comeback in the 1990s and prosperity as it globalized, could not separate itself from the industrial paradigms of Fordism and Sloanism. Recently, Ford's president said that it would adopt the flexible factory model of

European Ford in its factories in North America since its business was stagnating,[12] and GM was about to take the same action.

Though the Big Three were enjoying positive earnings in the 1990s, there are many questions about how much effort they were making in order to raise the total productivity of their cars. In particular, almost none of their passenger cars had hit sales targets in the 1990s. In the first half of the 1990s, Chrysler produced a compact model Neon and a medium LH-model, which were considered hits, but their popularity did not last very long. Neither Ford nor GM managed to produce successful passenger cars. The main profit for Ford and GM came from pickup models, such as Ford's Explorer and GM's S-10 series, and from strategic models in the long-life light truck segment, from a kind of modular architecture or open-architecture type, such as the SUV model, with high added value. This shows that productivity did not increase, despite the high profits of the 1990s. Most of that high profit was injected into M&A with other makers overseas, redundancy payments and retraining costs for downsizing the employees, including white-collar workers, and IT-related e-business services, and so spending huge sums of money on factory reform and products development, which was essential, was put off.

The biggest problem was that the Big Three generally put off the development of new engines, which are the heart of an automobile, and any real investment in factories to build engines. As a result, they did not produce any fuel-efficient engines. Table 10.1 compares the average fuel efficiency among car makers in the US. You can see that the numbers for Toyota and Honda are high, especially for passenger cars. This shows the negative aspect of the strategic behavior of the Big

Table 10.1 *Projected growth of new driveline technologies (thousand new vehicles per year)*

	2000	2010	2020	2030	2040
Hybrid cars/LTs	–	–	2,700	22,500	50,500
FC taxis	–	35	200	450	550
Hybrid LCVs	–	350	2,500	8,000	14,500
Hybrid local trucks	–	30	350	1,300	2,500
FC urban buses	–	1	35	100	150

Source: Autopolis, 2010

Three's managers, who were constantly considering cash flow and market share in order to obtain short-term profits. In contrast, Japan's automobile makers had concentrated on business in North America while bearing the difficulties of the 1990s, and laid great importance on the development and production of fuel-efficient engines. Eventually, Japan's automobile makers took the lead in the fuel-efficiency of gasoline engines and exhaust-emission control. Even while the Big Three were making high profits in the 1990s, the market share of Japanese cars in North America did not fall, and the price of Japanese used cars remained high in comparison with US cars. This is probably one of the hidden reasons why the market share of Japanese cars reached 30 percent in the twenty-first century.

The global strategies of Ford and GM impacted on European makers as well as Japanese makers. Global restructuring was advanced by the mergers between Daimler and Chrysler in 1998 and Renault and Nissan in 1999, by the participation of Mitsubishi Motors in the DaimlerChrysler group, by the acquisition of Volvo and Range Rover by Ford, and by the participation of Fuji Heavy Industries in the GM group (later in 2006 GM sold Fuji Stock to Toyota). In this restructuring fever, the former president of Ford, Jacques Nasser, stated that the number of the world's automobile makers would be reduced to four or five in the future. As a result, the 4 million car survival theory was trumpeted.

One of the main reasons for this global restructuring was the investment burden of tackling global environmental issues, such as the problem of CO_2 emissions, technologically. This has had two positive effects. One is to reduce the huge investment risk for projects such as developing fuel-cell vehicles and transitive fuel-efficient engines, including common-rail diesel engines, which are mainly seen in Europe. The other effect is to make it possible to respond quickly to environmental issues. However, it cannot be ignored that Fordism was the biggest reason for global restructuring in the automotive industry. That is to say, two ideas, one to standardize global platforms and the other to effect a dramatic cost reduction by large-scale parts purchase through expanding global sourcing, lay at the bottom of global restructuring. Standardization of platforms would certainly reduce development costs per platform, which is said to take up 40 percent of total development costs. However, any platform standardization that emphasizes only this could create a huge danger of destroying the identities of products as well as brands, depending on how it is conducted. In order to assure the differentiation of goods while standardizing platforms, it is important to define components, parts, and the interface for platforms in a way that assures architectural strategies and brand identity based on those strategies. Brand identity is the corporate culture of each automobile maker, so if this were lost by the standardization of platforms, the risk of losing brand power would be beyond our ability to imagine. Ironically, makers that have been successful in both standardizing platforms and brand identity are European makers that did not participate much in global restructuring – such as PSA, with two big brand models in Peugeot and Citroën, and VW, with the affiliated companies of Skoda and Seat. Though US makers hammered out their platform strategies openly, they have not produced major results yet.

Global sourcing, another promise for global restructuring, also presents various problems. Though the global procurement and group purchasing of commoditized standard parts is meaningful, local purchasing and adjustment of parts in order to protect brand identity has problems. Even in the procurement of module parts, a difficulty exists in matching brand identity and the needs of local markets. Global sourcing can produce a good integrated result when local procurement is systematic, but it is impossible for a company that just merged and jumped onto global procurement without any premise to achieve a good result.

Global restructuring which is unilaterally about economies of scale will not necessarily be successful all the time. Subjective integration of companies and unilateral imposition are extremely dangerous, and this could result in spin-outs even if companies manage to merge. A good example is the spin-out of Daimler to Chrysler. The future of the alliance between Renault and Nissan is worth paying great attention to, since they have been trying to cooperate through common benefits and to make snazzy cars while respecting the corporate culture and brand identity of each company. Both companies, for example, have agreed on the standardization of platforms for low-cost models such as the Micra and Clio, but they are careful about standardizing platforms for high-class models. For global, central purchasing of parts, too, both are considering each other's brand identity and architectural strategies carefully before making decisions.[13]

The fever for merging, at one time exclusively aimed at popular economies of scale, has cooled down, and now the content of restructuring has become more important. The merit in restructuring and merging is not just about scale, it is also about facing every market and providing consumer value while respecting diverse corporate cultures and brand identities. If major reforms to create flexible production systems are conducted in the light of these kinds of strategies, then restructuring can produce real and positive outcomes. The bigger mergers and restructurings are unlikely to happen now because of their high risk when the content and strategies of global restructuring are being revised. From now on, a partial alliance for specific strategic reasons that respects the identity of each company, such as those between Toyota and PSA and Honda and GM, will be more important than bigger mergers.

Global restructuring is now in a period of self-questioning and reconstruction. Are new global automotive makers likely to emerge from developing countries in the future? We recall the entry of the Korean Hyundai and Kia groups, but the next maker to try to enter the global market will probably be Chinese. As a national strategy, China will want to foster two or three automotive makers that can join the global players. However, there are plenty of problems to be solved. First of all, it is difficult to participate in the global market without having strong reserves of foreign capital. This is because, in contrast to China's successes in appliances and two-wheelers which could be imitated with the right modern equipment, automobiles are complex and cannot be so easily copied. In order to be a global manufacturer, environmental technology is essential for domestic cars produced in China, and this is as essential as establishing electronic components and other high-level parts industries. For this to be possible, a partnership with foreign capital is essential, but such tie-ups require a constitutional reform of automotive makers as state-owned enterprises, eventual privatization, and then going public. It is difficult for publicly owned automotive makers to join the market since they have to maintain the national industrial policies set by the government, but it is possible that they could create a separate, merged company with foreign capital and then go public.

The conditions for tie-ups with foreign capital are becoming more favorable, but China's automotive makers have no other way forward than to develop as local makers for a while, supported by an increase in demand at home. In this case, the problem is how to produce and expand the low-price popular automobiles which are standard cars in China. Users in the expanding market for passenger cars are mainly the wealthy, and the market for popular cars has not developed yet. In this situation, how Chinese users will accept commercial cars and low-price passenger cars, which are the Chinese standard and have rather open architecture, will decide the direction of China's automotive makers as local manufacturers. However, how China's standard cars will be accepted by their users in China also depends on competition with imported cars, for which tariffs will be drastically lowered.

What we can say is that it is possible for China's makers to be independent if they expect to develop only as local manufacturers, but it is impossible for them to participate as global players without total collaboration with the advanced makers, which have the necessary environmental, developmental, and production technologies. Competition among the global automotive makers, which are aiming to strengthen their presence in China by merging with China's automotive makers in the future, will become more severe.

We have observed the historical development of the global automotive industry over the past quarter century and the changeover in industrial paradigms during that time. We started with the reversal of Japan and the US at the beginning of the 1980s, followed by the globalization of the Japanese automotive industry, the Big Three and European and US makers displaying their own way of learning of lean production, the comeback in business performance and the development of global strategies by the European and US makers in the 1990s, their globalization and restructuring, and the dynamic changes and innovation which aim to review global restructuring and to focus on Chinese and Asian strategies. The shifts in industrial paradigms, a constant feature of the past twenty-five years in the global automotive industry, are still happening, and the arrival of IT innovation and globalization could promote further paradigm shifts. Though the Japanese automotive industry took the lead with lean production, it overcame the maturation and stagnation of the automotive industry unintentionally and opened a new path for growth. Now the Japanese automotive industry is expected to raise this industrial paradigm to a higher level through IT innovation and the global era. This means the development of an industry which is responsible for social and global civilization, including global environmental and traffic problems. Under this situation, a slim, fast R&D system that integrates various kinds of advanced technologies to directly face environmental issues, and a production system that can reduce losses in market production, will be pursued (see Table 10.1, Figure 10.1, and Figure 10.2). This

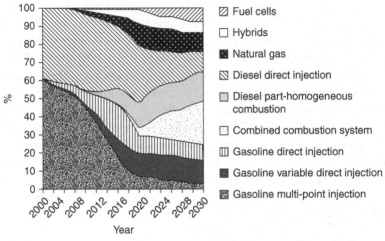

Source: Dobson, "The future of vehicles and fuel," in Maxton and Wormald, *Time for a Model Change* (Cambridge University Press, 2004)

Figure 10.1 Share of engine technologies in new light vehicles, 2000–2030

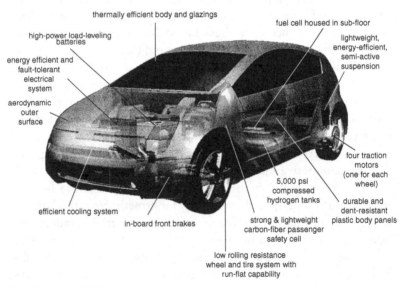

Source: Hypercar, Inc. 2002

Figure 10.2 The hypercar

Table 10.2 *A comparison of the average fuel consumption for cars made by makers in the US*

Model		Passenger car					Small-size truck				
Year	(mpg)	1998	1999	2000	2001	2002	1998	1999	2000	2001	2002
Average fuel consumption											
TOYOTA	D	27.5	27.5	27.5	27.5	27.5	20.7	20.7	20.7	20.7	20.7
	I	28.0	28.3	33.3	34.2	33.6	23.5	22.9	21.8	22.1	22.1
NISSAN	D	30.7	29.9	28.9	28.9	29.3	22.3	21.2	21.1	20.7	20.7
	I	29.9	29.9	28.3	27.7	28.9					
HONDA	D	32.7	33.5	35.4	36.3	35.0	26.9	26.1	25.3	24.9	25.2
	I	28.1	29.4	29.0	29.3	29.6					
GM	D	27.8	27.7	27.9	28.1	28.6	21.2	20.3	20.9	20.5	21.1
	I	29.4	25.5	25.0	26.5	27.7					
FORD	D	27.8	27.6	28.1	27.5	27.8	20.4	20.4	20.9	20.5	20.7
	I	28.9	30.1	27.5	27.8	28.1					
CHRYSLER	D	28.8	–	–	–	–	20.6				
	I	25.4	–	–	–	–					
MERCEDES	D	27.2	–	–	–	–	21.3				
	I										
DAIMLER–CHRYSLER	D	–	27.2	27.5	27.7	27.6	–	20.8	21.3	20.7	21.2
	I	–	26.5	25.3	27.1	26.5					

Notes: (1) Made in the US, I = imported

(2) The figures for Mazda are included with Ford from 1999

Source: Toyota Motor Corporation Research Division

production system will have to be more flexible and more human, in the sense that it will be able to collect intelligence. A dynamic supplier system has to be built which can guarantee design and development, innovative and creative technical capabilities, capacity-building of QCDE, and the formulation of effective supply chains. A sales and distribution system has to be built that can offer high service and consumer value, backed by thorough consumer consciousness and clear brand power, and which can remove wasted distribution stock and costs.[14] Furthermore, the building of global, cross-border, and balanced value chains is a big item on the agenda. Though global restructuring is in progress, you cannot find an automotive maker which is assured of balanced earning capacity in China, Asia, and any other countries in the world.

I talked in my previous book about the necessity of being responsible for the automotive civilization that had been created by the automobile industry itself and the social and environmental changes that it brought, but I ended with a simple, idealistic theory. I would like to conclude this book by saying that that simple, idealistic theory is becoming more realistic, rather than less so, as the paradigms of globalization and the automobile industry progress.

Notes

1. K. Tomiyama, "Nihonno Jidousha Sangyo" (Japan's automotive industry), *Toyokeizai-shinposha*, 1973, p. 220. In this book, Mr. Tomiyama pointed out that the era would come of the growth of Japan's domestic automotive demand, of new demands, and of the renewal-of-order-oriented slowdown.
2. W. J. Abernathy, *Productivity Dilemma*, Johns Hopkins University Press, 1978. W. J. Abernathy, K. B. Clark, and A. J. Kantrow, *The New Industrial Competition*, Basic Books Inc., 1983.
3. K. Shimokawa, *A Business History of the US Automotive Industry*, Toyokeizai-shinposha, 1977.
4. E. Rothschild, *Paradise Lost: The Decline of the Auto-Industrial Age*, Random House, 1973, pp. 97–112. K. Shimokawa, *A Business History*, pp. 318–322.
5. E. Rothschild, pp. 107–109. K. Shimokawa, pp. 319–320.
6. E. Rothschild, pp. 248, 247–248, 249. K. Shimokawa, pp. 325–327.
7. J. P., Wormack, D. J. Jones, and D. Roos, *The Machine That Changed the World*, Rawson Associates, 1990.
8. Ibid., pp. 85–86.

9. T. Fujimoto, "Seisan Manegimento Nyumon II" (Introduction to production management II), *Nihon Keizai Shinbun*, 2001, pp. 202–211.
10. T. Negishi, "Toyota niokeru IT o katsuyoshita korekarano kurumazu-kuri" (Toyota's car building with IT in the future), *Nikkei Mekanikaru (Nikkei Mechanical)*, September 2001.
11. In an interview with the author, Mr. Scheele, the president of Ford, said that they carried excessive plant and equipment of up to 2.9 million units for the production of 4.8 million cars, even in the time of the boom. "Interview with Ford's Nick Scheele," *Nikkan Jidosha Shinbun (Daily Automotive Newspaper)*, December 4, 2002.
12. Ibid.
13. Based on the hearing at Renault Technical Center in March 2002. K. Shimokawa, T. Fujimoto, et al., "The strategic moves of European automotive makers which are trying to strengthen their global strategies and environmental strategies, and the strategies in Europe of Japanese automotive and parts makers and research on their factories," *Keieishirin*, vol. 39, no. 4, 2003.
14. In recent years, some automotive makers inside and outside the country are trying to produce some models by the build-to-order system. This trial is drawing attention as a way to reduce distribution stock.

Epilogue

The writing of this book culminated in 2008, just as the global automotive industry was hit by the world financial crisis and a global recession. The automotive industry reigned as a leading global industry during the twentieth century – an especially remarkable phenomenon. The fall of the US Big Three, which had led the global reorganization of the industry until ten years ago, is alarming. GM and Chrysler both received public-funds assistance from the government. However, many people doubted the effectiveness of such an immense injection of about 3 trillion yen from public funds.

The causes of the downfall of the Big Three are described in Chapter 7 of this book and were anticipated at the time of writing. However, to summarize simply and without fear of repetition, they are as follows.

The first factor is that the Big Three devoted themselves to short-term profits, finance, and M&A and forgot the origins of manufacturing. This tendency was strong in GM, and the profit structure depended on financial income (consumer finance earnings + sub-prime loans, various financial risk hedging), which rode on the wave of global expansion of credit, which was raised by the sales financing subsidiary of GMAC. Although they are automotive companies, they did not earn their profits from cars but from earnings made through finance, and the stock that was raised.

The second factor is that the basic technology of the engine and the platform did not evolve because too many management resources were concentrated on light trucks, represented by large SUVs, and not on the development of passenger cars, which is the foundation stone of the automotive industry.

The third factor is a neglect of environmental technology. The United States gave priority to fuel-consumption regulation, but although it enacted the Muskie Act first, it delayed effectuation for ten years. One round of fuel-consumption regulation finished in 1985, and since then there has been no change in fuel-efficiency standards. In the meantime, the average fuel consumption has decreased in China. Also, the fuel efficiency of light trucks is very low in comparison with passenger cars. Environmental and energy-saving measures were the only way forward for the Big Three. When consumer awareness converts into action and environmental conservation becomes a major issue, it cannot be overstated that a company with such an attitude cannot hope to adapt to the market environment. The GM chairman, Mr. Wagoner, admitted this mistake by congressional testimony. However, at present, he is able to expect only venture companies to take up the challenge concerning future environmental technology.

The fourth factor is a lack of concern for factory reform and improvement (*kaizen*) activities, and it can be said that manufacturing techniques and R&D failed to evolve.

The fifth factor is the improvement of pension and health insurance benefits through negotiations with UAW and the profitable conditions of the 1990s, resulting in a legacy of greater cost burdens. Although this point has been fully negotiated with UAW, there is doubt whether an infusion of public funds is really possible.

The sixth factor is ruin triggered by the simple mistakes of global M&A. It may be said that, after all, restructuring has culminated in a global bubble of money games by investment banks.

As the decline of the Big Three continued, a huge crisis also occurred in September 2008 for auto makers in Japan, which had previously been the only winners in the global markets. Ignited by the collapse of Lehman Brothers, the effects of a global recession hit home. Eight main auto makers, including Toyota, Honda, and Nissan, fell into deficit, which had not been anticipated. The profitability of exports to North American markets, which had previously contributed 60–80 percent of overall profits, declined with the appreciation of the Japanese yen. There has been a reduction in sales of 5 million vehicles to North American markets per year because of the vicious circle of overproduction and overstock. For example, although the financial return went into the red and Toyota saw signs of a crisis in quarter earnings ending in March 2008, it continued to increase production and there were no production adjustments. Therefore, stock circulation came to exceed 100 days for Toyota and Honda, compared with the previous acceptable time of 30–40 days.

Thus Japanese manufacturers are facing a recovery period at the time of a reduction in the size of the North American market. So, for the time being, inventory adjustments should be planned to extensively decrease domestic and overseas production, and also an adjustment of stock due to the reduction and postponement of overseas factories. It is necessary to return to the starting point of the Japanese production system, to curb excess production and the build-up of excess inventory, and to convert to a lean management structure in which profits can be made by operating at 60–70 percent of capacity as at the time of the first oil crisis. If so, it is necessary for production technology to adapt to flexible production volumes in the market, and not only flexibility in the kind and type of car that Japanese automotive makers have pursued so far.

The North American automobile market has witnessed not only quantitative reduction but also a criterion shift in the mind of consumers toward value for money. Therefore, a re-examination of product strategy for the extensive promotion of a small-size vehicle with low fuel consumption or an environmentally friendly vehicle, and further strengthening of environmental strategies are needed. It is necessary to maintain R&D investments, and this is a big paradigm shift in corporate strategy.

For Japanese automotive makers, another important strategic paradigm shift is to give more emphasis to developing countries, such as India, China, and ASEAN, rather than to North America or to the global strategies led by advanced nations. Also, a shift of global strategies toward an environmental society and wider demand is needed. Although, until now, such a change was thought to be for the future, due to the impact of the world financial crisis, the timing may have been brought forward. It is believed that Japanese automotive makers misread the world financial crisis and thus lost half or more of the cash flows accumulated during the past ten years. Although in a stage of recovery, if the two aforementioned strategic paradigm shifts are successful, there is still a chance of renewed development. There must be a shift from the old paradigm of the twentieth century-type "mass production – mass marketing – mass consumption," and we must question whether a new paradigm of social use for an automotive society that can coexist with the natural environment can be realized.

Index

absolute value of production equipment, Japan–US comparison 20–22
AFTA (ASEAN Free Trade Area) 231, 237, 238, 239, 249–250, 252
AICO (ASEAN Industrial Cooperation) 231, 238–244
American auto industry *see* US auto industry
American Motors 137
ASEAN (Association of Southeast Asian Nations) region
  automobile industry in Thailand 252–255
  complementary division of labor 237–245, 250–252
  current options for Japanese auto makers 231
  impact of China's automotive industry 257–258
  impact of the Asian economic crisis (1997) 230–231
  Japanese auto makers' strategy before the currency crisis 231
  potential automobile market 230
  presence of Japanese auto makers 234, 235–237
Asia
  automobile industry in Thailand 252–255
  complementary division of labor 237–245, 250–252
  current options for Japanese auto makers 231
  history of local production 231–237
  impact of China's automotive industry 257–258
  impact of the Asian economic crisis (1997) 230–231
  Japanese auto makers' strategy before the currency crisis 231

  potential automobile market 230
  presence of Japanese auto makers 231–237
Asian economic crisis (1997)
  impacts of 230–231
  measures taken by Japanese auto makers 246–250
Aston Martin 205, 210
Automotive Industry Action Group (AIAG) 83–84
auto-parts industry
  changes in component procurement systems 155–160
  formation of a global procurement system 185–194
  mergers and acquisitions (mid 1990s) 155
  modularization trend 161–163
  restructuring and globalization 155–163, 185–194, 226–227
auto-parts standardization, Japanese restructuring (early 1990s) 102–103, 105–106
auto-parts suppliers
  changing supplier relationships 161–163
  cooperation with 106–108
  development of skills 170–171
  emergence of global suppliers 155
  impacts of auto industry reorganization 155–163
  influence of global platform and sourcing strategies 185–192
  module building 194
  need for strategic management 194
  participation in design and development 161
  quality issues related to cost reduction 197–198
  strategic M&A activities 194

317